Full praise for America's Midlife Crisis

"*America's Midlife Crisis* is an important book. It is a book that both Americans and non-Americans alike need to read as they grapple with the massive changes taking place in global geo-politics. Gary Weaver and Adam Mendelson, two leaders in the field, bring profound cultural insights to their analysis of the challenges the United States faces and the choices the country has made. The insights from *America's Midlife Crisis* will support each of us in making the myriad decisions that will ultimately lead to the success of our global society."

—Nancy J. Adler, S. Bronfman Chair in Management, McGill University, Montreal, Canada, and author of *From Boston to Beijing: Managing with a Worldview*

"This book is a must-read and provides pragmatic insight into America's complex role here at home and aboard. Rigorously researched, this is a truly remarkable contribution, a rare and enormously useful study offering fresh and compelling views of our diverse and racial identities. Splendid scholarship prevails; Weaver and Mendelson discuss how history has helped shape our domestic and international policies, ideals, culture and values. It is a pleasure to read, and I highly recommended it for scholars, students, policy makers and general audiences alike."

—Dr. Jack G. Shaheen, author of *GUILTY: Hollywood's Verdict on Arabs after 9/11*

"In this era of spin and hyperbole, it is refreshing to read such a calm, insightful and cogent analysis of this critical period in our history."

—Harriet Fulbright, president of the J. William & Harriet Fulbright Center

"*America's Midlife Crisis* is a provocative, thoughtful book offering a multifaceted and compelling understanding of America at the dawn of the new century. This book is essential reading for anyone — within or beyond America's borders — who is trying to understand the country's foreign policy and the culture behind it. Weaver and Mendelson show us where we have been, and also where we are headed. It is a timely book, yet one that will continue to be well thumbed through by readers for years to come."

—Wendy Chamberlin, former US Ambassador to Pakistan and Laos and president of the Middle East Institute

"The prism of culture, particularly when focused on changing values, beliefs and attitudes, presents a revealing vehicle for gaining new insights into the American experience. Gary Weaver and Adam Mendelson make the most of this intriguing approach to understanding America's successes and failures—and its prospects."

—Lawrence E. Harrison, Director, Cultural Change Institute, The Fletcher School, Tufts University

11/22/08
To Ros,
Great spending the evening with you! Enjoy! Gary Weaver

AMERICA'S MID★LIFE CRISIS

The Future of a Troubled Superpower

Gary R. Weaver

Adam Mendelson

INTERCULTURAL PRESS
A Nicholas Brealey Publishing Company

BOSTON • LONDON

First published by Intercultural Press, a division of Nicholas Brealey Publishing, in 2008.

Nicholas Brealey Publishing	Nicholas Brealey Publishing
20 Park Plaza, Suite 1115A	3-5 Spafield Street, Clerkenwell
Boston, MA 02116, USA	London, EC1R 4QB, UK
Tel: + 617-523-3801	Tel: +44-(0)-207-239-0360
Fax: + 617-523-3708	Fax: +44-(0)-207-239-0370
www.interculturalpress.com	www.nicholasbrealey.com

Printed in the United States of America

12   11   10   09   08   1   2   3   4   5

ISBN: 978-1-931930-07-9

Library of Congress Cataloging-in-Publication Data

Weaver, Gary R. (Gary Rodger), 1943–
    America's midlife crisis : the future of a troubled superpower / Gary R. Weaver, Adam Mendelson.
        p. cm.
    Includes bibliographical references and index.
    ISBN 978-1-931930-07-9
    1. United States—Civilization—1970–   2. National characteristics, American.   3. United States—Social conditions—1980–   4. Social change—United States.   5. Social values—United States.   6. Political culture—United States.   7. United States—Foreign relations—1989–   8. United States—Politics and government—1989–   I. Mendelson, Adam. II. Title.   III. Title: America's mid-life crisis.

E169.12.W38 2008
973.92—dc22

                                                    2008018778

Acknowledgments

*I*t seems that every book has some kind of acknowledgments statement. Some authors thank their husbands, wives, children, and the family dog. Others thank their editors, co-workers, and lawyers. Thus, we must acknowledge the support others have given us over the past year or so. We are indeed very grateful to many friends and family members who helped us write this book.

The one person without whom this book would never have been written is Trish O'Hare. Her endless patience, encouragement, enthusiasm, and support kept us writing in spite of a few setbacks. Her ongoing commitment to this book made it happen. Most of all we value her friendship.

Thanks also go to Chuck Dresner, Erika Heilman, and the rest of the team at Intercultural Press. Their professionalism and infectious enthusiasm helped to bring about the successful completion of the book. We also owe a debt of gratitude to Karen Santiago, for her conception and creation of the "new" iceberg graphics included in this book, and to Dan Deming for his crack proofreading job. We would also like to thank everyone who reviewed the book for their time and their comments.

In addition, Gary would like to thank his family and friends who put up with his crankiness during the ups and downs of this project. His wife Marte, daughter Alia, and friends Les Fox and Gary Wright were incredibly tolerant and understanding.

Adam would like to thank Gary and Trish for the confidence they displayed in him by bringing him on board for the book. It's been a wonderful experience for which he is deeply grateful. A tremendous amount of gratitude goes to his friends and family, not only for their enthusiasm and suggestions, but also for their promises to buy lots of copies once the book came out. Their excitement about this book has been heartfelt and humbling. Special thanks are due to Katie, whose encouragement and support was infallible and beyond value in this project, as it is always; to his parents, Barbara and Peter, who are the best role models, parents, and friends that one could hope for; and to his grandmother Ruth, a perpetual inspiration to all whose lives she has touched to do, learn, and live as much as and as well as possible.

Contents

INTRODUCTION

9/11 — A Challenge to American Culture

ALMOST EVERY WEEK FOR THE PAST 30 YEARS, I have spoken to foreign audiences of diplomats, government officials, journalists, scholars, and students about various aspects of American culture. I have tried to explain how and why Americans see the world the way they do, why we behave as we do on both the personal and public level, and how we communicate with each other and the rest of the world. Most important, I'm often asked to explain American public policy.

Whether I'm overseas or speaking to groups in the United States, I usually don't feel obligated to defend American behavior or public policy. Instead, the ultimate purpose of my talks is to provide some understanding of Americans. I want to help others to understand why we do what we do within the context of American historical experiences and traditional cultural values.

I find that most people from other countries know a great deal about American history, the economy of the United States, and our political issues. They are very aware of American foreign policy because it impacts people around the globe. While it is certainly true that their sources of information, especially movies and television, often distort their understanding of the United States, still they know more about my country than most Americans know about any other country beyond their own.

Over the years I've discovered that people from other nations admire many of the "good things" Americans have done, such as assisting countries to get on their feet after World War II or defending and supporting the economically and politically oppressed around the world. Citizens of other countries even share and emulate many of our traditional values such as egalitarianism, individual freedom, and democracy. Of course, from the perspective of their own national experiences, they are also critical of many of the "bad things" the United States has done such as military, political, and economic intervention in other countries' internal affairs or flooding the world with our entertainment media. They are also quick to note that, given its enormous economic, military, and political power, the United States has not helped others enough.

On balance, I have found that people are fair. They realize that any country will do good and bad over time and they realize that when a powerful country makes a mistake, it impacts the rest of the world. For example, because of its myriad ties with the American economy, many people in Latin America know the old saying that "When the United States gets an economic cold, the rest of the hemisphere suffers economic pneumonia."

Most people in foreign countries are able to separate the policies and behavior of the United States government from the values and beliefs of individual Americans. When others criticize some aspect of American foreign policy, I often hear the comment, "We really like the American people and we know they are good people, but we can't accept the policy of your government." To an American, this comment often sounds rather strange because we Americans have trouble making this kind of distinction, but I have usually taken it as a compliment. Quantitative data has backed up my own anecdotal experiences. Over the last several years, one of the countries that the U.S. has had the most difficult relations with is Iran. Tensions have been high, and negative popular and official portrayals of each country have been commonplace in the other. It may not be surprising, then, to learn that in a December 2006 poll, only 5 percent of Iranians viewed the U.S. government favorably. In the same poll, however, 45 percent of Iranians still viewed the American people favorably, showing that even the population of one of our supposedly most intransigent antagonists clearly distinguishes between the people of the U.S. and its government.[1]

President Clinton was well-liked by people around the globe and viewed as a world leader who supported international organizations and collaboration with other countries to limit the nuclear arms race. He worked diligently to bring Israelis and Palestinians together in peace talks and he supported global efforts to protect the environment. While he did engage in military action in Kosovo, he won the support of many nations around the world as he tried to build and strengthen new nations in the former Yugoslav Republic.

Especially in Europe, people were surprised by the political reaction of many Americans to President Clinton's sexual affair with an intern. This was viewed as a personal matter and certainly not a reason to impeach the leader of the most powerful nation in the post–Cold War era. Throughout the famous Lewinsky hearings before Congress, Clinton's popularity actually grew around the world and even in the United States.

I think it is fair to say that most people outside the United States were mystified and even shocked with the election of President George W. Bush in 2000. He seemed to be inexperienced with world affairs and campaigned against "nation building" and international treaties such as the anti-ballistic missile treaty and the Kyoto Accords on climate change. For many around the world, it was not entirely clear that he was actually elected to the presidency because of his razor-thin—and controversial—electoral victory.

Immediately after the terrible tragedy of September 11, 2001, when about 3,000 innocent people were killed by terrorists, most of the world supported the American people and endorsed President Bush's global effort to find those responsible. Almost all people worldwide wanted to stop terrorism—not only in the United States, but around the globe. Both as a catch-phrase and an idea, 9/11 will go down in history as a turning point for Americans because we no longer felt safely protected from enemies by the two vast oceans bordering our country. The rest of the world understood this.[2]

Following 9/11, the United States developed policies that made it more difficult for foreigners to get visas, and people suspected of aiding terrorists were arrested or questioned using practices that seemed to violate many basic civil rights protected by the U.S. Constitution. I found that many people from other countries understood that when people in any country feel threatened, their government will develop policies aimed to restore security but at the same time restrict individual freedom. However, after a few months or years, people assume these restricted rights will be restored.

During President Bush's first term of office, following the events of 9/11, and the wars in Afghanistan and Iraq, I still met citizens of other countries who expressed the clear distinction between their opinion of the American government and their opinion of the American people. However, they wanted to know if the American people really supported President Bush and his policies. The clear demarcation between "the American people" and the "policies of the government" was beginning to blur.

Following the reelection of President Bush in 2004, people began to ask me, "Why did you reelect him? What's wrong with you people?" On the day following Bush's reelection, the headline of the British paper *The Daily Mirror* read "How can 59,054,087 people be so DUMB?" For the first time in my life, people in other countries were not making the previously common distinction between the American government and the American people. People from other countries could not understand how the American people could accept the torture and humiliation of prisoners by American military personnel at Abu Ghraib prison in Iraq or the detention and interrogation of prisoners at Guantanamo Bay prison in Cuba without respect to the Geneva Convention. People from other countries could not understand why the American people would give their federal government the authority to invade their privacy and even arrest and hold people while ignoring the rights guaranteed under their own Constitution. Of course, part of the answer is because the American people were insecure, particularly on the heels of 9/11.

Deep down I know that most people around the world understand that the United States government and the American people are still reacting to the attacks of 9/11. For the first time in over a generation, we Americans are afraid that our enemies can destroy our cities and our way of life. *Fear* is the single word that best characterizes the sentiment of the American people and is used to justify many government policies since 9/11. The security that Americans felt after the end of the Cold War disappeared within hours with the collapse of the two towers at the World Trade Center, the passenger plane slamming into the side of the Pentagon and another nosediving into a field in rural Pennsylvania.

During the Cold War in the 1950s and 1960s, the fear of a nuclear attack against the United States was as great as the present fear of terrorists after 9/11. In most cities, buildings that possibly could withstand the destruction of atomic bombs were designated as air raid shelters. School children went through air raid drills during which they would respond to civil defense sirens by hiding under their desks. Many Americans constructed underground fallout shelters in their basements and backyards, fully equipped with ventilation, water, and food to last for an extended period. During that fear-filled time many innocent people were accused of being traitors or Communist sympathizers. With the collapse of the Soviet Union, this fear of domestic destruction evaporated. Yet in the space of a few hours on September 11, 2001, a similar fear reemerged with a vengeance. No longer did the two oceans and the tremendous economic and military power of the United States protect us. While this insecurity may be unfounded and almost paranoid, it has changed the United States and its policies. To understand the nature of these changes, to predict if they are only temporary or long-term, and to understand how these changes occurred, we have set out in this book to examine the history, and most important, the culture of the American people.

—Gary Weaver, April 2008

CHAPTER 1

American National Culture

A Matter of Culture and History

The longer you look back, the farther you can look forward.

—WINSTON CHURCHILL

SINCE THE VERY BEGINNING OF THE NATION, Americans have always been confident that their economic and political system was better than those of most other countries, and that theirs was an exceptional nation. In 1630 John Winthrop, among the early Puritan leaders of settlers in Massachusetts, borrowed a phrase from the Book of Matthew to inspire his compatriots. "We shall find that the God of Israel is among us," Winthrop promised. "He shall make us a praise and glory that men shall say of succeeding plantations, 'the Lord make it like . . . that of New England.' . . . We shall be as a city upon a hill. The eyes of all people are upon us." The subsequent continual economic growth and political stability in this very young nation was considered as evidence that somehow the United States indeed *was* an exceptional country with exceptional people.

The phrase "city upon a hill," and the idea behind it—that America should be a beacon for all humanity—has echoed down through the ages, always finding resonance within the American sense of exceptionalism. Ronald Reagan described his vision of the city as "a tall proud city built on rocks stronger than oceans, wind-swept, God-blessed, and teeming with people of all kinds living in harmony and peace, a city with free ports that hummed with commerce and creativity, and if there had to be city walls, the walls had doors and the doors were open to anyone with the will and the heart to get here." While Reagan emphasized the city's inclusiveness and prosperity, John F. Kennedy drew parallels between the difficult task of creating a model government in an unforgiving world in both Winthrop's time and his own: "But I have been guided by the standard John Winthrop set before his shipmates on the flagship *Arbella* three hundred and thirty-one years ago, as they, too, faced the task of building a new government on a perilous frontier. 'We must always consider,' he said, 'that we shall be as a city upon a hill—the eyes of all people are upon us.' . . . For we are setting out upon a voyage in 1961 no less hazardous than that undertaken by the *Arbella* in 1630. We are committing ourselves to tasks of statecraft no less awesome than that of governing the Massachusetts Bay Colony, beset as it was then by terror without and disorder within."

Between Winthrop's time and the present, the American civic culture has endured through many national crises. There were economic recessions, a very violent Civil War, and numerous wars overseas, yet it seemed that after each national crisis the nation only grew stronger. In his second inaugural address, President Bill Clinton described this as a process of becoming "a more perfect union." The traditional national values and beliefs have proven to be very resilient and have been firmly held throughout the history of the United States, and these values and beliefs have resulted in a very unique nation, much as Winthrop predicted and Reagan and Kennedy confirmed.

Nevertheless, all national cultures change and grow, and certainly the United States and its people have been dramatically impacted by the terrorist attacks of September 11, 2001. But, how much has the country changed since that tragedy? Are these changes likely to be short lived or long term? Has the confidence of the American people been undermined by the events of 9/11? Has the civic culture been permanently altered following the creation of the new Department of Homeland Security and the passage of the Patriot Act?

American historian Arthur M. Schlesinger Jr. wrote that "History is to the nation as memory is to the individual. As persons deprived of memory become disoriented and lost, not knowing where they are . . . going, so a nation denied a conception of the past will be disabled in dealing with its present and its future."[1] We cannot tell where we are today, or where we will be tomorrow, unless we know from where we have come. Therefore, to consider how the United States has changed since the terrorist attacks on September 11, we must first consider traditional worldviews, values, and beliefs that shape the public policies of the United States. Traditional cultural values and historical experiences shared by the nation shape the way its people respond to a traumatic national event.

The purpose of our book is to place in a cultural context the behavior and public policy of the American people. Many books have been written for American business people, government officials, diplomats, and scholars to help them understand other countries. These books range from a list of dos-and-don'ts and business etiquette, to more substantive historical, sociological, and anthropological books that try to explain the underlying cultural values and beliefs that motivate the behavior of people and their governments.

Of course, there are also books such as these written about the United States. Ironically, some of the very best are quite old and were written by foreigners, such as the French political thinker and historian Alexis de Tocqueville's classic *Democracy in America* written in two volumes in 1835 and 1840, and the Swedish economist, sociologist, and Nobel Prize winner Gunnar Myrdall's 1944 book *An American Dilemma: The Negro Problem in Modern Democracy*. It is difficult for people in their own country to objectively write about its history or basic cultural values, In fact, most people are unaware of their own culture until they leave it and this is especially true for Americans because the vast majority have never left the shores of the country. Foreigners have an outsider vision, which allows them to be very perceptive and perhaps more objective observers of a host culture. While our book in no way comes close to either the comprehensiveness or the depth and breadth of the analysis of these famous foreign authors, it is nevertheless intended to modestly give some insight into contemporary American behavior on both the individual and public levels.

Many of the books written about the United States have been either primarily historical or cultural in nature. Very few bring the historical and cultural approaches together to explain contemporary behavior.

The overarching framework for this book is a combination of historical sociology and cultural anthropology. To explain why people behave as they do, we must understand their psychological and anthropological makeup. Our approach must be interdisciplinary because it requires us to examine American sociological, economic, and political systems. This also requires an exploration of American historical experiences in the context of the nation's physical environment and resources. All of these factors are completely interconnected, and no single factor can adequately explain the American people's behavior or the public policies of their government.

The Importance of Culture

We first need to consider some cultural concepts that will allow us to frame much of the interpretation and analysis of American public and personal behavior. There are thousands of definitions for the word *culture* because it is an abstraction or a concept, not a thing. It is intangible and inside our heads. We cannot see or touch a culture, yet we know it exists because people within the same society tend to view the world in similar ways. They share many basic values and beliefs. They even seem to think alike and solve problems with common approaches or strategies. Culture makes this happen.

When most Americans use the word *culture* they are referring to a way of life, including basic values, beliefs, and worldviews, which is passed down from one generation to another through learning. No one is born with a culture. While a person may be born in America or in Malaysia, they are not born with a set of preprogrammed American or Malaysian cultural characteristics. Rather, we acquire our primary culture very informally by growing up in a particular family in a particular society. Parents do not sit down at the dining room table and tell their children, "These are our values in the United States." Rather, the children learn their basic cultural values through their interaction with and observations of others, beginning with their family. Moreover, children's and folk literature are usually filled with cultural traditions, mores, and admonitions shared by almost everyone in a particular culture.

For many people the word *culture* also means art, music, literature, and history. But, these are really the relics or results of culture. We can examine the art, music, literature, and history of a people and infer that they have a system of values, beliefs, and behavior but these artifacts are not what we usually mean when they say the word "culture." Nevertheless, these products of a culture provide us with a way to begin to understand the underlying values, beliefs, and worldview of a people.

External and Internal Culture

Culture is like an iceberg.[2] The tip protruding above the surface is only a tiny fraction of the total size of the iceberg. Most of it is under water and hidden. The same is true of culture. That which you can easily see—the behavior and products of people including their customs, language, food, art, and so forth—is actually the smallest part of culture. This might be considered *external* culture, while the most significant part of culture is *internal* or inside our heads.

This internal culture encompasses our way of thinking or how we organize information to solve problems, how we perceive or interpret reality, and most importantly, the values and beliefs that were unconsciously learned while growing up in a particular society. These values, beliefs, and ways of thinking in turn shape or determine most of our behavior. We are unaware of our internal culture because it is learned through the process of informal socialization during our formative years. We become aware of our internal culture when we experience the disorientation and confusion of leaving our own culture and entering another. Many sojourners report that they first became aware of their own culture and how it controlled their behavior, beliefs, and values when they left home to go to college, the military, or to live in another culture.

We could add other dimensions to this model. For example, beliefs are slightly above and below the water level of awareness. Some of our beliefs are learned consciously or explicitly and some are acquired unconsciously or implicitly and they are not always in agreement. For example, in a village in the Middle East, we might discover children learning their Muslim religious beliefs by formally reciting and memorizing the Quran just as many Christians learn their religious beliefs through the process of Catechism or Jews through preparing for their bar or bat mitzvah.

On the other hand, any five-year-old Iraqi child knows that God exists long before learning to read. This is because this belief was acquired informally and implicitly simply because the child can speak Arabic. Many greetings or expressions of gratitude have the word *God* in them. For example, a student might say, "I will pass this examination, *insha'allah* (God willing)" and "I passed the examination, *al-hamdulilah* (thanks be to God)." Because the child has learned to speak Arabic, he has already acquired a belief in the existence of God. Specific religious beliefs learned overtly can change with new experiences or information, but the belief in the existence of God seldom changes because it is so deeply internalized and unconscious.

It is possible to hold inconsistent or conflicting beliefs. For example, one might profoundly believe in the sanctity of human life and still support the death penalty for murder out of a belief in justice or order.

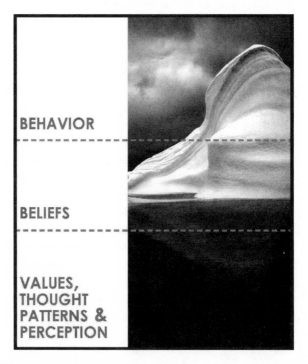

FIGURE 1.1 The image of an iceberg illustrates the relationship between internal and external culture. Copyright Gary R. Weaver.

While the respect and reverence one holds for human life may never change, it is possible that with the information that the death penalty does not deter crime or large numbers of innocent people have been put to death, a person may oppose the death penalty. Americans value both freedom and order, and yet these values often conflict. During times of stability and peace, individual freedom becomes more salient than public order whereas during times of military threat and insecurity, public order becomes more important than individual freedom.

At the base of the iceberg, "thought patterns" refer to *conceptions* or systems of logic: how we organize information to solve problems and deal with the world.[3] In addition, which information gets into our head is in large part determined by our culture.

Culture Shapes Perception

Internal culture must include *perceptions*. What information we pay attention to and how we organize and interpret that information depends upon our culture. In fact, Marshall Singer believes that culture can be understood in terms of shared perceptions.[4] People from the same culture usually perceive the world in similar ways and give similar meanings to symbols. Thus, people from different cultures might look at the same object and derive entirely different meanings.

Singer also believes that when we share a way of perceiving reality with others, we also shares their culture. Culture could be understood as a group who share a way of looking at the world and give similar meanings to the same messages or symbols. In turn, these people share an identity. When we say, "as Americans we look at the situation this way," we are also claiming that we belong to a group called "Americans," who shares a worldview and we identify with this group.

In a classic perception study conducted by James Bagby, Americans and Mexicans were asked to look into a stereoscope where the picture of a bullfight and a baseball player were projected simultaneously, one to each eye. Their description of what they saw almost always corresponded to one of the monocular fields, with the result that only one of the two images was seen by most participants in the experiment. The typical Mexican saw a bullfight, the American a baseball player.[5]

Thus, our experiences condition us to notice some things and ignore others: to see or perceive reality in a particular way. The image that forms in our mind is a combination of "objective" reality and our own cultural expectations, which filter that reality. Selective awareness or perception is just one example of the pervasive influence of culture on the individual.

The terms *culture* and *civilization* are often used interchangeably and yet they are very different.[6] Samuel Huntington writes about seven contemporary civilizations[7] that are in conflict, but his civilizations are defined primarily by a common religion such as Islam, Christian Orthodox, or Confucian whereas other scholars would consider these typical of "cultures." He is certainly correct in assuming that cultures (or civilizations) are not necessarily restricted to national boundaries but, on the other hand, a civilization contains many cultures and a single nation could have a wide variety of cultures.

A *civilization* usually spans hundreds or thousands of years, it includes many different cultures and it is not restricted to national boundaries. For example, one might speak of a Western civilization, which includes many different cultures that have existed over thousands of years. While there may be an "American culture," it would be difficult to conceive of an "American civilization," because of the youth of the U.S. and the fact that the culture is mostly restricted by its national boundaries.

Many people from other areas of the world also see these as interchangeable terms and concepts. In fact, this often leads them to ask a question such as, "How could you begin to compare Egyptian culture with American culture?" You can't. There is an Egyptian civilization, which has existed over thousands of years with hundreds of cultures, but there is not a similar American civilization. There is, however, an American culture, which is certainly part of Western civilization.

To understand the external or overt aspects of the culture such as typical American behavior, customs, public policy, and even communication, we must begin with the internal aspects of traditional values and beliefs. We need to examine individual and public behavior within the context of Western civilization but, more specifically, within the unique historical experiences and values shared by most Americans in the United States. Of course, while there is an overarching dominant or mainstream culture shared by most Americans, we must continually remind ourselves that in a country of over 300 million people living in a continental landmass that is over 3,000 miles wide, there are a great many regional, racial, ethnic, and religious differences amongst various groups of Americans.

In the 1950s and 1960s, many authors wrote about American "national character."[8] While these studies have lost favor because they were often too sweeping in scope and were often overly stereotypical, it is possible to consider the basic values, beliefs, and worldviews shared by most Americans and across generations as part of the character of its people. Today, most scholars would simply use the term *culture*. When we speak of values, beliefs, and ways in which we identify and perceive ourselves as members of a nation, we are focusing on a national civic culture.

Culture is always a *generalization*. Whatever we might say to describe members of a culture could never apply to everyone, at all times, in every situation. However, just because we find exceptions to our generalization, there is no reason to discard the concept of culture. It is still very useful for explaining and predicting the behavior of people within a particular society, as long as we acknowledge these exceptions.

There is a vast difference between a cultural generalization and a *cultural stereotype*. When we stereotype, we make our generalization apply to everyone in the society without exception. Generalizations can be discarded when they are no longer useful or accurate for explaining the behavior of most people in a society. Stereotypes, on the other hand, are usually retained long after they have lost their accuracy or usefulness.[9] This book will be filled with generalizations that will help the reader to understand American political, social, economic, and personal behavior. But, we will try our very best to avoid stereotyping.

Primary and Secondary Cultures: Enculturation and Acculturation

No one is born with a culture. Rather, it is an unconscious phenomenon that we learn simply by growing up in a particular family in a particular society. Because it comes from our childhood experiences, we are usually unaware of its existence until later in life when we must interact with those who are culturally different. This *primary culture* tends to stay with us throughout our lifetime and is probably acquired long before we go to school. The process of learning our primary culture is usually referred to as *enculturation*.

Our culture gives us a sense of attachment or belonging; it defines who we are as a member of a group, and gives meaning to both the world and to our place within it. In other words, it is a primary source of our *identity*. This identity could be limited to a village or a civilization and it may include religion, class, region, or all of these characteristics. If that culture is contained within a single nation and shared by others in the state, we can even speak of a *national identity*. Furthermore, most Americans may have similar perceptions of the United States and the rest of the world, which we could refer to as a "national image."[10]

As we go through life, we join various other groups that also shape our perceptions, values and beliefs. These affiliations are *secondary cultures*, which we acquire or learn through the process of *acculturation*. They also give us a "sense of belonging" or identity. When we say, "as a Catholic, we look at the situation this way" we are actually saying "as a *member of the group we call Catholics, we share certain views, beliefs, and values*." No two human beings belong to exactly the same secondary cultures at exactly the same time. Thus, we are all culturally unique.[11]

One might assume that people join a political party in the United States because it best represents their interests, beliefs, and values. However, most research shows people inherit their party affiliation from their parents, or they join one in early adulthood because it is composed of people like themselves, and they stay with that party the rest of their lives. Party affiliation usually shapes interests, beliefs, and values, not the other way around.[12]

Once party affiliation is established, they bend their philosophies and perceptions of reality to fit this secondary culture. Membership in the party and even voting is no longer rational because partisanship becomes a filter that selects or levels out facts that are inconsistent with the party's accepted worldview and exaggerates or sharpens facts that confirm it. To this extent, a political party is like a religious denomination or any other secondary culture.[13]

While secondary cultures have a very powerful impact on the individual, the primary culture remains the most important because it is acquired much earlier, it is more deeply buried in our unconscious mind, and it shapes behavior and perception throughout our lives. This is a psychoanalytic way of viewing culture.

In Edward Hall's book *Beyond Culture*,[14] he defines culture as "mind" because it is inside our heads and includes the ways in which our society shapes our basic values, beliefs, thought patterns, perceptions, and even our feelings. How we learn and what we learn, how we use our senses to gather information, and how we organize that information to solve problems and cope with life, depend upon our culture.

Of course, we are all individuals. Each tree in the forest is different. Still, we also find commonalities between trees: *pine* trees, *maple* trees, *oak* trees, and so forth. We can acknowledge the individuality of each tree and still accept the reality that there exist categories of trees.

Internal Culture and Psychoanalysis

The iceberg model is actually a very psychoanalytic model of culture. Sigmund Freud often suggested that our personality is like an iceberg. The conscious part, which is observable, is the smallest part. The largest part is totally unconscious and yet it is the most important because it controls conscious behavior. To truly understand our personalities, we must focus on the unconscious.

Freud believed that traumatic events that occur during childhood fixate us at an immature stage of emotional growth and control our feelings and behaviors as adults. These events are repressed or buried in our unconscious. In Victorian times, these childhood events often involved sexuality which was greatly repressed and a source of tremendous guilt. This was by far the most sensational aspect of Freud's theory. However, the principles of psychoanalysis go far beyond childhood sexuality. The belief in the primacy of the formative years for shaping an individual's personality, including his or her basic values, attitudes, and worldviews, leads to an explanation for much of our behavior.

The motivations for our personal, social, political, and economic behavior and the attributions we give for the behavior of others were learned so early in life that we are unaware of their origins. For example, if someone had an authoritarian father, it is possible that later in life that person will have an irrational fear and dislike of all males in authority—teachers, police officers, or a boss—because they represent that person's father. This person is said to have an authoritarian personality. Very early in life, they learn to obey authority figures and assume that there is a great power distance between superiors and subordinates. Furthermore, when they become adults and have power or authority over others, they expect obedience.

Some political psychologists claim that if an entire society raises its children in a similar way, and the child-raising practices are authoritarian, you can actually have an authoritarian society that is very hierarchical, where there is great distance between subordinates and superiors, and people tend to obey orders and expect others to obey them when they have power.[15]

As adults, we can only escape the childhood traumas and fears that control our lives when we can remember these experiences. Through a process of free association, the psychoanalyst helps us to enter the unconscious and raise these memories to conscious awareness where, as adults, we can rationally understand what happened to us during our formative years and transcend these experiences. We then are free of the irrational fears of the past and can resume emotional growth. This is an interesting paradox—we find our self when we leave our everyday life and enter into a relationship with the psychoanalyst where we analyze and interpret those experiences and fears that are deeply buried in our past and our unconscious. We move to the future by remembering the past and we escape childhood irrational fears that have imprisoned us by using rationality and the conscious awareness of an adult.

We are all prisoners of the culture of our childhood and yet we are usually unaware of that prison until we leave it. The best way to find one's own internal culture is to interact with people in other cultures. The icebergs of each person's culture collide not at the tip but rather at the base. Through this collision of cultures, we raise to conscious awareness the values of others and our own values, and we naturally contrast and compare these values and ways of thinking. We ask the question "why"—"Why do they do and say those things?" At the same time we must also ask ourselves, "And, why do we react the way we do?" The only way to answer these questions is to focus our attention on significant internal cultural values. More importantly, this process allows us to escape or transcend the cultural prisons that we were born into.

Throughout American history, Americans have been very domestic-centered rather than concerned with international issues. Except during times of international conflict or to promote American commerce, domestic political interests have been much more important than international affairs. Few Americans have even sojourned overseas in their lifetime. For most Americans, because their national cultural iceberg so rarely collides with others, we can understand their relative lack of awareness of their own culture and many other cultures.

Fela, the famous Nigerian jazz artist, once commented that he was unaware of what it meant to be an African until he left Africa. Similarly, the renowned Irish writer James Joyce went into voluntary exile in order to better understand his home country and culture. On the other hand, most Americans have never left the United States. Only around 21 percent have passports.[16] In 1998 a journalist asked Congressman Dick Armey, one of the most powerful members of the House of Representatives, if he intended to go overseas. He answered,

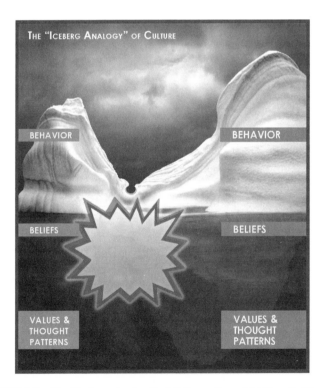

FIGURE 1.2   The "Iceberg Analogy" of Culture. Copyright Gary R. Weaver.

"I've been to Europe once. I don't have to go again."[17] As late as 2003, President George W. Bush had never traveled to Berlin or Paris. But, this is typical of most Americans. The American iceberg rarely collides with others.

As a country, the United States has had a very prolonged and sheltered childhood and adolescence. The newly emerging nation was initially populated by white, Anglo-Saxon Protestants (WASPs). Others gave up their home languages and customs to fit into the dominant WASP culture. The dominant culture did not actually encourage cultural pluralism. Rather, the immigrant had to assimilate to the mainstream society by giving up their differences.

In the West, there was a strong Spanish colonial influence that still exists today. However, even in areas that today comprise the states of Texas and California, English became the dominant language. Although external cultural characteristics of the Spanish and Mexican cultures are certainly present today in terms of food, music, and even the presence of Spanish as a second language, most immigrants in the West shared many of the basic values that are attributed to mainstream Americans. In addition, most of these early Americans were economically successful within one or two generations and, protected behind two enormous oceans, the country grew without much influence from the rest of the world.

Eventually, as the United States went out into the world in terms of commerce and military adventures, Americans became aware of their national culture and developed a clearer national identity. They have begun to see themselves as part of an international system of nations and they have developed realistic empathy toward other nations. This new adulthood has emerged very slowly, however, and with many growing pains. Americans are becoming seasoned by their interactions with other nations and only in the last century has the United States grown into a real adulthood.

Culture Is a System

Culture is not simply a collection of unrelated customs, rituals, ceremonies, values, beliefs, attitudes, and thought patterns but rather an integrated composite of all of these elements passed down from generation to generation. Each element is associated with the others and together forms a dynamic whole.

A system is a group of elements interrelated by communication links and the whole operating as one to reach a goal. If we add more elements to the system, we must add more communication links. This definition would apply to any system: social, physical, or biological. Both the parts and links between the parts are important; if any of these elements fails, the entire system shuts down.

The American society is a social system where status is determined by a person's economic achievement (or perhaps ancestry) and is a set of elaborate spoken and unspoken rules regarding appropriate behavior that are commonly accepted. The introduction of new technology changes social systems in ways that are not always anticipated. For example, consider the introduction of the automobile in the United States. It was not simply a vehicle that allowed for increased physical mobility. Certainly, people could easily travel to other parts of the country, but the car also became a status symbol, and it provided a way for teenagers to escape the watchful eyes of their parents. The size or price of the automobile was often equated with power and success, and even manhood. When a son had to ask to use the family automobile to go on a date, the father's role as "keeper of the keys" was firmly established. When the son could own his own automobile, he was now independent and self-reliant and a grown-up man. Furthermore, parents no longer knew what their adolescent children were doing when they went on dates or where they were doing it.

The automobile allowed people to leave their hometowns and move to nearby cities or take jobs tens of miles from home. This meant that they had to establish new ways of maintaining communication with loved ones. The use of the telephone increased but people still had difficulty keeping in touch with family and friends and the amount of face-to-face communication decreased. While it gave everyone a greater sense of freedom and independence, it also created more social distance between loved ones. In many ways, the automobile changed the American society as much as airplanes and modern electronic communication and information have changed the world.

The penetration of new inputs usually changes any system: economic, social, or political. Elements rearrange themselves and new links between elements often develop. As a cultural system becomes more complex, the number and types of communication links between individuals must increase. If the system becomes overloaded, some individuals may feel cut off or alienated from the total culture.

We must, therefore, consider very carefully the total system and its overall stability when we introduce inputs from other cultures. If we understand the makeup of a culture, we can loosely predict what a foreign input will do. Most importantly we must understand that cultures are constantly changing and, of course, increasingly interacting.

Change is clearly one of the foremost characteristics of the American cultural system. The earliest settlers coming from Europe wanted change—a new way of life or culture—and the continual influx of immigrants throughout American history has contributed to the diversity of the overall culture today. Each group brings about some change to the overall cultural system. Increasing urbanization, demographic shifts, and dramatic changes caused by modern technology and communication have all been hallmarks of the American culture. And yet these components are interrelated and impact each other. The whole is much more than simply the sum of the parts. It is this "whole" that will be referred to as the "mainstream" or "dominant" culture of the United States.

Realistic Cultural Empathy

The economic, political, social, and personal behavior of the American people can only be understood within the context of their unique culture. The traditional beliefs and worldviews of the American people, and even the way they think and solve problems, are all shaped by their shared historical experiences and their common cultural values.

It is almost impossible to explain or predict a person's behavior unless we know how they perceive the world and how they solve problems. In other words, we cannot understand what an individual says or does until we get inside that person's head. Most importantly, we cannot predict how a person will respond to what we say or do without knowing how that individual thinks.

The ability to understand the perceptions of others, and their beliefs, values, and ways of thinking, is *empathy*.[18] When we are empathetic we can put ourselves in the "psychological shoes" of others. It would be impossible to realistically explain the behavior of another person without some empathic skills.

To explain the public behavior and policy of any society we must have *realistic cultural empathy* or the ability to put ourselves not only into the people's psychological, but also their cultural, "shoes." From a psychological perspective, we all understand the importance of getting inside another person's head to fully explain his or her behavior. People from the same culture share many customs, values, beliefs, ways of communicating, patterns of thinking, and worldviews, and this in turn shapes their aggregated, collective public behavior and policy.

Consider an example to illustrate this point. The word *freedom* to an average American usually means individual freedom. Among the early Calvinist settlers, there was a strong belief that the individual is paramount and has a direct relationship with his or her God. This fit nicely with the later belief that in a capitalist economy every individual ought to be free to excel economically. In the American version of democracy, not only should each individual's vote count equally, but the rights of individual Americans must be protected from an overly powerful central government. This is what Americans mean when they use the phrase "individual civil rights."

During the June 1989 student rally in Tiananmen Square, the symbolic center of China, many Americans pointed to the image of a student standing before a line of Chinese tanks as epitomizing the concept of individual freedom. It appeared that this young man was bravely risking his life and standing up to overwhelming power. Posters of this famous "Tank Man" photo can be purchased in many stores throughout the United States today. Yet for many Chinese this was simply some young man who was either incredibly self-centered and egotistical or crazy. In their culture, standing out from the group decreases the significance of the unity of a shared effort. It would be viewed as look-at-me showboating *and* taking an irrational risk.

In China, a more poignant image that became very popular was that of a group of three students—some of them on their knees—ascending the steps of a government building to present a petition to their government "elders." This reflected the practice of honoring elders and respecting the collective values of traditional Chinese culture instead of individualistic grandstanding. However, to an American audience, this image—emphasizing collectivism and respect for authority—was met with little attention or cultural resonance. For an American or Chinese person to interpret each picture according to their own cultural values takes little effort. However, for them to understand how and why each picture resonates in the other's culture, realistic cultural empathy is required.

It is important to realize that *empathy is not sympathy.*[19] Empathy is primarily cognitive, not affective. Empathy requires understanding how another person thinks and perceives the world. It is very realistic and practical; unless we know how an individual thinks, we cannot explain or predict his or her behavior. On the other hand, sympathy is affective and primarily external, rather than internal. For example, we may feel sorry for another's misfortune without really knowing how that person thinks or feels—without *empathizing* with him or her.

We should also note that *empathy is not agreement with.* We do not have to agree with another person's political or religious beliefs, worldview, or system of logic, yet we can still explain and understand his or her behavior. Muslims may not agree with Christians on many religious matters, and yet they can still understand why Christians might find certain comments offensive.

Unfortunately, we are often confronted with incidents betraying a lack of cultural empathy. For example, in 2006 the Danish newspaper *JP* published 12 satirical cartoons featuring images of the Prophet Muhammad and various symbols of Islam. These provoked outrage, violence, and condemnation in many parts of the Muslim world. For many non-Muslim Westerners, this was a matter of free speech and freedom of the press, and the Muslim reaction was granted little empathy. For many non-Western Muslims the publication of these drawings was an insult to their religion and highly disrespectful, and the justifications offered for their publication similarly did not receive much empathy.

And finally, *empathy is not identification with or being like the other person.* Most Mexicans would find it very odd to encounter an American living in a village who tries to act more Mexican than a native by wearing sandals made from tire treads or eating such spicy Mexican food that tears stream from his eyes.

When they relate to one another, people from different cultures often use some sort of cultural profile as a sort of shortcut for empathy. These sketches or profiles might list characteristic behaviors or customs, religions, ethnic compositions, and so on. They offer a great deal of information but little understanding. Information usually means simply knowing *what* people in the culture do; understanding includes knowing *why* they do it. To understand why people in a particular culture or society or nation behave as they do, we must have realistic cultural empathy—not a list of dos-and-don'ts.

Understanding Americans

A list of American customs and taboos may be useful for describing general American behavior, but it will never be accurate for all Americans. The word *culture*, by definition, is always a generalization, and it usually refers to national culture or the set of perceptions, values, beliefs, and behaviors shared by most people in a nation. We attempt to subsume regional and ethnic differences into a set of universally shared behaviors and customs. While there are certainly a great many customs and taboos shared by most Americans, the United States is also very ethnically diverse and has many regional differences. The list of our customs and taboos is useful as long as it is accurate and we accept that it would never apply to every American, all of the time, in every situation. But it is only a beginning and really does not give us complete understanding. When this list is no longer accurate for *most* Americans, it ought to be discarded because it is a stereotype. When we base our thoughts and actions on stereotypes we act as though our generalizations apply to everyone all of the time, without exceptions, and we often hang onto these generalizations long after they have lost their usefulness or their accuracy.

The Importance of History

Henry Ford once said "History is bunk." His comment does indeed reflect a common American attitude toward the past—that it is irrelevant. What is important to Americans is the future. Early immigrants left their pasts, in their native countries and began anew looking to a better future for themselves and their children and, as we shall discuss, this focus on the future has developed into a key cultural value of

Americans. All the same, how can we really understand where we are going unless we reflect upon from where we have come? Can we really disconnect the past from the present or the future?

It is almost impossible to explain national behavior without referring to the history of the nation. Their ahistorical and future-time orientation puts Americans at a great disadvantage in understanding other people and their cultures.[20] On the other hand, Arthur Schlesinger Jr. warns that all "historians are prisoners of their own experience." Because they view history through the lens of their experiences, they cannot claim to represent the absolute truth. "So the historian is committed to a doomed enterprise—the quest for an unattainable objectivity." Nevertheless, Schlesinger asserts, a great power cannot ignore history because it "is the best antidote to delusions of omnipotence and omniscience. Self-knowledge is the indispensable prelude to self-control, for the nation as well as for the individual, and history should forever remind us of the limit of our passing perspectives."[21]

As we write this book, the United States is caught up in one of its gravest foreign policy crises since the Vietnam War. To truly understand the Iraq War and predict where the United States will be in the near future, we must humbly attempt to understand our own history and to place our policy in historical perspective. As Schlesinger has also written, "The great strength of history in a free society is its capacity for self-correction . . . in the end, a nation's history must be both the guide and the domain not so much of its historians as its citizens."

CHAPTER 2

What Is the American Culture and What Is a "Typical" American?

Let every nation know, whether it wishes us well or ill, that we shall pay any price, bear any burden, meet any hardship, support any friend, oppose any foe in order to assure the survival and success of liberty.

—JOHN F. KENNEDY

IF YOU STOPPED AN AVERAGE AMERICAN WALKING down the street and asked him or her, "What is *the* American culture," the person would probably be very surprised by the question. It is not the kind of question an American would ask another American, because generally we don't think about our culture very much. We can easily picture Parisians sitting in cafes having endless discussions about what it *really* means to be French. But, it is highly unlikely that you would hear Americans having this kind of conversation in a restaurant, or anywhere else.

Most Americans take their own culture for granted. Just as a fish is probably unaware of its aquatic environment until it is taken out of its pond, most people are not cognizant of their cultural environment as long as they are immersed within it. Americans seldom leave their own country. The earliest settlers sojourned thousands of miles from their homelands, and once they arrived, they found themselves isolated and insulated from the rest of the world by two large oceans. Few returned to their homeland or traveled to other countries. Even today, while it is true that the average American relocates at least 14 times in his or her lifetime, these moves are usually within the borders of the U.S. Most Americans never move their families overseas.

One can travel over 3,000 miles from the East to the West Coast of the United States and find that almost everyone still speaks the same language and eats basically the same food. In spite of many regional, racial, and ethnic differences, America is remarkably homogeneous. This explains, in part, the relative lack of awareness most Americans have of their own culture and other cultures. In Europe, and many other parts of the world, if you travel more than 500 miles in any direction, you will end up in another culture where people speak a different language and eat different food. Consequently, Europeans seem to be more aware of their own culture and the rest of the world.

Americans are often a bit sensitive or thin-skinned when it comes to hearing others making critical comments about the U.S. Although most Americans can be very self-critical and have little difficulty making disparaging comments about their government or its leaders, they often become very upset when people from other countries make the same remarks. The French are accustomed to hearing Germans make critical comments about French policies and the French people. Conversely, Germans often hear the French criticize Germany and its policies. But, Americans are unaccustomed to hearing people from other countries make critical comments about the U.S. Thus, we often find ourselves being very defensive even if others say the very same things that we have said about ourselves. Somewhat like a close-knit family, we don't mind when relatives say negative things about the family or a family member, but the neighbors ought not to say those things.

A question that has been raised by Americans since 9/11 is "Why do they hate us?" It is understandable for Americans that much of the Arab world would hate the U.S. because of its foreign policy (even if the reasons why, and the depth of these feelings, are generally not understood), but Americans do not understand why other people around the globe, including some of our closest allies in Europe, dislike

America. People from other countries often point out that they admire Americans and their ideals, but disagree with the foreign policies of the U.S. government. Furthermore, many of the comments that our friends have made about U.S. foreign policy are the same as those we have made about ourselves. Nevertheless, most Americans tend to consider negative comments about the U.S. government, or a specific leader, as hostility toward Americans in general and they simply are uncomfortable when foreign nationals make critical observations.

Most Americans want others to "like" them. They view the U.S. as a peaceful country that only fights wars to defend itself and others from tyranny and aggression. The criticism of the U.S. as an aggressor or even a hegemonic bully is seen as unfair. Many Europeans would view this as overly defensive, naive, even childish or narcissistic. All countries view themselves as peaceful nations that only use aggression to defend themselves and others. However, one result of the Iraq War, and the Vietnam War in the 1960s, is that Americans may find that they are similar to other mature nation-states and have foreign policies that primarily benefit their own national interests. And, with the best of intentions, all nations over time make mistakes. People in many other countries would say that it is time for America to "grow up."

Americans Are Not Europeans

If you pressed an average American to answer the question "What is *the* American culture?" the first answer might be "Americans are just watered-down Northern Europeans." Americans are "watered-down" because of the years of separation from Europe, but otherwise there is little difference between Americans and Northern Europeans.

The first immigrants who voluntarily came in large numbers to the Atlantic Coast were certainly from Northern Europe—the British Isles, France, and Holland—and they quickly established the dominant or mainstream society. These Northern European pilgrims established the original American colonies and nearly 300 years later, their ancestors fought the Revolutionary War that established the United States of America. The so-called "founding fathers" of the new nation were of Northern European stock who applied Enlightenment reason and

British concepts of democracy and jurisprudence to establish the new nation.

At the same time that Northern Europeans were landing on the East Coast, Spaniards also arrived on the Pacific Coast and in the Gulf of Mexico; but, the new nation grew from the East to the West. The Spanish influence on the national culture was greatest only after the mid-1800s. Indigenous or aboriginal natives, who were mistakenly labeled "American Indians" by the Northern European settlers, were here when the Europeans first set foot on the new land, but they were soon outnumbered by the waves of Europeans. There were at least ten times as many American Indians here when Columbus came as there are today. Over 90 percent died from diseases that Europeans brought with them and many were killed as newcomers took over their land. And, the very first slaves were brought from Africa to Jamestown in 1619 but they were marginalized by white Europeans and not considered full citizens. The Spanish, African, and American Indian cultures all contributed to the overall national American culture, but the dominant or mainstream culture was clearly Anglo-European.

A new wave of immigrants arrived by the mid-1800s. Between 1840 and 1880, large numbers of Irish came, fleeing starvation and British persecution. Germans also began to flood into America at this time because of war and political turmoil in Germany. In fact, during this period there were so many German immigrants in Chicago that German was used in public schools. Lastly, for the first time great numbers of Chinese arrived on the west coast, where they worked building the transcontinental railroad.

Southern, Eastern, and Central Europeans did not really arrive in large numbers until the end of the nineteenth century, and many found the conditions so harsh that they returned home. (Between 1880 and 1921, it is estimated that, of the number who immigrated to the United States, at least a third later emigrated out of the country.[1]) Northern Europeans came earlier and they stayed. Consequently, Northern Europeans shaped the dominant or mainstream American culture that included the values, beliefs, and customs that later immigrants adopted through acculturation.

The assumption that Americans are watered-down Europeans is a very common one, held by many in the United States and around the globe. When American businesspeople are trained for relocation overseas to a non-European country, about half of the Fortune 500 companies provide weeks or months of cross-cultural orientation training prior to their departure. Before they leave the United States, they will often learn about the basic religious beliefs, traditional values, and customs of the people in the country in which they will work. However, if they are going to work in Northern Europe, the most common type of training is simply a language course. In other words, many Americans think that there is little difference between the typical American and the typical German, except that Germans speak German and have better beer and coffee. Otherwise, we assume our cultures are fundamentally the same. Closer examination, however, shows that this is not true. In fact, the highest incidence of culture shock occurs when Americans relocate to England, a culture that superficially and linguistically may seem quite similar to America. One of the explanations for this high incidence is that most Americans assume that the British are basically the same as Americans and therefore they do not anticipate the difficulties of adapting to a new cultural environment.

Most Europeans would remind Americans that their nation is very young: the Anglo-American culture is about 500 years old and the nation itself is only 232 years old. Every European country is thousands of years old from a cultural viewpoint and most nations have existed since the nation-state system was first created with the Treaty of Westphalia in 1648. By contrast, some Americans think an antique is anything over 100 years old. While Europeans may admire the youthful idealism and exuberance of Americans, there is also the perception that we are upstarts who have not really "grown up" and lack the seasoning, discipline, and humility that a long history gives a people. Like untrained, wild horses, we are full of energy but unpredictable and likely to go in all directions.

It is also important that even the early waves of immigrants who came to America were not at all "typical" Europeans in terms of their values and worldviews. They already valued individualism or they would never have left the collective security of their extended families and communities in Europe. Rather than glorifying the past, they believed that the future would get better if they came to the New World and they were willing to leave the past. And many wanted a more democratic society without the political oppression of monarchs.

European Tragedy versus American Melodrama

If an average American went to Europe and watched the popular movies and television shows, read the popular novels, or even went to a few operas, he or she likely would conclude that when Europeans look at world events they see tragedy, like the old Greek tragedies where good people sometimes do bad things and bad people sometimes do good things. There's a great deal of gray area—an in-between area away from the extremes of good and bad. Most human events or conflicts are not simply black or white. Usually things are gray. Most importantly, the tragic reality (many Germans might term this *realism*) is that bad people often win out. They do become successful.

It may not be an accident that the most popular movies in Europe and Russia are tragedies.[2] The least popular movies in the United States are tragedies. Americans prefer melodramas, not tragedies. The *leitmotivs* of a melodrama are exemplified by the old American cowboy movies where the bad guys and good guys are absolutely identifiable. The bad guys wear black hats and the good guys wear white hats. These films embodied the American sense of melodrama, epitomized by John Wayne, who starred in many such movies, and who said: "If everything isn't black and white, I say, 'Why the hell not?' " There are no gray hats because there is no area in between good and bad. Of course, Americans are also inherently optimistic. In those old cowboy movies, the good guys always win.

Just as the European tragic worldview is surely a result of their historical experiences, the American melodramatic way of looking at the world must, in part, be a result of our relative youth and lack of experience with the adversity of war on our own soil and the continual threat of external invaders. But, this worldview is also perhaps a result of an atypical way of thinking that was brought from Europe. The Calvinists, Puritans, and other early Protestant settlers tended to look at the world in terms of dualistic opposites. They believed that we can easily distinguish between good and evil, the body and soul, or angels and devils, and that these forces are at war with each other; they are totally incompatible and mutually exclusive. These religious beliefs held that there was Heaven and Hell, and that there were no in-betweens such as Purgatory and Limbo as were described in Roman Catholicism.

This dualistic way of looking at the world was brought from Europe and, combined with American youth and lack of adversity, it explains why there is a dominant, black or white, melodramatic, dualistic way of thinking in the United States today.

Since the attacks of September 11, 2001, President George W. Bush has not only used the word *evil* many times to describe the nation's enemies, he has also used war metaphors quite freely. He has spoken of a "crusade," "smoking them out, dead or alive," and the "war on terrorism." The label "Axis of Evil" provided a handy image for placing the proverbial black cowboy hat on other countries deemed to be clear-cut enemies of the U.S. Many Europeans believe that Bush's use of the word *war* in such a cavalier manner in his declaration of a "war on terror" diminishes the tragic reality of such truly catastrophic wars such as World War I and World War II. Of course, they have experienced countless wars, with millions of lives lost just during the twentieth century alone. Cities were destroyed and almost everyone has lost a loved one fighting some other country. However, for Americans, "war" is often used rather melodramatically and casually.[3]

Our melodramatic image of the world and the national self-image that we are good and our enemies are evil is perhaps stronger in the United States than many other countries because of the traditional perceptions Americans have held about the rest of the world. Indeed, the new nation was founded by people fleeing religious or political persecution and they wanted to create a society isolated and insulated from the wars going on in Europe.

The tragedy of war has not been personally experienced by many American families in recent history, at least not within the borders of the continental United States. Homes have not been destroyed in warfare, and cities have not been leveled by bombs dropped by foreign powers. Unlike Europeans, Americans have not fought lengthy wars on their own soil when neighbors invaded and killed hundreds of thousands or even millions of innocent civilians and destroyed major cities. We certainly have not experienced world wars on our soil and therefore see the world in a very different way than most Europeans. The Civil War was bloody and the longest war Americans have ever fought on their own soil. But, this was a matter of Americans killing Americans. No one invaded the U.S. Even though the tragedy of September 11,

2001 may have changed the mindset of Americans, it may not have directly touched the personal lives of most people who did not live in the Northeast.

On 9/11 the entire world watched endlessly repeated film of the two planes flying into the World Trade Center. Early reports showed pictures of office workers jumping to their deaths to avoid the conflagration. To respect the feelings of family members and friends of these victims, many television networks in this country shortly stopped showing these images. Ironically, because most of us never saw the bodies of those who perished in New York that day, or in Washington, D.C., or Shanksville, Pennsylvania, this may have made it easier for the world, and Americans, to avoid accepting the tragic reality of the violent death of so many innocent people. For many, repeatedly watching the two planes slamming into the skyscrapers was almost like a video game or a movie, without human victims. A form of psychic-numbing probably occurred, which was abetted by not showing dead bodies.[4] Melodrama is very different than tragedy because it allows us to escape or avoid a painful reality. When the human consequences of war remain unseen, it is easier for war to remain a melodrama.

On the other hand, earlier, when the Federal Building in Oklahoma City was blown up on April 19, 1995, by fanatical right-wing Americans who hated the United States government,[5] we saw the victims on television. One especially poignant image was of a firefighter holding a child's broken body in his arms. The realistic tragedy of this incident was fully appreciated by everyone.

This effort to sanitize images of the tragic reality of war has been extended into coverage of the U.S. occupation in the Afghanistan and Iraq wars. Not only have few dead bodies been shown on television, Americans were not even allowed to view flag-draped coffins of dead soldiers being transported back home. During the Vietnam War, the Korean War and World War II, there were efforts to avoid showing dead Americans. However, these efforts failed because journalists were not restricted as they are by current government policies and they believed it was their duty to show war as it really happens, including the tragic reality of death. Today, American journalists cannot freely move about in battle zones and there are restrictions on images of dead Americans imposed by both the self-censorship of news organizations and by some federal regulations.

Our melodramatic worldview is reflected in and reinforced by mass entertainment as well as the news media. For example, one of the most popular movies in 1996 was the science fiction movie aptly named *Independence Day*. It was not simply a science fiction movie—it was cowboy melodrama. The bad guys were the aliens from outer space and the good guys were the Earthlings. President Whitmore of the United States—who just happened to be an ace jet fighter pilot—led the air attack that destroyed the alien spaceships. As the alien craft fell to the ground, many American theater audiences broke out into spontaneous applause in a celebration of the triumph of the forces of human goodness over alien evil.

Even the movie *Titanic* (1997) turned a historical tragedy into a very melodramatic love story, which was later turned into a Broadway musical. The movie *Saving Private Ryan* (1998) began as a tragedy, but ended as a melodrama with good overcoming evil. It also delivered the very American message that the individual is as highly valued as an entire patrol of soldiers, all of whom were charged with trying to save one low-ranking private from being killed. Nevertheless, *Saving Private Ryan* was actually a very European movie in that it portrayed war in a more realistic and tragic way than most traditional Hollywood movies.

Most Americans liked the movie, and it won the Academy Award as the best motion picture that year, despite the barrage of horrible images in the first 20 minutes of the film. The movie opened with scenes of the landing of American troops at Omaha Beach, a real historical event during which over 5,000 Americans died. Director Steven Spielberg strove to show the landing as it actually occurred, with the tragic carnage of battle, the sea red with blood, arms blown off soldiers, and the beach strewn with mutilated bodies.

Films that depict the violence or gray area of the morality of war often have aroused controversy. Movies like *MASH* (1970), *Platoon* (1986), and *Full Metal Jacket* (1987), while often critically praised, were not received without controversy. And non-melodramatic depictions of cowboys and frontier life—such as the Academy Award–winning *Unforgiven* (1992)—have met with similar controversy.

Perhaps the first movie to present violence both tragically and realistically was *Bonnie and Clyde* (1967). The "bad guys" were a husband and wife team of bank robbers whose characters were very well developed. We saw them playfully interacting and even making love.

The audience was allowed to get inside the killers' minds. Until this movie, the bad guys were almost always portrayed as caricatures of evil beings while the good guys were not only angelic, but their characters and personalities also were very fully developed. Of course, the bad guys were killed but there was little blood spilled.

Bonnie and Clyde ended with a scene that seemed to last for at least five minutes in which they were violently machine-gunned by law enforcement officers. Blood and gore was spread across the cinemascope screen. There were many reports of Americans who walked out of the theater in the middle of this scene because they were appalled by the portrayal of real violence and the tragic death of real people.

This dualistic, melodramatic image of the world is also reinforced and perpetuated by the American news media. Most Americans get their national and international news from network television broadcasts in the early evening. If you take out the commercials, this amounts to about 20 minutes worth of news a day on ABC, NBC, CBS, and more recently, Fox. About one-third of Americans read a newspaper every day and these are mostly local newspapers. Only 12 percent read national newspapers. Although Americans are increasingly using the internet to find national and international news, most are not viewers of cable newscasts.

Most news in the U.S. is supported by advertising. Major newspapers make more money selling advertisements than newspapers. This, of course, influences what gets covered as news and the priority of these events. To attract more readers with a high disposable income, newspapers tend to focus on the local news and the sensational events. This means that they also want readers with a high disposable income to attract advertisers. To this extent, one could argue that American news media is an example of class, rather than mass, media. The American television news media is also supported almost exclusively by the advertising it sells and the commercial networks depend upon maintaining a large number of viewers. The more viewers, the higher the fees charged for each minute of advertisement. Thus, in 1995, when CNN—at that time, the premier cable news network—carried the O.J. Simpson trial live and its viewership went up over 600 percent, it was a superb business decision.

There are a number of possible explanations for the fascination Americans had with this trial. To begin with, Americans have always enjoyed trials and many are prominent in American history. The Scopes Monkey Trial (1925), The Lindbergh Kidnapping Trial (1935), *Brown versus the Board of Education* (1954), and other famous trials are significant benchmarks in the twentieth century and occupied the headlines for weeks. Many national newscasts today features some contemporary trial of a famous figure, and each afternoon there are at least a half dozen reality courtroom shows featuring a judge who adjudicates a civil dispute on national television. At one time, this even included a judge on Animal Planet Network who decided disputes regarding pets.[6]

It is not simply that the United States is a nation of laws rather than men. These trials are highly entertaining because they are so melodramatic and oppositional. Trials are not held to reach compromises. One side wins and one side loses, and most Americans assume that in the end it is justice or goodness that wins out.

Of course, another reason that Americans may have watched the O.J. Simpson trial is that Simpson is black while his murdered wife and the man killed with her were white. Race still matters to many Americans, and only served to increase the explosiveness of the trial. In addition O.J. Simpson was a well-known celebrity. He was an outstanding football player and perhaps a mediocre actor. Yet the most important reason that Americans were glued to their television sets during the Simpson trial was because of the way in which it was presented by CNN. It was not information or news. It was melodramatic entertainment or, using a newer term, "infotainment."[7] In the courtroom, the lawyers played to the camera with catch phrases such as the now-famous assertion by defense lawyer Johnnie Cochran "If the glove doesn't fit, you must acquit." Several of the attorneys wrote books about the trial, appeared in various televisions shows, and have become media celebrities.

To make it even more melodramatic, at the end of each day of the trial, CNN featured legal "experts" from academia or celebrities from radio and television talk shows. They would engage in very spirited "debates" taking opposite viewpoints regarding the trial. While these debates were oppositional, melodramatic, and very entertaining, they were not very informative or educational.

Since the financially successful coverage of the Simpson trial, the evening national network newscasts (ABC, CBS, NBC, and Fox) have featured more stories about violent crime and trials.[8] Before the Simpson trial, if there was a murder trial in Denver, it was not considered a national or international news event. Because of the large audience CNN attracted by covering the Simpson trial, the networks began to cover similar events. Unfortunately, the result is that many Americans and people around the globe believe that violent crime has gone up in the past decade in the U.S. whereas it has actually gone down dramatically. In most major urban areas it is now around the lowest since records have been kept. According to annual statistics released by London's Metropolitan Police department, in the period of 2001–02, Londoners were about six times more likely to be mugged than New Yorkers.[9] People believe there is more violent crime in the United States because it is featured more often in the evening national television newscasts.

In 1998, three years after the O.J. Simpson trial, Americans tuned in to a different sort of television melodrama: the Congressional hearings regarding an affair between a White House intern and President Clinton. While the Monica Lewinsky affair could have led to the impeachment of the president, the constitutional and legal experts featured on the evening newscasts focused their discussions in graphic and sometimes pornographic detail on what sex acts may or may not have taken place. Kenneth Starr's Office of Independent Council allowed the sordid details to be heard by Congress and the entire world when it issued its report to Congress. Power, politics, and puritanical attitudes toward sex were all mixed together in one of the most entertaining and embarrassing episodes in recent American history. The only television network that refused to carry this melodramatic and titillating story as a news event was the Public Broadcasting System (PBS).

As with the Simpson trial, television networks, and especially cable networks, featured lively debates between so-called experts who were best known for their emotional tirades and the firmness with which they held their positions. A debate is not an opportunity for dialogue— it is a format that often leads to simultaneous, oppositional monologues. While the debate format is entertaining, the object of any debate is not to educate, to inform, or to find the truth. The primary goal is to defeat your opponent. It is a game, a contest. Debaters often ridicule or exaggerate the positions of an opponent and, even when an opponent makes a valid point, no debater would say, "Well, that's a very good point. You're right. I will reconsider my facts and conclusions."

Another common debating tactic is the creation of a "straw man" when you caricature your opponent's argument and then knock down the straw man you created. Using this technique, a debater defines his opponent's position in the most extreme or absurd terms possible. For example, in a debate, the opponent of someone who advocates the public funding of medical care for everyone might create a "straw man" by saying that this policy is the same thing as communism. Then he will go on to argue against communism, rather than universal health coverage. Of course, most straw man techniques are much more subtle than this, but once such a charge is made, the other debater is forced to defend against it and the defense of his or her real position is sidetracked— along with his or her own attack on the opponent's position.

For example, on April 30, 2004, President Bush was discussing Iraq and said: "There's a lot of people in the world who don't believe that people whose skin color may not be the same as ours can be free and self-govern. I reject that. I reject that strongly. I believe that people who practice the Muslim faith can self-govern. I believe that people whose skins . . . are a different color than white can self-govern." While there were certainly many Americans who doubted the ability of the United States to easily spread democracy in the Arab world, they were hardly advocating such a sweeping, and easily discredited, racist position.

The debate format seems to be very popular with Americans because it is entertaining and melodramatic. Views are clearly and eloquently stated for the audience and there is very little nuance or subtlety in a debate. Presidential candidates often appear in a series of nationally televised debates. However, it is uncertain how many Americans actually watch these debates in order to be better informed voters, to find "truth," or to even be persuaded to change their votes. Many may view the debates as melodramatic entertainment and hope that the candidate they support will say something very clever and his or her opponent will, in turn, say something incredibly foolish.

Trials and debates are inherently adversarial and dualistic. There is a wide-spread belief that opposition is the best way to get anything done. It has come to be accepted in this country that the best way to discuss an idea is to set up a debate; the media have fostered this fallacy. As sociologist Deborah Tannen has written, the view is widely held that the best way to present the "news" "is to find spokespeople who express the most extreme, polarized views and present them as 'both sides'; the best way to settle disputes is litigation that pits one party against the other; the best way to begin an essay is to attack someone; and the best way to show you're really thinking is to criticize."[10] Tannen believes that the foundation for this oppositional "argument culture" can be traced all the way back to Aristotelian dualistic thought. In Europe, this way of thinking has been tempered by tragic realism. The American tendency to see the world in terms of dualism and melodrama may be a unique combination of Western Aristotelian thought, Protestantism, and especially Calvinism, mixed with the American youthful experience.

E Pluribus Unum—*"Out of Many, One."*

Although most Americans share a national image and many common values, beliefs, and ways of looking at the world, the United States is also a country of enormous ethnic, racial, religious, and regional diversity. Each region of the United States has its own geography and history of immigration. Texas and New Mexico have a Spanish heritage; Louisiana and Maine have strong French influences; and Michigan has a very large Arab population. For more than four centuries, Europeans, Asians, Africans, Middle Easterners, and Latin Americans have all brought their own cultural values, beliefs, and worldviews, and especially such unique external cultural contributions as music, food, customs, and dress.

New waves of immigrants arrive and often start out in urban areas where entire neighborhoods change within a short period of time as previous immigrants find success and move elsewhere. Harlem in New York was originally Dutch, but later it became the home for African-Americans who were displaced from the South during the Civil War. More recently, large waves of immigrants from Puerto Rico and the Dominican Republic have arrived in what is now called Spanish Harlem. A hundred years from now, Harlem will likely become associated with yet another ethnic group. As with the coastline of any continent, the waves seem to come ashore forever.

Ethnic neighborhoods change when the wave of immigrants from one region crests and a new wave of immigrants from another area of the world begins to enter the neighborhood. A neighborhood that at one time was predominantly Italian now may have many Asian residents and few of the young Italians still living there can speak Italian. Within these changing ethnic immigrant communities, young people meet and marry with those of other racial and ethnic backgrounds.

Within the past century increased mobility within the United States, and the influx of new immigrants, has brought not only greater diversity but also greater commonality. Mexican immigrants, for example, can be found in every community in every part of the country, and someone originally from New York City can be found in a small Mexican-American town in Texas. As they reach adulthood, many immigrant children move out of ethnic enclaves such as Little Italy or Chinatown. Even regional accents are disappearing.

It is very important to remember that, despite being a very diverse, very large country that is constantly changing with the influx of new immigrants, *there have almost always been more similarities than differences among the American people.* Almost all Americans, including recent immigrants, shared common American internal cultural values and beliefs even before they arrived. In fact, many came because they were highly individualistic and believed in the so-called American dream of a better future with economic mobility. When they arrived, each group had a different immigrant experience, but at the same time they all had many similar historical experiences of a struggle to move up the economic ladder and, often, of facing discrimination. And within a generation or so, most became American citizens. The country's coins carry the motto *E pluribus unum*—"out of many, one." While the motto originally referred to the unification of the many states, it can also be interpreted as the general unity of values of Americans, regardless of their many origins.

In most countries, nationality is determined by some kind of ancestral linkage. Ancestry (*Jus sanguinis*—"right of blood"—meant that the country of citizenship of a child is the same as that of his or her parents), ethnicity, religion, and language combine to give people their national identity and citizenship. If you are the child of an American, you can be American, but it is also a matter of *jus soli* ("right of soil"). If you are born in the United States, you are automatically entitled to be an American if you want to be. In addition, any immigrant can apply for citizenship.[11]

Many urban areas in Western Europe have almost as many foreign-born citizens as there are in metropolitan centers in the United States. This is a very recent phenomenon and until the past four or five decades, most were Europeans who were displaced by wars or political upheavals within Europe. The vast majority of newly arrived immigrants in Europe today are non-white and non-Christian. But countries in Europe do not view themselves as immigrant nations. The mainstream institutions of European society remain tightly knit, insular, and largely homogeneous. Discrimination against immigrants still exists in many parts of Europe. A 2005 French study found that job applicants with French-sounding names had 50 times the chance of being interviewed as those with Arab- or African-sounding names.[12]

Being an American today means that identity is based on ideas and values, and it is a matter of choice rather than historical legacy. The American system mandates that individuals share a social contract that assumes they can determine and take responsibility for their own economic and social well-being. To many traditional collectivistic societies around the world, this American belief in free will, choice, and the celebration of self seems to be very selfish. However, Americans also freely choose to accept a number of social or civic obligations to provide for the common good. They have not eliminated a sense of social responsibility for others but rather have replaced its hereditary basis.[13]

Volunteering to help others and joining together in civic organizations to promote the good of the community—or even the nation— is a tradition going back to the earliest days of American history. Furthermore, this help was usually given to others regardless of class allegiance, ancestral ties, religious affiliation, or extended family obligations. In many other countries, generosity is extended no further than the family, tribe, or village. For others in need, the nation assumes the responsibility through centralized social welfare programs. In the United States, the local community comes together to help others and there has always been a healthy reluctance to allow the federal government to provide nationalized social welfare except when it is not provided by the local community. There is no American national education or health care system for similar ideological reasons.

Americans also believe in the equality of opportunity and fairness. When individuals are not given the same opportunities to achieve or to educate their children, when they are discriminated against without the protection of their individual civil rights, then the federal government is expected to step in. The Civil Rights Movement of the 1960s is a clear example of this expectation. Nevertheless, much of the movement began at the local level when religious groups, grassroots organizations, nonprofits, and others joined together to demand freedom and equal rights.

Fairness in America is not simply a matter of eliminating discrimination. It is also a matter of providing equal opportunities for everyone to succeed. Often this can only come about through governmental intervention at the federal level.

While some Europeans and some domestic critics label the American programs of affirmative action in the 1960s through the 1980s as "positive discrimination," the practical reality is that programs that allowed those who were victims of discrimination to succeed have created an enormous black middle class that previously did not exist in America. Furthermore, these programs have benefited all Americans who have suffered from discrimination because of their national origin, ethnicity, race, gender, religion, and so on.

Americans would strongly object to the phrase "positive discrimination" because there was very little discrimination against anyone, including white people. While there were surely some cases in which a white person did not get a job or enter a medical school because of the decision to give a member of a disadvantaged minority group a chance, these cases of reverse discrimination were very small and the overall social, economic, and political benefit to the society was enormous. And today, almost none of these programs exist because they are no longer as necessary as they were in the mid-1960s when there was rampant discrimination against minorities. In addition, most companies, universities, and public organizations found that diversity tended to result in greater productivity and creativity with decreased turnover of personnel.

"Affirmative Action" Becomes a Matter of "Managing Diversity"[14]

The United States has changed dramatically over the past half century. Segregation and discrimination are against the law, and, although racism still exists, it is no longer widely acceptable. Racial incidents have decreased and the opportunities for everyone to succeed economically and politically have increased. (Although the income gap between whites and non-whites is wider than in the 1960s.) The society has become more racially diverse and cultural pluralism, or multiculturalism, is not only accepted, but celebrated by most Americans.

In June 1965, President Lyndon Johnson gave one of his most significant addresses on civil rights at Howard University in Washington, D.C. In this commencement address, titled "To Fulfill These Rights," Johnson suggested that it was more than just a matter of freedom or giving African-Americans the rights of all other Americans. He said,

> But freedom is not enough. You do not wipe away the scars of centuries by saying: Now you are free to go where you want, and do as you desire, and choose the leaders you please. You do not take a person who, for years, has been hobbled by chains and liberate him, bring him up to the starting line of a race and then say, 'you are free to compete with all the others,' and still justly believe that you have been completely fair. Thus it is not enough just to open the gates of opportunity. All our citizens must have the ability to walk through those gates.
>
> This is the next and the more profound stage of the battle for civil rights. We seek not just freedom but opportunity. We seek not just legal equity but human ability, not just equality as a right and a theory but equality as a fact and equality as a result. For the task is to give 20 million Negroes the same chance as every other American to learn and grow, to work and share in society, to develop their abilities—physical, mental and spiritual, and to pursue their individual happiness.
>
> To this end, equal opportunity is essential, but not enough . . .[15]

What needed to be added to freedom and opportunity was affirmative action—public policies and initiatives designed to help eliminate discrimination based on race, color, religion, sex. or national origin. The phrase was first used in Johnson's 1965 *Executive Order 11246*, which required federal contractors to "take affirmative action to ensure that applicants are employed, and that employees are treated during employment, without regard to their race, creed, color or national origin." In 1967, Johnson expanded the Executive Order to enclude an affirmative action requirement to include women.

To make up for over 300 years of racism and discrimination, and to provide an opportunity to succeed, programs were developed to ensure that the federal government and its contractors—in public housing, education, law enforcement, the military, and every other facet of life—actively recruited minorities and ensured that they were represented in all jobs. This initially required the establishment of quotas, which meant hiring a minimum number or percentage of minorities (though all applicants and employees had to have relevant and valid job or educational qualifications). Under President Nixon, the federal government established racial quotas, but by the mid-1990s a series of court cases made them illegal.

Some white Americans opposed affirmative action because they believed quotas created so-called "reverse discrimination." Quotas, they said, were inherently undemocratic because everyone was not treated equally. In fact, only 1 or 2 percent of the hundreds of thousands of employment discrimination cases brought before the Equal Employment Opportunities Commission (EEOC) since 1965 were reverse discrimination cases. And, according to one poll, while over 78 percent of whites believed that white people were being hurt by affirmative action, only 7 percent claimed to have been personally affected in any way by affirmative action.[16] Very few personally knew anyone who actually was prevented from being admitted to a university or from securing a job because of affirmative action. To a large extent, reverse discrimination has been shown to be a myth.

European and American National Identity

Just as a federation of separate states evolved into the confederation known as the United States of America with its own singular national identity, a United States of Europe appears to be emerging from the loose confederation of states in the European Union (EU).

Brussels is sometimes already referred to as the capital of Europe because NATO and two of the main institutions of the European Union—the European Commission and the Council of the European Union—are located there. Furthermore, the city is a mixture of French and Flemish-speaking Belgians, thus reflecting the linguistic pluralism of European states. Gradually, a new European identity is developing.

In Europe, as in the newly independent United States, numerous articles and treaties have been signed between states to form a federation that will allow for a common currency, free trade, free travel across state borders, and shared labor practices. A weak central government is necessary to guide foreign policy and provide for the common defense. Just as the United States agreed that there would be no national religion in its new confederation, the EU also has decided that there should be a separation between government and religion.

A political entity usually evolves from such practical necessities as providing a common defense against external enemies, developing a shared currency, insuring internal order, and protecting citizens and their trade with other entities. Technology often changes the political unit. The feudal lord with a small army of men with crossbows could no longer protect his people and territory when gunpowder was invented and large armies were amassed. In a small village, everyone shares a common language and culture, but with increased trade and more modern transportation, urban centers form with a heterogeneous population. Gradually, villages become cities; cities become city-states; and city-states join together to become nation-states. As the new entities become more effective in meeting people's economic, social, or security needs, they gain legitimacy: People begin to identify as members of the broader unit. Political nationalism seems to be the last stage in this progression.

Ironically, a national identity and nationalism also often result from having a common enemy or knowing who we are not. The United States has defined itself as *not* being a European country with a state religion, a strong central government, or a parliamentary system. The nation is governed by the people, protected by a system of law rather than the rule of a powerful leader. The majority will of the citizens rules through free elections; individual civil liberties of the minority are protected—such as freedom of speech, the press, and religion.

World War I and World War II deepened American patriotism and nationalism, and, during the Cold War, the American national identity was very much shaped by anti-Communism. When the Cold War ended, there was no readymade, concrete enemy. In 1992, Francis Fukuyama wrote *The End of History* and *the Last Man*, in which he argued that the progression of human history as a struggle between ideologies ended when the Berlin Wall fell in 1989 and the world reached a general agreement that political and economic liberalism was best for all peoples.

Samuel Huntington provides a clear, simplistic enemy in two of his books, *Who Are We?* and *The Clash of Civilizations*. In both cases, the enemy is a threat to the so-called American way of life. In his more recent book *Who Are We?* published in 2004, he claims that *we* are certainly not undocumented Mexicans who will eventually destroy the American culture. In his earlier 1996 book, *The Clash of Civilizations*, Huntington neatly breaks down the world into homogeneous religious civilizations that threaten Western civilization. China and the Arab world are seen as particular threats to Western civilization. Yet, there is great diversity within all religions and Chinese and Arab nationalism and the desire for economic development are certainly greater determinants of their public policy than Confucianism, Islam, or any sort of anti-American ideology. All the same, Huntington provides a simple, ominous enemy image in both books and offers Americans a clearer self-definition during a period of enormous insecurity and ambiguity.

It is interesting to note that Huntington's simplistic perception of the world is remarkably similar to that of Osama bin Laden, who also takes the position that another civilization—Western civiliation—is seeking to destroy the Islamic world. Thus, Bin Laden argues, Muslims must unite to destroy the infidels before they contaminate the Islamic world.

Since the end of the Cold War, many Europeans also have been defining their own identity in terms of who they are *not*. Especially since the occupation of Iraq, most Europeans are defining themselves as *not* Americans. In 2003, Jeremy Rifkin, president of the Foundation on Economic Trends, wrote:

> President Bush's Iraq policy has helped millions of Europeans, who often find themselves at odds with each other on the most banal considerations of life, to find their common identity in opposition to the war. . . . The Iraq crisis has united Europeans and armed them with a clear sense of shared values and future vision . . . Europeans are finding their identity. . . . While Brussels is far from most people's minds, what united Europeans is their repudiation of the geopolitics of the 20th century and their eagerness to embrace a new "biosphere politics" in the 21st century. . . . A growing number of Europeans see the U.S. government openly opposing these things they so ardently care about.[17]

We can see this opposition in many different areas. No states within the EU have the death penalty, and Europeans support the International Criminal Court, which the Bush Administration refused to join. Many public opinion polls show that Europeans are more concerned than Americans about such environmental issues as global warming, and they are more likely to support cooperation between nation-states to solve problems. On the other hand, President Bush began his first term of office with an isolationist and unilateralist foreign policy. He refused to sign the Kyoto Accords whereby countries agreed to reduce the amount of greenhouse gases. Most European countries signed them. Bush withdrew from the antiballistic missile treaty before 9/11, while Europeans support nuclear disarmament and the increased use of the United Nations to settle disputes among nations. Conversely, the United States bypassed the UN Security Council to act almost unilaterally in Iraq.

Although most Americans may view themselves as peaceful, the country has often used war as a means of obtaining justice. Even in the past few years, surveys commissioned by the German Marshall Fund consistently show that 80 percent of Americans agree with the proposition that "under some conditions, war is necessary to obtain justice." In France, Germany, Italy, and Spain, less than one-third of the population agrees with this statement.[18] While this may seem very new, the American willingness to use military force has always been a part of American foreign policy. Some Europeans believe that the U.S. is trapped in a Hobbesian world of endless chaos and war, believing that only the use of military force maintains security. Europeans, who have had centuries of tragic wars and conflict, appear to be in search of some kind of Kantian pacifist vision of universal peace and order. Of course, on the other hand, it also can be argued that the American willingness to use power has probably maintained order and prevented local conflicts from boiling over to become major world wars.

A national identity cannot arise simply from sharing some kind of superordinate goal or a common enemy. Once the goal is achieved, or if the common enemy no longer exists, and if a positive and long-term social fabric has not been developed, the confederation will not hold together. In many countries, we have seen that the temporary unity between discordant ethnic or religious groups resulting from a shared hatred toward a colonial power or occupying army dissolved into a civil war once the common enemy has been defeated or has withdrawn. No European identity can last if it is primarily based upon *not* being American, unless the real needs of people are effectively met and the central authority gains some legitimacy.

While there is talk of postreligious, postnational identities in Europe, most of the European identity is still a matter of family, community and territory. At this point, Brussels is not the Washington, D.C. of Europe. The "Europeanness" or collective identity has not yet evolved to the level of connecting with a formal EU structure. All that really exists is a single trading market and a unified currency. Europeans engage in endless debate regarding foreign policy and, in the end, the EU takes no position or very weak positions on many world issues. Moreover, there is no united European military presence.

What Is an Average American?

We've established that Americans are not "watered down" Europeans. We've also provided a rough sketch of a number of American cultural attitudes, and will continue this discussion throughout the later chapters of this book. Yet at this point, one might ask, "This is all well and good, but what is a typical American like?"

When we refer to an average American, from a statistical standpoint we are speaking of someone who considers himself or herself as middle class. In fact, this is the vast majority of Americans: A 2006 poll by the Economic Policy Institute found that 62 percent of Americans—the vast majority of them regard themselves as middle class, while only 2 percent define themselves as upper class and 8 percent as lower class. The remaining 27 percent label themselves as working class.[19] The United States if often referred to as a middle-class society. If this means that most Americans are not rich or poor, but somewhere in between, it is true. However, the United States is not the most middle-class society in the world. For example, the middle class in Japan is a much greater part of the overall population and the gap between the rich and the poor in that country is much smaller.[20] And, income is distributed much more equally in most European countries, as well as Australia.

We suspect that most Americans don't even like the word *class* because they consider the United States to be classless.[21] It is generally believed that one's social or economic class is never fixed, and each individual can pull himself or herself up the economic and class ladder through their own individual hard work. As the old saying goes, you can simply pull yourself up by your bootstraps. However, this very egalitarian assumption is unfair to those who have never had boots or who have suffered discrimination because of their racial or ethnic background.

The average American is probably a Protestant Christian. If we force Americans to select a religion out of a list of religions, about 50 percent would categorize themselves as Protestants, 23 percent as Roman Catholics, 2 percent Jews, and about 1 percent as Muslims.[22] Interestingly, the majority of U.S. presidents have been Episcopalians—the American version of the Anglican Church or the Church of England.[23]

Racially, according to the U.S. Census, about 80 percent of Americans are white. African-Americans make up a little less than 13 percent of the population, and Asian-Americans represent about 4 percent of the U.S. population.[24] The census regards Hispanic-Americans as an ethnic rather than racial group, which makes up roughly 12.5 percent of the U.S. population.[25]

American National Identity in the Post–Iraq War World

Theo Sommer, former editor in chief of Germany's *Dei Zeit*, has said, "Underneath every America-hater is a disappointed America-lover."[26] It is abundantly clear that most of the world is profoundly disappointed that Americans don't seem to live up to their own founding ideals, especially when it comes to foreign policy. During the first half of the twentieth century, many newly emerging states— including many Arab countries—saw America as a beacon of anticolonialism. America, that "city upon a hill," was seen as the home of liberty and democracy and a state powerful enough to help them spread throughout the world, to many countries ruled by illiberal, undemocratic means. Yet, with every "stable" dictator or status quo supported to the detriment of international democracies, there is a sense in these same countries today that the United States has betrayed them and the very ideals that Americans seem to want to promote around the globe.

The good news is that the world is mostly disappointed with American governmental public policy and not the cultural and national values that are shared by most Americans. Furthermore, it is apparent to the global community that much of foreign policy since 9/11 has been a result of fear and insecurity. As this fear dissipates, and as the United States moves out of its unilateral protectionism into a more internationalist foreign policy, and most importantly, as it returns to its basic values and principles, this perception of the United States should change. But Americans must earn the respect of the world based upon what they do, rather than their rhetoric.

There is the possibility that with new leadership and changed public policy, the United States could again become a beacon. There is an international perception that this process may have already begun, with the sweeping changes to Congress in 2006 to a Democratic majority and the international recognition that most Americans believe that the Iraq War was a tragic mistake. The issue is not one of should the United States leave Iraq, but rather how fast can it leave and how to do so in a way that will not make the situation even worse.

Of course, the United States must close the prison at Guantánamo and agree to abide by the Geneva Convention regarding the interrogation of prisoners to show the world that the United States does believe in the rule of law and the fair treatment of all humans. There is the belief that America should live up to the highest standards of its ideals and foundational values, rather than come down to the lowest standards of the terrorists upon whom the country has declared war. There are other steps that can be taken to ameliorate America's image problem, such as becoming more involved in environmental efforts to control carbon emissions, restoring full involvement in international organizations, and moving from the use of force to negotiation and diplomacy. Surely, future Americans will move away from unilateralism and especially the unilateral use of military force rather than face increasing unpopularity and isolation in the global community.

While American exceptionalism has been twisted recently to justify self-interested interventionism, it originally was intended to serve as an example within a community of nations that shared the liberal ideals and values of liberty, equality, self-governance, and tolerance. A move toward humility as a member of the world community, rather than hubris and arrogance, may be one result of the Iraq War, and, if America practices what it preaches, it ought to be able to earn the respect given to all members of a peaceful world community and even potentially regain its position as a beacon of progressivism.

CHAPTER 3

Melting Pots to Mosaics

Race and Immigration

All societies have a dream and a nightmare. And our nightmare has been, I think, our racism. We practically committed genocide on the people who were here, the Native Americans. We enslaved another race of people, the Africans. And then we dropped the atom bomb on Asians. We would have never dropped that bomb in Europe in my view. And I think that's what proves the racism of it. That's the nightmare of America. The dream of America is enunciated by the great speech by Martin Luther King, I Have a Dream. The dream is that there is no country on earth that has tried to actually embrace all the people that we have tried to embrace. All you have to do is walk through New York City to see that or any of our cities and not a few of our country sides at this point. We could be called the most racist. Or we could be called the least. We are both. And it always remains a tension and a question as to which side of us, the good side or the bad side, will win out in the end. And I think that's true for every society.

—Thomas Cahill[1]

*W*E HUMAN BEINGS HAVE AN UNCANNY ABILITY to forget painful or embarrassing events from our childhood and to remember or highlight those that were pleasant and good. Thank goodness for repression or we would all find it difficult to go on after having endured the normal traumas, trials, and tribulations of our early years. This is also true of nations. The ways in which people perceive their own nation and other nations in the international system often involve both conscious and unconscious distortions. National images level out that which is demeaning and ugly while sharpening or exaggerating that which is noble. All nations seem to suffer from this kind of historical amnesia.

In addition, every country has a legacy of contradictions, paradoxes, and hypocrisy. Civic values often clash with the actual behavior or policies of the government. A government may paradoxically claim to believe in certain principles and yet engage in practices that clearly contradict those principles. We find that we can easily identify immoral behavior in others while at the same time denying the immorality of this behavior when it becomes part of our public policy. Citizens will change their beliefs to conform to the actions and policies of their government, especially during times of war. Before we engage in military action there may be great dissent, yet once the armed conflict begins, we rally around the flag and patriotically support our nation. We even begin to believe that military action not only is justified to defend ourselves and others, but even more, that there are few other ways to deal with a hostile and threatening enemy.[2]

People are quite capable of holding contradictory beliefs and values. Americans cherish individual freedom, but they also value public order, and these two values are often in conflict. One of the most obvious paradoxes is that although Americans have always claimed that they strongly and sincerely are advocates of individual freedom, liberty, and egalitarianism, the country has an obvious historical record of slavery and racial or ethnic discrimination. Today, there seems to be no way any rational and fair-minded American could have defended slavery or taken any pride in the country's long centuries of racism. Nevertheless, we must acknowledge that many of our forefathers did just that. Although the practices of racial segregation and discrimination are illegal today, and bigotry and racism may be less lethal, overt, or apparent, they still exist in America. As the old saying goes, "They are as American as apple pie."

Many of the founders—including Thomas Jefferson, George Washington, and Benjamin Franklin—had slaves and yet they all grew to abhor the institution of slavery. While these men sought to escape the enslavement of Parliament and a British king and late in their lives spoke out against the slave trade, they each held slaves until the day they died. Franklin, who rose from a printer's apprentice to become a world statesman, publisher, and inventor, eventually became an antislavery voice only shortly before he died. Also, despite his progressive stance, he was always fearful that some immigrants would destroy the newly emerging nation. His bigotry toward Germans and other non-Anglo-Saxon immigrants is well documented.

Of course, racism exists in many countries around the globe even today. The percentage of the population of Aborigines in Australia is roughly the same as the percentage of American Indians in the United States, and the two nations' histories of racist public policies and discrimination are very comparable. The Afrikaners in South Africa were Dutch Calvinist settlers who developed the racist public policies of apartheid to enslave the native tribes. In many parts of Germany, Russia, Latvia and other countries, there has been a recent dramatic rise in incidents involving assaults and even the murder of people of color. Skinheads in Europe are just as violent and racist as skinheads in the United States.

The United States Is Not Just a Mixture of Many Different Cultures

We stress the American Muslim identity, that home is where my grandchildren are going to be raised, not where my grandfather is buried.

—SALAM AL-MARAYATI, EXECUTIVE DIRECTOR OF THE MUSLIM
PUBLIC AFFAIRS COUNCIL

Let us return to the question, "What is *the* American culture?" If the average American is most likely to answer this first by saying that it is some kind of watered-down Northern European culture, a second equally common answer could be that there is no such thing as *the* American culture. This is because the United States is a mixture of many different cultures *without a dominant or mainstream culture.* Just as Americans often view themselves as class*less* because they believe that everyone can easily move up and down the socioeconomic class ladder, they also tend to view their country as culture*less* or a nation without a dominant or mainstream culture. The U.S. is just a hodge-podge of various cultures. We have been taught that people came to these shores from around the world and brought their cultures with them and, if there is a "typical" American culture, it is simply a com-bination of all of these cultures.

The metaphor that is used to reflect this viewpoint is commonly referred to as "The Melting Pot," a phrase that became popular fol-lowing its use in a play produced in New York City in 1907, Israel Zang-will's *The Melting Pot: The Great American Drama.*[3] At one point, a character proclaims, "Understand that America is God's Crucible, the great Melting-Pot where all the races of Europe are melting and re-forming! A fig for your feuds and vendettas! Germans and French-men, Irishmen and Englishmen, Jews and Russians—into the Crucible with you all! God is making the American." The melting pot idea—redolent with undertones of American exceptionalism—seized the popular imagination, and thus a sustaining metaphor for our culture was launched.

During the first two decades of the 1900s, waves of immigrants came from Eastern and Southern Europe. Very few were Protestants—most were Roman Catholics, Orthodox, or Jews. They did not speak English and therefore tended to begin life in America in a community of co-nationals who spoke their own language and provided social sup-port, such as Little Italy in Philadelphia or Little Poland in Milwaukee. Many had darker hair and darker skin than most Northern Europeans. Theodore Roosevelt, who was president during this period, was a fanat-ical advocate for restricting immigration from countries that were not Northern European and he led an English-only not only movement not only to make English the national language, but also to require it of all immigrants. Roosevelt often used the metaphor of a melting pot to describe his vision for an ideal America and he had seen and highly praised Zangwill's *The Melting Pot*, which in fact was dedicated to him.

Although the following quote is often cited as something Roosevelt said in 1907, it is actually from a letter he wrote shortly before his death in January 1919, just as the Ku Klux Klan was beginning to reemerge as a violent racist, anti-Semitic, and anti-Catholic movement in America and laws were being enacted making it illegal for a white person to marry someone of another race.[4]

> In the first place, we should insist that if the immigrant who comes here in good faith becomes an American and assimilates himself to us, he shall be treated on an exact equality with everyone else, for it is an outrage to discriminate against any such man because of creed, or birthplace, or origin. But this is predicated upon the person's becoming in every facet an American, and nothing but an American. . . . There can be no divided allegiance here. Any man who says he is an American, but something else also isn't an American at all. We have room for but one flag, the American flag. . . . We have room for but one language here, and that is the English language. . . . and we have room for but one sole loyalty and that is a loyalty to the American people.

When Roosevelt used the term "melting pot" he was not envisioning a country that was truly a mixture of all the cultures brought to its shores and he definitely was not what we today would call a multiculturalist or a cultural pluralist. He firmly believed in assimilation where immigrants were expected to give up their differences. To "Americanize" meant to lose one's ethnic identity. Roosevelt opposed any kind of hyphenated identity such as Irish-American or Asian-American. He certainly would never accept the possibility of any citizen referring to himself or herself as an African-American, Mexican-American, Muslim-American, or gay-American. He would detest any American flying an Irish flag on St. Patrick's Day or a Mexican flag on Cinco de Mayo. And, chances are that he would enthusiastically support efforts today to build a fence between Mexico and the U.S.[5]

The Melting Pot Myth versus the Cultural Cookie-Cutter

Many of these "nativists" believed the early natives (white, Anglo-Saxon Protestants—WASPs) were superior to all other groups. These "others" should be prohibited from immigrating but if they do come, they should give up their differences and adopt both the external and internal aspects of the dominant WASP culture.

The metaphor of the American melting pot is mostly a historical myth if it is viewed as a claim that there is cultural equality for all races, ethnic groups, nationalities, or even religions in the United States. There are some truths embedded in *all* national or cultural myths and they usually offer explanations for a people's history and provide direction for the future, but overall they are false and amount to oversimplified distortions of reality. Furthermore, the concept of the American melting pot is especially unfair to those who did not historically melt into the mainstream pot, particularly people of color. Even if they tried, they could not change their skin color or their hair texture.

Each racial or ethnic group has not been allowed to contribute its own cultural traits proportionally to the whole or mainstream culture, especially when we consider such internal cultural characteristics as beliefs, values, worldviews, and thought patterns. These are the most important aspects of any culture. Most of the contributions were merely parts of their external culture. While we could clearly say that American culture, and Western civilization, has been immeasurably enriched by Arab scholars, scientists, and philosophers of the Middle Ages and the Greco-Roman heritage of Southern Europe, there is also no doubt that Northern European, Protestant culture has placed the dominant stamp on American culture. There are very few direct, foundational contributions from Middle Eastern, Asian, Latin American, and even Southern Mediterranean cultures in mainstream America. The pot probably melted no further than shish kebab, chop suey, tacos, and pizza—and, two of these foods were invented in the U.S. Although there are many cities with American Indian names today, and between 1913 and 1938 an American Indian appeared on the "Buffalo" or "Indian Head Nickel," the major contribution of Native Americans, in the minds of many American citizens, is a food—corn. Ironically, they were the true "natives" who were actually excluded and oppressed by those who called themselves "nativists." Obviously, racism is a major part of American history, and although it is not as overt or sanctioned by public policy, it still exists today.

This is especially true when we examine such institutions as the United States government, businesses, or even academia where the traditional and mainstream internal cultural values, ways of thinking, and worldviews are dominant rather than those of racial and ethnic minorities. As opposed to a melting pot, a more accurate historical metaphor to describe the immigrant experience is a *cultural cookie-cutter* with a white, male, Protestant, Anglo-Saxon mold or shape. [6] Those who could easily fit this mold simply blended into the dominant or mainstream culture while those who could not were often excluded. In this country, differences have been shaped or *leveled*, rather than simply *melting* and being stirred into some generic pot of American stew.

America began as a group of colonies and, as with many former colonies, before independence and even for decades after independence, those citizens who best resembled the original colonists often found it the easiest to advance socially, economically, and politically. They could easily assimilate or give up their cultural differences to fit the dominant cultural cookie-cutter mold. This was surely true of most French, Spanish, Portuguese, Dutch, or British colonies. In many former French colonies, those who spoke French well and were lighter skinned often became the elite of their post-colonial societies.

All immigrants can *acculturate* by adopting the values and behaviors of the dominant culture. However, the power to *assimilate*, or to be accepted as an equal within the dominant or mainstream cultures, ultimately rests in the hands of the dominant culture.[7] In former colonies, these hands were European and white. Ironically, in the case of the United States, those who had been on the soil the longest— American Indians, African-Americans, and even many Mexican-Americans—are still not fully assimilated. However, in today's more multicultural America, they at least have the opportunity of being truly American while retaining aspects of their ethnic or native cultures.

Consider the following hypothetical example of the cookie-cutter assimilationist process. In the early 1900s, a German Catholic immigrant, Wilhelm Schmidt, arrives in the United States without a penny in his pocket. He knows only a few words of English. He soon changes his name to William Smith or simply Bill Smith[8] and becomes a Protestant. While he never learns much English because most of his friends are German immigrants, he refuses to allow his children to speak German outside their home. He works very hard as a laborer in a factory in Milwaukee and insists that his children get a good education. Today, all of his grandchildren are college graduates, they live in the suburbs in middle-class neighborhoods, and they affectionately refer to Wilhelm as "Grampa Bill."

A logical question might be, "If Grampa Bill could raise his family from dire poverty to the upper middle class within two generations, then why can't Puerto Ricans, African-Americans and American Indians be just as successful?" This is a fair and reasonable question if the United States is truly a pluralistic melting pot where everyone has an equal opportunity to succeed. Some might answer by saying, "It's because *these people* lacked Wilhelm's willingness to work hard and his determination to succeed."

But, how did he become so successful? Was it simply a matter of "throwing his culture in the pot" and working hard? Of course it wasn't. Wilhelm easily gave up those cultural characteristics that did not fit the American cookie-cutter mold: his name, his religion, and his language. Many Northern European religious groups easily adapted to the dominant American culture. For example, the Danish Lutheran Church decided to conduct religious services in Danish. However, after less than ten years, it was decided that all services would be in English. It was not this easy for Roman Catholics who conducted masses in Latin, Jews who prayed in Hebrew, Greek Orthodox Churches with masses in Greek, or Muslims who pray and read the Quran in Arabic. Even today, the most economically successful Arab-Americans are Lebanese Christians who more closely fit the cookie-cutter mold. On the other hand, American Indians, Mexican-Americans, and African-Americans could not fit the mold. Regardless of how much they acted like white, Anglo-Saxon Protestants, they could not change their skin color. Even if they mastered English and behaved like Anglo-Americans, they were identifiably different and therefore were easily excluded. They are often subjected to being called pejorative names, such as Oreos (African-American on the outside, white American on the inside), bananas (Asian-American on the outside, white American on the inside), or apples (Native-American on the outside, white American on the inside).

American Identity Movements: A Challenge to the Melting Pot Myth and the Cultural Cookie-Cutter

A cookie cutter is an accurate metaphor for assimilation into the dominant culture throughout the first two hundred years of United States history (and the image still fits today to a certain extent), and yet it is important to also acknowledge that members of all racial, ethnic, and religious groups have contributed to the development of the United States and have left their mark on the mainstream culture. Most of these contributions have been to the external culture in terms of words found in American English coming from American Indian and various African languages, food, music, the arts, sciences, and even architecture. However, many of those who could not fit into the cookie-cutter mold also challenged Americans to create the structurally and culturally pluralistic society it claimed to be.

The country has greatly changed in the past half century. School segregation was legal until 1954, when the Supreme Court outlawed it in the famous *Brown v. Board of Education* case. In 1955, Emmett Till, a fourteen-year-old boy from Chicago who was visiting his relatives in Mississippi, was kidnapped, beaten, and shot in the head by two white men because he may have whistled at or said "Bye baby" to a white woman. His mutilated body was found three days later in the Tallahatchie River. The two men were tried for Till's murder and acquitted by a jury of 12 white men, and the egregiousness of the incident helped to spark the nascent Civil Rights movement.

As late as the 1960s, it was illegal for a white person to marry a black person in 17 states. In 1967, the Supreme Court unanimously ruled in *Loving v. Virginia*[9] that anti-miscegenation laws were unconstitutional in Virginia and all other states. As far north as Washington, D.C., most restaurants, public schools, and neighborhoods were segregated well into the mid-1960s. The 1964 Civil Rights Act made it illegal to discriminate against people within the United States, or people coming to America, because of their race, ethnicity, or religion. Not only did segregation become illegal in public restaurants and schools, but it also became illegal to discriminate against "classes of people" in the workplace.[10]

Certainly, the most dramatic cultural challenge to both the melting pot myth of cultural pluralism and the cultural cookie-cutter of assimilation to a dominant cultural mold took place in the mid-1960s during the Civil Rights Movement in the United States. Cultural imperialism (not cultural pluralism) was a result of racism, but also a consequence of liberalism. The dynamics of racism are very apparent, but the more subtle effects of liberalism are less apparent. In fact, the idea of a community of equals found in American liberalism seems to be contrary to any sort of racism or cultural imperialism. Yet, the belief that all men are equal is perhaps as responsible for this cultural leveling as any sort of overt racism, primarily because it denies the reality of physical and cultural differences among and between people.

In the 1960s, many white liberals argued that their position was the polar opposite of the racist. They would actually say, "I can't be a racist because I'm a liberal!" One very fundamental problem with this assertion is that it posits that only conservatives can be racists[11] and this is untrue. Many liberals are, in fact, racists, and many conservatives are totally opposed to racism.

Let us contrast the position of the overt racist and the liberal in the 1960s. The racist would maintain that whites and non-whites are inherently genetically *different* and therefore non-whites are *inferior* to whites. The racist position would hold these two premises:

Racist They are different; therefore they are inferior to us. Some African-Americans would say that only white people can be racists because they have political power. This is perhaps sociologically and politically true, but all people are capable of holding racist beliefs. For example, in the 1960s an African-American psychiatrist at Howard University claimed that white people are genetically inferior to black people because they lack melanin in their skin. She concluded that this is why they lay out in the sun all the time to make their skin appear to be darker. And, Elijah Muhammad, a leader of the Black Muslims, encouraged the belief that whites were created by a mad scientist as a race of "blond, pale-skinned, cold-blue-eyed devils—savages, nude and shameless."[12]

The liberal would claim that whites and non-whites are basically the same, except that non-whites have not been treated equally or fairly. This contention seems to be very humane, yet could easily be interpreted to mean that the only reason non-whites are different is they simply have not had the resources to succeed because they are pathologically white or underdeveloped white people. In other words, they are deficient in some way.[13]

A white liberal in the 1960s might say the following: "There are no differences between black and white people. All men are created equal. It says so in the Constitution. Given an equal opportunity, they would be just like us." This position would hold these two premises:

Liberal There are no differences; they are (or could be) just like us. To begin with, if we are claiming that everyone is the same, this is clearly untrue. There are biological differences between men and women, there are racial differences, and there are certainly cultural differences between people. Secondly, there is nothing in the Constitution stating that all men are equal. It is in the Declaration of Independence, a document created to dissolve a relationship between a colonial power (England) and the newly independent country (the United States). The Constitution does indeed create a government and a body of law and procedure, and it contains no mention of equality. Thirdly, no matter how many opportunities are given, black people cannot become white. And, why should they become white?

Until the mid-1960s, most groups that were excluded from the mainstream culture and society fought to get into the middle class and have an equal opportunity to succeed economically. That is, their social movements were *quantitative*—the objective was to gain a piece of the socioeconomic and political pie. This was true of the labor movement or the movement for the right of women to vote. No one really questioned the cookie-cutter process.

In the mid-1960s, a clenched black fist become a symbol of "Black Pride" and an assertion of the right to retain one's racial and cultural difference and still become part of the mainstream American culture. The Black Identity Movement was a cultural movement. "Black Power" amounted to a rejection of both the melting pot and the cookie cutter. It was no longer a matter of demanding to be allowed into the mainstream by giving up differences to fit a mold. Rather, black Americans asserted their right to keep their differences and still be treated fairly and with an equal opportunity to succeed. This new position demanded not only structural pluralism (desegregation and treating everyone the same) but also cultural pluralism (where all cultures are accepted and valued), or what would later be termed multiculturalism.

This movement was truly culturally revolutionary because it was *qualitative*. Black leaders began to question not only the quality of the pie, but also the process of getting their share. They saw no reason to give up or deny their racial and cultural differences. They couldn't become white even if they wanted to. The new position held the following two premises:

Realistic Humanism   We are different; there is no need to give up our differences. This third position became the basis for the women's liberation (feminist), Chicano (Mexican-American), American Indian (AIM), and gay pride movements. Members of each of these groups acknowledge and celebrate their differences from the mainstream society, but they also want to be accepted equally as part of the overall American society and culture.

No longer are members of these minority groups willing to pay the price of the loss of individual and cultural identity to get their fair share of the systemic pie. If gaining a quantitative advance means a qualitative loss in lifestyle to accommodate the mass-society cookie-cutter, then the alternative is no longer to withdraw, but rather to alter the dominant cultural system to allow for the retention and enhancement of cultural identity while still getting a fair share of the pie.

These three different positions regarding race can be outlined in this manner:

RACIST: *OTHERS ARE GENETICALLY DIFFERENT; THEY ARE THEREFORE INFERIOR*

LIBERAL: *WE ARE ALL BASICALLY THE SAME; GIVEN AN EQUAL OPPORTUNITY, THEY WOULD BE JUST LIKE US*

REALISTIC HUMANIST: *THERE ARE PHYSICAL AND CULTURAL DIFFERENCES; NO ONE NEEDS TO GIVE UP THESE DIFFERENCES TO SUCCEED*

To better understand the melting pot and cookie-cutter myths in action, we will next consider the history of the interaction of American Indians, African-Americans, and Asian-Americans with the dominant American culture. Unlike European immigrants, these people were identifiably different, and they could not simply melt into the pot or give up their differences to fit a mold even if they wanted to become a part of the mainstream culture. They were often excluded and experienced discrimination.

Next, with the experience of these groups in mind, we will discuss if the melting pot and cookie-cutter are no longer accurate analogies for multiculturalism in America, whether there is a more accurate analogy that we can make? Finally, we will discuss the current hot button racial topic: the immigration of Mexican-Americans and its impact on American culture.

Manifest Destiny: American Indians and Ethnic Cleansing

> *Toward the aborigines of the country no one can indulge a more friendly feeling than myself, or would go further in attempting to reclaim them from their wandering habits and make them a happy, prosperous people.*
>
> —ANDREW JACKSON

The treatment of the American Indian[14] and the institution of slavery are among the most unsavory aspects of American history. Andrew Jackson, a war hero and land speculator, was called "Long Knife" by American Indians because of the sword he carried as he fought in a series of bloody wars against various Indian tribes. As president, Jackson created a policy of removal that amounted to the forced eviction of almost all of the Indians on the East Coast. Jackson gave eloquent speeches before Congress in which he claimed that it was impossible to protect American Indians and to preserve their cultures. He argued that it was therefore in their own best interests that they should be relocated inland—far away from perhaps the most fertile land in the country, which they currently occupied, and onto barren, scarcely cultivatable land west of the Mississippi River.[15]

In 1830, Jackson gave a speech on Indian removal in which he said,

> It gives me great pleasure to announce to Congress that the benevolent policy of the government, steadily pursued for nearly thirty

years, in relation with the removal of the indians [sic] beyond the white settlements is approaching to a happy consumation [sic]. . . . It will seperate [sic] the indians [sic] from immediate contact with settlements of whites; enable them to pusue [sic] happiness in their own way and under their own rude institutions; will retard the progress of decay, which is lessening their numbers, and perhaps cause them gradually, under the protection of the government and through the influences of good counsels, to cast off their savage habits and become an interesting, civilized, and christian [sic] community.

In his fifth annual message to Congress on December 3, 1833, Jackson defended his policy as a way of protecting Indians, and yet it ended with their total removal from land on the East Coast on which they had lived for tens of thousand of years.[16] This policy destroyed their traditional ways of life. This policy today would clearly be described as ethnic cleansing.

Over a ten-year period, more than 70,000 Indians gave up their homes. In 1836, tens of thousands died of famine and disease during the deadly forced march westward, which is referred to as the Trail of Tears by American Indians. Of course, the removal of Indians freed up very valuable land for white settlers; land that could be cultivated for crops and some land on which valuable resources were found. In 1838 and 1839, the Cherokee nation was forced to give up its lands east of the Mississippi River and to migrate to an area in present-day Oklahoma. Over 4,000 out of 15,000 of the Cherokees died during their march to Oklahoma.

This policy was a consequence of Manifest Destiny, another variation on the theme of American exceptionalism. The phrase was invented by the journalist Timothy O'Sullivan and it described the widely held belief that Divine Providence had given white settlers the entire continent from the East to the West Coast. It was the "Will of God." James Polk,[17] who followed in Jackson's footsteps, used a political platform built on the concept of Manifest Destiny to get elected to the presidency in 1845.[18]

In 1851, Congress created the reservation system, which moved the remaining American Indians to lands allotted to them by the government. The land they were given was often quite barren and this placed the Indians in a difficult economic situation from the start. Originally, white religious leaders were placed in charge of the reservations, so that the Indians could be taught Christianity and essentially made to fit the Anglo-American cookie-cutter model. Eventually, in 1934, American Indians were granted self-government rights on a tribal basis, although for many, the quality of life on reservations remained exceptionally poor.

Today, American Indians have among the highest rates of malnutrition, alcoholism, suicide, and poverty of any racial or ethnic group in the United States. They have among the highest levels of unemployment and illiteracy. They are less than 1 percent of the overall American population, and over half still live on reservations. While some of the more than 500 different tribes and clans are doing better than they did a few decades ago because of the discovery of oil or minerals on their land or the establishment of casinos,[19] overall they are still economically, socially, culturally, and politically marginalized.

Most Americans really do not give much thought to the fate of American Indians. At a press conference at Moscow State University in May 1988, a student asked President Reagan about American Indians. He was taken aback by the question and paused for a few moments, after which he responded that the government provided land for *preservations* and they were "humored" by being allowed to keep their kind of "primitive lifestyle."[20] Of course, he misspoke with the word "preservations" and corrected himself with the word *reservations*. It is not exactly clear what he meant by the word *humored*. Perhaps he meant that Americans tolerated their unwillingness to blend into the overall mainstream culture. The point, however, is that the president of the United States was unprepared to answer this question. Even he had not given much careful thought to the history or current situation of the native peoples of America.

Slavery, African-Americans, and the Civil Rights Movement

No other racial, ethnic, or religious group has encountered the same level of systematic brutality, discrimination, dehumanization, and overt and legalized racism that African-Americans have experienced for nearly four hundred years. Slavery, a bitter Civil War, Jim Crow laws that allowed for legalized discrimination, lynching, and the economic and educational inequality that still exists between African-Americans and white Americans are all familiar to people around the globe.

The first Africans arrived as indentured servants in Jamestown, Virginia in 1619. By 1640, Maryland had become the first colony to legalize slavery; legally Africans were property to be bought and sold by their masters. In 1790, when the first census was taken, slaves and so-called "free Negroes" numbered about 760,000 or nearly 20 percent of the overall population. In 1860, at the start of the Civil War, the black American population was about 4.4 million and by 1900 it was 8.8 million. In 2004, the African-American population was approximately 36 million or about 13 percent of the overall population.

Following the freeing of the slaves in the Civil War, African-Americans were not immediately ensured their civil rights as citizens. It was not until the Civil Rights and Black Identity Movements in the late 1960s that their status in the society approached real equality, at least in the eyes of the law. Not only was racial discrimination made forcefully and fully illegal, but people who had been regarded for so long as inferior human beings because of their race now could take public pride in their race. This movement was the basis of every identity movement since the 1960s, including the Feminist, American Indian Movement, Chicano or gay liberation movements. People who were different than mainstream white Americans were now able to take the position that they were not only different but also proud of their difference. They could become hyphenated Americans and could demand to be given the same opportunities to succeed that white Americans—those who fit more neatly into the American cookie-cutter—had been accorded for hundreds of years.[21]

One result of the Civil Rights Movement and other identity movements that followed was that after years of discrimination and oppression, special opportunities had to be given to allow people of color to catch up with white American males. Beyond making it illegal to discriminate against people in terms of race when it came to jobs, housing, the use of public facilities, or education, in the 1960s the federal government developed affirmative action programs to close the gap between racial groups. To a large extent, these programs succeeded and many have been discontinued, but gaps still exist and racial incidents still occur.

On August 23, 2005, one of the costliest and most damaging hurricanes in American history slammed into New Orleans and destroyed much of the city. At least 1,836 people died in Hurricane Katrina, and the aftermath of the hurricane exposed the reality that black Americans are disproportionately poor. In the low-income areas of New Orleans, many could not leave the city before the hurricane arrived because they did not have the financial resources to escape. They were trapped in poor neighborhoods where floods destroyed their homes. Images of poor black Americans struggling to stay alive in polluted flood waters were broadcast around the globe. There were very few white Americans forced to swim for their lives in New Orleans.

Racism and discrimination still exist in the United States and incidents still occur in which African-Americans are harassed, assaulted, and even killed by racist white people. African-Americans are much more likely than white Americans to be unemployed and below the poverty level, and the percentage of African-Americans in jail is far in excess of their proportional numbers in the overall population. There also remains a significantly large education gap between black and white Americans.

Nevertheless, there have been great improvements for African-Americans in recent years. The income and unemployment gap has narrowed; it is illegal to engage in racial discrimination, and the education levels achieved by African-Americans have improved greatly over the last 50 years. More African-Americans hold public office today than at any other time in American history and many hold or have held very powerful positions in the government. Colin Powell served as head of the Joint Chiefs of Staff and the Department of State, Condoleezza Rice is the Secretary of State and fourth in line to the presidency, and many African-Americans have conducted credible, widely supported campaigns for president, including Jesse Jackson, Al Sharpton, Allen Keyes, and Barack Obama.

A paradox exists that while matters have gotten objectively much better for African-Americans over the past 40 years—and many white Americans think that racism no longer exists—a significant proportion of black Americans think things have gotten worse.[22] When we see the statistic that African-American per capita income has increased

125 percent in the last 40 years, we may be inclined to believe that racism is a thing of the past. Yet, when we also see that the per capita income among whites is nearly twice that of African-Americans, the picture becomes much grayer.[23] Great progress has been made, but work remains to be done.

The Yellow Peril

Asian-Americans have the highest per-capita income and the highest level of education of any racial or ethnic group in America today, including white Americans.[24] The success of Asians in America suggests that race has not been a factor when it comes to the economic or educational success of this group of people. Some would even consider Asians as a model minority and raise the question, "Why can't black Americans do the same thing?"

Of course, all Asians do not succeed and there are many who live in urban areas in absolute poverty. Nevertheless, although the Asian population in the United States is only 4.7 percent, the incoming Harvard class of 2011 was 20 percent Asian.[25] In 2007, at the Massachusetts Institute of Technology, 26.4 percent of the undergraduate and 11.7 percent of the graduate student body was Asian-American.[26] The range of abilities of Asian students is roughly the same as any other group of students. However, many Asian families live in communities that lend social, cultural, and economic support—the China Towns or Korea Towns in the urban areas of the East and West Coast. Most Asian families emphasize the importance of education and regard individual success as success for the sake of the family.

It would be extremely unfair to compare African-Americans to Asian-Americans. Slaves were brought to America involuntarily. They were denied their culture and were often mixed together on the slave ships and the plantations with other slaves who spoke different languages and came from different tribes. Prior to emancipation, it was against the law to teach a slave to read or write. No other ethnic or racial group suffered under the systematic and government approved discrimination that African-Americans experienced for over 400 years.

Despite the fact that Asian immigrants did not suffer the same discriminatory experiences as African slaves, the notion that Asian success has come easily assumes that Asian immigrants were just like European immigrants who could work hard, throw their culture in the melting pot, and become mainstream Americans. This denies the historical reality that the first race riots in the United States actually were Asian, and they occurred in California and Hawaii. During World War II over 120,000 Japanese-Americans were interned in camps in California because the government did not trust their loyalty to the United States. Their property was seized by the government or stolen by neighbors, and yet over half of those interred were legally American citizens. Many had children or siblings who served in the military during the war with Japan. The same mass round-ups and internments did not happen in large numbers with Italian-Americans or German-Americans, despite the fact that the U.S. was simultaneously at war with their countries of origin.

Most Americans have surely forgotten the degree, scale, and extent of the hatred toward Asians in American history. We romantically recall the adventures of the frontiersmen and cowboys of the nineteenth-century Old West. We forget what happened to the American Indian and Asian-Americans during that time. In her book, *Driven Out: The Forgotten War Against Chinese Americans*, Jean Pfaelzer describes "thousands of Chinese people who were violently herded into railroad cars, steamers or logging rafts, marched out of town or killed," from the West Coast to the Rocky Mountains.[27]

Immigrants have often been considered a threat to the American way of life, but this has been especially true of non-white immigrants. In many cases, they became scapegoats for the many economic failures of lower-class white Americans. Even Irish Catholics, who are clearly "white," were considered non-white by many nativists shortly after the arrival of the first enormous wave of Irish immigrants during the Great Famine of 1845.[28] They worked as manual laborers using shovels and hammers to dig ditches and tunnels, build roads, and construct office buildings. As long as they were designated as lower on the class ladder than poor native-born Americans, they could be looked down upon. This, in turn, elevated these poor nativists, in just the same way as poor whites in the deep South often were the most racist toward

THE YELLOW TERROR IN ALL HIS GLORY

FIGURE 3.1 "The Yellow Terror In All His Glory." A racist 1898 editorial cartoon.

black Americans. For Irish Catholic immigrants, being labeled non-white was a matter of social and economic class, not skin color or hair texture. This is surely a classic example of how race has little to do with biology and is instead very much a social construct.

The best thing that ever happened to the Irish was when the first large wave of Italian immigrants came. There has been a longstanding historical pattern of Americans looking down upon the most recent waves of immigrants. This same pattern is repeated today with the current attitude toward Mexican immigrants. Unfortunately, one of the ways immigrants have often raised themselves up the socioeconomic ladder is by putting down people of color. Although Irish Catholics were discriminated against in Ireland, they often "became white" by supporting discrimination and racism against African-Americans. In many countries, words that designate racial color are much more based upon social or economic class than skin color. For example, in Brazil, the word *preto* literally translates as "black," yet it is used to describe someone of a low social class. An upper class person with dark skin might not be described as *preto*. In many parts of Europe, people from India with dark skin are described as *black* whereas in the United States they would not be.

After gold was found in California in 1848, many Chinese came there to find their fortunes, but most were unsuccessful and left California for work elsewhere. In the mid-1800s, they worked as laborers to build the railroad connecting the East and the West coasts. As laborers and people of color, like the Irish, they were viewed as an inferior race of people. When the railroad beds were finally laid across the country, Chinese laborers were no longer needed and they were viewed as a threat. The Chinese Exclusion Act of 1882[29] was initially a ten-year law excluding Chinese from immigrating to the United States or becoming naturalized citizens. The Geary Act extended the act for another ten years in 1892, and the Extension Act of 1904 made the law permanent. In 1943, China became an important ally of the United States against Japan, so the Chinese Exclusion Act was repealed.

The racist idea of a "yellow peril," which was popularized by the Hearst newspapers and manifested itself in the Exclusion Act, did indeed reduce Chinese immigration from 30,000 per year to just 105. The labor leader Samuel Gompers argued: "The superior whites had to exclude the inferior Asiatics, by law, or if necessary, by force of arms." Even Irish Catholics looked down upon the Chinese- and African-Americans and became the most vocal members of labor unions who fought to exclude people of color.

The Chinese were perhaps the first people to engage in massive civil disobedience and staged the earliest Civil Rights Movement. The Geary Act of 1892 required Chinese immigrants to carry an identity card, proving that they were in the country legally, or else face deportation. Thousands refused to comply with what they termed the Dog Tag Law. Furthermore, Chinese immigrants filed more than 7,000 lawsuits in the decade after the Chinese Exclusion Act of 1882. As with the 1960s Black Civil Rights Movement, they challenged what they viewed as unfair and unconstitutional legislation that violated their civil rights. Most importantly, both African-Americans and Chinese-Americans forced the nation to obey its own laws.

Salad Bowls, Mosaics, and Tapestries

Few Americans today would refer to the United States in terms of melting pots or cookie-cutters. For over 20 years the Department of Commerce has described contemporary America as a *salad bowl*. While this metaphor reflects the assumption that each vegetable adds to the salad and there is some sort of common dressing, the idea of groups of people as carrots and lettuce is not very flattering. A much more artistic metaphor might be that the United States is becoming a *mosaic* or a *tapestry*.

The splendor of a mosaic or tapestry is found in its contrasting colors and textures, and if you were to remove one piece from the mosaic or one thread from the tapestry you would destroy its beauty and integrity. Today, most Americans would say these metaphors aptly describe the United States. It is not a matter of melting cultures together into some sort of tasteless stew or giving up cultural differences to fit into some mold, but rather one of retaining the unique contributions and character that each cultural group brings to the whole.

American society is moving from a structurally pluralistic society (the melting pot) to a culturally pluralistic (mosaic) one in which the mainstream culture becomes much more than simply the sum of its parts.[30] Desegregation, affirmative action, and laws that protect civil rights all are important aspects of *structural pluralism*. This means more than simply freedom from oppression. It also requires providing equal opportunities for education, housing, and employment, and removing the barriers that prevented minorities from realizing the American Dream. *Cultural pluralism* means moving to a higher level of integration by accepting and valuing the differences that each group brings to the overall society.

The Mexican Threat

Today, some politicians want laws passed that would require Mexican[31] immigrants to carry identity cards. Some counties and cities have even passed laws that allow local police to stop Mexican immigrants, ask for their identification, and if they have nothing to prove that they are legal immigrants or citizens, to turn them over to federal authorities for deportation. Just as Chinese immigrants went to court because these types of laws were unfair, discriminatory, and a violation of civil rights, it is possible that Mexican-Americans soon will organize to challenge the constitutionality of such laws that are obviously racist. No one would consider requiring white people or even other non-white immigrants to carry identity cards. Although it is possible that nearly 20 percent of Korean immigrants are undocumented, there seems to be no movement to require Koreans to carry identity cards.[32] Mexicans, the most recent wave of immigrants, have replaced Irish Catholics, Italians, and Asians as scapegoats.

Harvard Professor Samuel Huntington argues that Mexican immigrants, especially those who are undocumented, are a threat to the American culture because they refuse to learn English or adopt the values of mainstream Americans. In his opinion, Anglo-Protestant values and institutions have made the country what it is today: "Throughout American history, people who were not white Anglo-Saxon Protestants have become Americans by adopting America's Anglo-Protestant culture and political values."[33]

Huntington claims that Mexican-Americans refuse to *assimilate*— they are unwilling to learn the values, customs and behaviors of mainstream Americans. Learning the behavior and values of another culture is usually termed *acculturation*, not *assimilation*. There is no evidence that Mexican-Americans refuse to learn the values and behaviors of mainstream America. In fact, it is rare to find the child of a Mexican immigrant who speaks fluent Spanish rather than English.

The power to assimilate rests in the hands of mainstream white America, the dominant culture.[34] It literally means to be accepted as equal or as a full participant within the society. Regardless of how much a person of color tries to acquire the values of white Americans or to behave like them, because they are identifiably different, they can be excluded.

Just as other immigrants have adapted, Mexicans do indeed learn or acculturate to the dominant culture. While many children of immigrants may grow up in a home where a language other than English is spoken, research has shown that only about a third still speak it well by the time they are adults.[35] About 90 percent of Hispanic immigrants' children speak English at home.[36] About a third of these children marry non-Mexicans. Even illegal Mexicans commit fewer crimes than American natives. They are good Christians who come to work, raise their families, and have a better way of life than they had in Mexico. Is this any different than most other immigrants, such as Germans, Italians or Greeks?

The only significant differences between Mexicans and other immigrants is that they come from a country that is very poor and contiguous with the United States, and perhaps more importantly, they are Catholic and people of color. Huntington goes so far as to question the national loyalty of Mexican-Americans and suggests that when they fly the Mexican flag on Cinco de Mayo, it is a clear indication that their national loyalty is with Mexico. On St. Patrick's Day, it seems that the majority of Americans claim to have Irish ancestry and they wear green. Some even fly the Irish flag. And on Columbus Day, Italian-Americans proudly fly Italian flags. Yet, no one questions the patriotism or loyalty of Irish-Americans or Italian-Americans.

Television commentator, author, and former presidential candidate Patrick Buchanan shares most of Huntington's views and believes that a wall must be built between Mexico and the United States. Yet, he does not argue that a wall should be built between Canada and the United States. What is the difference? One obvious difference is that Canada is not as poor as Mexico and therefore Canadians are unlikely to illegally cross the border for jobs. But, it is also true that Canadians are white and most are Protestant Anglo-Saxons.

Both Huntington and Buchanan are staunch anti-Communists who saw Communism as a monolithic threat to the United States. During the Cold War, their version of patriotism was very reactionary and based upon fear of an imminent threat from Communism. Not only did Communism inform Americans as to whom they were not, it also brought about national unity and provided a very dramatic scapegoat. If the economy was bad, we could blame it on Communists. President Reagan often referred to the Soviet Union as the "Evil Empire." Moreover, his first Secretary of State, Alexander Haig, blamed all terrorism on Communists, including Iranians who took over the American Embassy in Iran in 1979. These Iranians were followers of Ayatollah Ruhollah Khomeini who certainly had no relationship with Soviet Communists, whom he would have viewed as "godless people" who followed an atheist ideology. In fact, prior to the seizure of the American embassy, the hostage-takers debated about whether the Soviet embassy would be the better target. Those who took the embassy surely hated the Soviet Union as much as they hated the United States.

When the Cold War ended, there was no overarching demonic enemy for the U.S. to oppose, and Huntington believes that a good enemy is necessary to maintain a sense of national identity.[37] In his book *The Clash of Civilizations*, he outlines his theory that the world is dividing into at least six civilizations according to religions, with the greatest threat coming from a monolithic Islamic civilization. Even worse, he says that Confucian Civilization (e.g., the Chinese) will sell arms to Muslims to attack the United States and the situation will degenerate into a clash "between the West against the Rest." This is carrying ethnocentric and xenophobic paranoia to a level unmatched since the medieval Crusades. But, it is also interesting that the civilizations that Huntington believes will be in conflict are the white Anglo-Saxon West against the non-white rest of the world. It is difficult to not conclude that racism is a factor in his warnings.[38]

Of course, the Islamic world is no more monolithic than the Communist world was, and most Muslims have no desire to destroy the West. The largest Muslim nation in the world is Indonesia, which is also one of the Muslim countries in which America's popularity is highest. But, Huntington's ideas have been very popular during the period of great and ambiguous threat since 9/11 because they give Americans a clear enemy and provide scapegoats. And, we seem to need clarity, enemies, and scapegoats. Whether we find these scapegoats for all or most of our ills in new immigrants, Islamic militants, or elsewhere, the need to define a clear and present enemy has been a crucial factor in American public policy following the Cold War, and especially following 9/11.

By all accounts, illegal or undocumented Americans represent no more than 13 million in a country of over 300 million people. They are a tiny minority who are overall peaceful, law-abiding, hardworking, family-centered people who long for a better way of life. As with other immigrants, Mexicans have often risked their lives to come here. They swim across the Rio Grande River or face the hardships of crossing a harsh desert. Many men, women, and children die in their attempt to find better education for their children and a future that will allow these children to become doctors, lawyers, or even presidential candidates.

They come to work at the lowest salaries and end up in backbreaking, manual labor jobs such as building roads and office buildings, picking fruit, housecleaning, or mowing lawns. These are jobs that many American citizens avoid.

Mexicans have never threatened hard-working Americans or the national economy. The unemployment rate has been under 7 percent for many years and there is a need for immigrants to not only provide labor, but to maintain the level of productivity that Americans have been accustomed to for centuries. While some would claim that the crackdown on illegal Mexican immigrants is a matter of fighting terrorism, there were no Mexicans in the planes that flew into the World Trade Center or the Pentagon on 9/11. In fact, none of the Arab terrorists came across the border from Mexico. Of course, all countries need to know who are legal citizens or visitors. But, one way to prevent illegal immigrants from coming across the border is to provide more visas for people to come legally. If they can come through the front door, why would anyone break into your house?

The Mexican Threat will recede in the minds of Americans just as the Yellow Peril and Communism have become innocuous historical bogeymen, and another group of people will probably replace Mexicans as an imagined threat and a real scapegoat. Of course, this group will be easier to depict as an enemy if they are not white Anglo-Saxon Protestants who fit the shape of the American cookie-cutter. Perhaps this is simply a rite of passage for newcomers, and perhaps the good news is that the rite is slightly less pernicious than in the past and every previously persecuted group has eventually made it into the mainstream. Moreover, the need to fit into the Anglo-Saxon Protestant mold is much less today than it was in the past, as the country truly becomes more of a tapestry in which more and more Americans are becoming hyphenated.

Americans think that we welcome immigrants as long as we can somehow force them to fit our cookie-cutter mold and share our so-called mainstream American values and practices. In reality, most of the immigrants who come here are probably not typical of people in their home cultures or they would never leave their homelands. Their choice to come to this country can be seen as an indication that they already must share such basic American beliefs and values as individualism and hard work, the idea of equality and earned status, a focus on the future, and an optimistic faith that life will get better if you do something to change yourself and the world. A 2007 Pew poll surveyed the Muslim population in America, and found some striking results to support this. The survey found that 64 percent of non-Muslim Americans held the quintessentially American belief that they could get ahead through hard work. The same percent of American-born Muslims shared that belief. However, 74 percent of Muslim immigrants to this country identified with this belief—making Muslim immigrants to the U.S. "more American" than native-born non-Muslim *or* Muslim-Americans.

This trend actually holds up across all immigrant groups.[39] Immigrants tend to put this belief in success through hard work into practice as well. A 2007 report by the Urban Institute shows that while 82 percent of the native-born population between ages 18 and 64 participates in the work force, 85 percent of legal immigrants are participants, as well as 93 percent of unauthorized immigrants.[40]

Returning to the Pew survey described above, twice the number of Muslim immigrants supported adopting American customs as those who preferred to "remain distinct" from American society. Conversely, of American-born Muslims, there was an even split between those who opted for adopting American customs and those who preferred to remain distinct.

Immigrants also tend to believe in the idea of American exceptionalism and the conception of the country as a city upon a hill. A recent survey of immigrants found that 80 percent believe that "America is a unique country that stands for something special in the world."[41] They also may have valued individualism more than collectivism, looked toward the future, and were willing to leave their extended family and the past behind, and shared many of the other typical American values and beliefs.

These immigrants not only were different than their compatriots who stayed home, they also shared a common experience of striving to get ahead in a new country. Italians, Germans, Poles, Jamaicans, Egyptians, and Mexicans all tell their children stories of coming to a new country with almost no money and managing to survive and excel based upon their own individual efforts. It is likely that every immigrant group believes that its people struggled more than others to succeed in the United States, and did so without much economic support from the government. They took jobs that most Americans would never do and they were paid pennies to perform menial labor. American immigrant literature is filled with these stories.

Along with the belief that they earned their place in the overall society, most immigrants have a sense of pride in the accomplishments of their own people. Popular ethnic movies such as *My Big Fat Greek Wedding* convey the message that "our people" are hardworking people who are now shopkeepers, lawyers, doctors, musicians, writers, and scientists who have contributed to the advancement of civilization and the new country that their children were born into. They are proud of their success, ethnic identity, and the fact that they are American citizens.

The mythology of immigrant struggle also explains why immigrants are not only among the most fundamentally patriotic Americans but also sometimes less likely to welcome any kind of economic or social support for recent immigrants. Psychologist Leon Festinger found that if we engage in a behavior that contradicts our beliefs we feel cognitive dissonance.[42] We can't deny the reality of the particular behavior, so the only way to restore consonance is to change our beliefs. It's an old marketing technique: Convince customers to try a product and they will often come to believe they like the product.

When immigrants leave their homeland and travel to another country, especially if they have done so voluntarily, they are likely to become even more convinced that the move was worthwhile. And, the longer immigrants stay in America, the more likely they are to identify themselves strongly as Americans.[43] Immigrants who have engaged in a struggle to survive in the United States often believe in the basic American principles more strongly than those who are born in the country, just as people who convert to a religion are often more fanatic about the religion than people who were born into the religion. Immigrants are thus often more fanatic patriots and nationalists than native-born Americans.

Despite the congruity of purpose between current immigrants to America and earlier immigrants to the country, immigration policy is a highly contentious issue in America. While we would expect that all immigrants, present and past, would identify with each other as immigrants, more recent immigrants are often looked down upon by those who have lived in the United States for many generations. It is not simply a matter of the earlier arrivals forgetting that they were treated in similar ways when they first arrived. Most tend to believe that their struggles were much greater, that immigrants today have far more economic support and social support from the government and their advocacy groups than they had, and they often share the perceptions of Buchanan and Huntington that recent immigrants do not want to become "good Americans." Indeed, a May 2007 New York Times/CBS poll found that about two-thirds of Americans believed that immigrants would either have no effect on American society or make it worse, and a similar percentage felt that the immigrants would make the economy worse.[44]

Two primary anti-immigration forces—nativism (immigrants are not "true" Americans, but rather an outside ethnocultural threat) and economic protectionism (immigrants will take "our" jobs)—have long driven the debate over immigration and likely will be present in future immigration debates as well. In fact, this is not surprising, as these forces are rooted in some of the American values and traditions that we have been discussing. Nativism bears a strong resemblance to the cookie-cutter theory of American culture. Nativist objections are essentially assertions that immigrants should slot easily into the cookie-cutter. The more immigrants have differed from the cookie cutter, the greater the outcry against them has been, historically speaking. So long as some Americans feel that the cookie cutter is essential to maintaining American culture, nativism will continue in this country.

Economic protectionism, on the other hand, stems from a fear that immigrants may in some way abridge Americans' economic opportunity and ability to earn status. Protectionists feel that Americans' avenues to individual opportunity and success may be constrained by immigrants entering the country and racing down those pathways ahead of native-born Americans. Indeed, polls find that the top fear of most Americans is that immigrants will hurt or take "American" jobs.[45]

Are anti-immigrant sentiments overwhelming in the United States? No. Many Americans support immigrants, authorized or not, in their acculturation to America. Only about a third of immigrants report encountering discrimination because of their immigrant status.[46] Yet, because immigration touches on sensitive issues about what the American Dream is, who can pursue it, and how and when they can do so, it will continue to be a divisive issue in America.

Should English Be the Official Language?

*[The immigrants] who come [to America] are generally of
the most ignorant stupid sort of their own nation. . . . Their
own clergy have very little influence over the people. . . . Not
being used to liberty they know not how to make a modest
use of it . . . they are not esteemed men till they have sown
their manhood by beating their mothers . . . now they come
in droves. . . . Few of their children in the country learn
English . . .*

—BENJAMIN FRANKLIN

There is no official national language in the United States today, and
immigrants have arrived speaking almost every language found on the
face of the earth. Nevertheless, the American version of English has
brought the country together and has a long history as a venue in which
the struggle over acculturation and immigration has been played out.

Cheque and *check. Cosy* and *cozy. Plough* and *plow. Favourite* and
favorite. Defence and *defense. Realise* and *realize.* While these differences
between British English and American English may seem quaint and
minor to many—and vaguely irritating to English editors every-
where—they are actually the heritage of a long debate over language
and its role as a social and cultural glue in America.

After the United States won its independence from Great Britain,
many Americans rued the fact that they spoke the same language as
their former colonial masters and yearned for a distinct language of
their own. As one said, "In most cases, a national language answers the
purpose of distinction: but we have the misfortune of speaking the
same language with a nation, who, of all people in Europe, have given,
and continue to give us fewest proofs of love."[47] John Adams believed
that legally establishing English as the official national language was a
way to set America apart from England and to make its citizens the
most eloquent and best English speakers in the world. (Great Britain
at the time had no official national language, and still does not today.)
However, not all early Americans felt that English should, as a matter
of course, become the national language. Some advocated for French
(the language of Britain's most powerful enemy), others for Greek (as

a nod to America's democratic forebears) and, tellingly, others for Hebrew (as a symbol of America's self-designation as the land of the new Chosen People, thus reinforcing notions of American exceptionalism and chosenness).[48]

Eventually, however, English won out. The early American educator and writer Noah Webster went to great ends to create a distinctly pronounced and spelled American English. "A *national language* is a band of *national union*," Webster wrote. "Every engine should be employed to render the people of this country *national*; to call their attachments to their own country, to inspire them with the pride of national character."[49] Writing at a time when roughly a quarter of Americans did not speak English as their primary language (compared to about a seventh today), Webster created a uniquely American speller (resulting in some of the divergent spellings noted above), which became one of the most popular books in the history of the country, while teaching millions of people to spell in an American manner.

Webster would be proud of the fact that language has played an important role in holding this country together. English is the *lingua franca* of the economic and scientific worlds, if not the entire world. Today, the economic incentives are enormous for one to learn English, in the world and especially in the United States. Some Americans believe it is un-American to use a language other than English in public discourse. One supporter of this position was Theodore Roosevelt, who said, "We have room for but one language in this country, and that is the English language, for we intend to see that the crucible turns our people out as Americans, of American nationality, and not as dwellers in a polyglot boarding house." More than two dozen states and many municipalities have made English their official language, but there is no national official language in America. And, there is no need for one because almost everybody speaks English. Although most Americans believe that English serves as a national unifier, nearly three-quarters of Americans do not feel that English is threatened by immigrants' use of other languages in their own communities.[50] Rather, this English-only push is an outgrowth of the immigration debate and the desire for all Americans to conform to the cultural cookie-cutter.

Over 96 percent of all Americans speak English, and over half of the children of immigrant parents who are born in the United States do not speak the language of their parents.[51] Why would any immigrant parent not want his or her child to speak English? If you are a Hispanic living in Miami, if your children cannot speak English they must remain in the ethnic Hispanic enclave in Miami or go on vacation to Los Angeles. Only about 10 percent of immigrants believe that it is "easy to get a job or do well without English," and over three-quarters of immigrants agree that "immigrants who speak good English have an easier time in the U.S."[52]

Thus, language unites Americans. It is one of the easiest ways for an immigrant to acculturate and begin to assimilate into American culture, and is a step that all immigrants do take sooner or later. It is nearly impossible to find in America a third-generation citizen—and likely not even a second-generation citizen—who does not speak English. Yet, this is not true in many other countries in the world. For example, if you put three Spaniards in the same room—one from La Coruña who speaks Gallego, one from Barcelona who speaks Castillian and one from Pamplona who speaks Basque—you would discover that they speak in quite different tongues. Similar Babels could be created with citizens from different regions of China, India, and many other countries. By contrast, the ability to speak and read English allows Americans of all stripes—new immigrants and Mayflower descendants alike—to join in the public discourse and become further ingrained in the country's culture.

CHAPTER 4

From John Winthrop to John Wayne

Exceptionalism, Self-Reliance, and Cowboy Values

Liberty is the proper end and object of authority, and cannot subsist without it; and it is liberty to that which is good, just, and honest.

—JOHN WINTHROP

Give the American people a good cause, and there's nothing they can't lick.

—JOHN WAYNE

*I*T SEEMS THAT THE BELIEF THAT AMERICA and its people are unique or special goes back to the very beginning of the nation.[1] We have discussed how John Winthrop and other early Puritan settlers wanted to create their "city upon a hill": a utopian society with exceptional people where everyone would prosper and live in peace and harmony. This would be totally different from the decadent and violent world they had left in Europe. Many early immigrants saw the U.S. as an opportunity, unique in history, to forge an idealized country in a land bountiful with resources and removed from the chains of tradition and oppression found elsewhere. Winthrop realized this on the deck of the *Arbella* as he launched into his famous speech, which we discussed earlier. The country did indeed become a unique experiment, with new and untested political and economic systems employed nearly from the start, which were enjoyed by people from a variety of social and ethnic origins.

As the country grew, its self-awareness of its own uniqueness never waned. For Lincoln, the U.S. was "the last, best hope on Earth." In the post–Cold War era, the U.S. became "the indispensable nation." Yet, we are left to wonder, what are the historical, sociological, and even geographical circumstances that have made the country and its national values exceptional? Where did this national culture come from? And, what impact has this legacy and conscious feeling of exceptionalism had on the course of American social and cultural development, and on America's place in the world?

What Country Is Most Similar to the United States?

If we ask the average American man or woman to identify the country that is most similar to the United States, the most common response likely would be Canada. Many Americans even jokingly call Canada the 51st state and suppose that it is like America, but colder and with more hockey. Of course, geographically Canadians *are* Americans, and both were originally colonies with early settlers coming from Northern Europe. From the perspective of Europeans, they are both young nations that were part of the "New World" settled by adventurous European explorers.

In both the United States and Canada, socialism as a political movement has never been as influential or as well-organized as in most European countries where social democratic parties are major players in national politics. There is certainly less class-consciousness among the working class of both the U.S. and Canada than in most other capitalist democracies and their concerns have been absorbed into two major political parties.

In contrast to many European countries where many countries that have had a national religion, in Canada and the U.S., the political system has been secular since the birth of both nations. One could go on and on listing the similarities that make both the U.S. and Canada very different from any nation in Europe.

On the other hand, Canada is very different from the United States when it comes to political and economic structure and many values and beliefs.[2] As Seymour Lipset has said, "Canadian intellectuals . . . frequently seek to describe what Canada is about by stressing what it is not: the United States." There are many ways in which Canada is much more "European." Canada has a very large national social welfare system whereas welfare in the United States is mostly a local matter. The United States' national social welfare system is one of the smallest in the industrialized world in terms of percentage of the federal budget. And, rather than throwing off its ties to its colonial motherland as the United States did in 1776, Canada is still part of the British Commonwealth.

When the United States was created, it was assumed that a free press would hold the government accountable and a balance of power between local and federal government and the three branches of government would prevent any leader or branch of government from becoming too powerful. There was a strong anti-statism in the U.S. and an almost obsessive fear of any overly powerful executive. Canada opted for a parliamentary system similar to most European countries.

The United States has never had a national police force similar to the Royal Mounted Police. (The FBI might be considered as somewhat similar to the Royal Mounted Police, but it only has jurisdiction over federal crimes or crimes that cross state lines.) Until recently, almost all criminal acts in this country were considered a concern of the local police force and even gambling has always been a local, not a federal, concern. As with all members of the European Union, Canada does not have the death penalty. It is much more secular than the United States. Emotional religious issues such as gay marriage and abortion are not as politically polarizing and explosive and, in fact, are legal in Canada.

In Canada, marijuana is legal for medical purposes and there is serious consideration for the legalization of marijuana for recreational use.

Following the 2000 Summer Olympic Games in Sydney, some Americans might have said that Australia is very similar to the United States. It is true that Australia was initially populated by British criminals as a penal colony, similar to the state of Georgia in the U.S., and it is also true that the Australians have historically treated the 1 percent of its indigenous or aborigine population in a manner very similar to the way Americans have treated the 1 percent of their indigenous or American Indian population.[3] Furthermore, the pioneer or frontier experience of Australia is often described as similar to the Wild West in the United States: Fearless pioneers built a nation with their bare hands in the face of starvation, an often rugged environment, and isolation from the rest of the world. Yet, like Canada, Australia is also much more European than the United States. It has a strong socialist party, a large federal social welfare system, and the Queen of England as the official head-of-state.

South Africa is another country that we could compare to the United States. Some South Africans might say that they had a frontier experience and while the United States had cowboys, they had their Boers. Afrikaners would argue that both the U.S. and South Africa were initially settled by Calvinists. Unfortunately in both countries, the Calvinist concept of predestination was sometimes used by white people to justify their oppression of black people. In South Africa and the United States some claimed that it was "the will of God" for white people to dominate black people.

But there are also great differences between South Africa and the United States. While the U.S. government supported the Afrikaner government of South Africa in the 1980s, the majority of Americans opposed its apartheid practices and supported sanctions until that government allowed for full political participation of all South Africans. The Afrikaner regime stood for everything that Americans claimed to be against since the passage of the American Civil Rights Act in 1964.[4]

Many Americans identified with the South African struggles against the racist practices of apartheid and saw a reflection of their own history of racism. Television news broadcasts of the fight of black and colored South Africans for democracy and freedom reminded Americans of the Civil Rights Movement in the United States. Despite the official policy of their government, American citizens realized that to fail to oppose apartheid would be the height of hypocrisy. Nelson Mandela is a hero to most Americans.

Thus, we can see that no country is entirely similar to the U.S. Indeed, most countries are unique to one another in many ways. So, where did the national culture of the U.S. come from? And why is it so exceptional, anyway?

American National or Civic Culture

Both individuals and nations develop their fundamental values, attitudes, and beliefs during their formative years. Over time, personalities and cultures may indeed change, but the change is much less than most of us would expect. Almost all psychologists and sociologists agree that patterns of values, beliefs, and behavior that were learned in childhood tend to last a lifetime. Political scientists and intercultural experts view national cultures the same way.

The *national culture* of the United States is a result of values and beliefs brought by early immigrants and shaped by their experience in the New World. Many of their values were reinforced and became even more important, while others died out because they were not rewarded. Even recent immigrants shared many of the traditional American cultural values, beliefs, and perceptions before they even came to the U.S. Thus, most of these original values are alive and well today, and they explain both the historical and contemporary behavior of the American people and their public policies.

When we speak of a *civic culture* we are usually focusing on the shared values and beliefs that shape and reflect the political and legal system of the society. They are the basis for governance. Historical experiences that people share within a nation, such as civil and international wars, economic crises, and natural disasters, give the government legitimacy and create a sense of loyalty or patriotism amongst the populace. In Europe and many other parts of the world, the people of a nation are often of the same religion, ethnicity, or race. However, in the

U.S.' national identity is really a matter of shared experiences and shared values and beliefs.

As we have mentioned in earlier chapters, the iceberg analogy of culture illustrates the relationship between values, beliefs, and behaviors. The largest part of an iceberg is hidden beneath the water level. The same is true of national or civic culture. Most of it is unconscious and hidden beneath the level of awareness. And yet this internal culture, which is inside our heads, is by far the most important aspect of culture because it allows us to explain and even predict behavior.

To understand the political, economic, social, and even personal behavior of Americans, we must first know the dominant values of their culture, which are passed down from one generation to another through both explicit and implicit learning. In the process of growing up in the U.S., children often acquire their basic civic cultural values and beliefs from their parents though the process of enculturation. But, they are also reinforced in school with formal classes on "civics" or through the process of socialization as they participate in various groups that use the legal, political, and economic principles shared by most Americans. And, while many immigrants already share many of these values before they arrive, which prompted them to come to the U.S., they and their children also learn these values through their participation in the American educational, legal, political, and economic system. These values have existed without much modification since the beginning of the nation. They are extremely resilient and long lasting.

Author and pollster Daniel Yankelovich conducted a nationwide survey of American traditional values and found that perhaps only one value going back to the early colonial period had changed in importance over time. This was the value placed on delayed gratification and saving money for one's children.[5] Early immigrants upheld the Calvinist values of hard work and frugality. Their hope was that through their efforts they would provide a better way of life and more opportunity for their children in the future. Yankelovich discovered that by the late 1970s, Americans were more likely to enjoy life and sought immediate gratification. Rather than saving for the future, they spent money to go on vacations or enjoy a new automobile. In turn, this meant that their children had to survive more through their own efforts. On the other hand, it is reasonable to assume that most of those in his survey were not recent arrivals and were born after the Great Depression of the

1930s. They did not have the memories or experiences of the privation and deprivation of earlier generations.

This new emphasis on the present and an unwillingness to invest for the future has major implications for the economy as we find that Americans often purchase goods with the expectation that they will soon become outdated and will need to be replaced. Furthermore, Americans save much less money than people in other countries, such as the Japanese. It is also reflected in the failure to maintain the infrastructure of the U.S.

Franklin Roosevelt developed federal programs to build monumental dams for hydroelectric power, and during the Eisenhower years Americans spent hundreds of millions of dollars to build an interstate highway system that is still the pride of America. Throughout the 1950s and 1960s, nuclear power plants and urban transportation systems were built. However, this system is falling into dangerous disrepair, bridges are collapsing,[6] subways are woefully inadequate to meet the demands of major cities and even the air traffic control system is completely out-of-date. However, because it appears that today most Americans seem to be more concerned about the present than the future, it is doubtful that any major political leader will call for massive federal spending to rebuild the infrastructure of the U.S. to preempt further deterioration of the national transportation system. Even worse, until very recently, few politicians would even consider such environmental issues as sustainable energy resources and protecting the environment for future generations. These issues have become of much greater concern in Europe.

The First Americans

To understand what constitutes the distinct, foundational characteristics of American culture we must first examine who made up the country's first immigrants. (First, however, a disclaimer: with apologies to the rest of the hemisphere, we are using the term *American* to mean citizens of the United States. Of course, anyone living in the Western Hemisphere is, by definition, an "American." And, both Canadians and Mexicans are indeed "North Americans." Unfortunately, there is no other way to describe citizens of the United States in standard American English. We cannot call them "United States-ians.") Understanding who these first immigrants were, and what type of society they wished to create, is crucial for understanding American culture and the course that the country has taken. As historian Arthur Schlesinger, Sr., noted, "In a large sense, all American history has been the product of these migratory movements from the Old World."[7] To understand who these first Americans were, we must ask ourselves: What kind of place were they leaving; what were the values that they held; why did they come; and what kind of place did they wish to create in America?

We sometimes forget that the first immigrants who came to the United States in large numbers were not typical Europeans. If they were typical, they would have stayed at home. In fact, most immigrants were quite atypical. The early settlers who embarked on the dangerous journey to the New World were fleeing religious and political persecution in countries where often corrupt and brutal tyrants ruled and where there were few individual rights and freedoms. These early immigrants set themselves apart from the majority of their fellow citizens because they rebelled against the persecution and limited rights and freedoms found in their countries. The Old World of Europe was a violent and warlike place, where absolute monarchs rather than laws ruled the people. Fear, hopelessness, and despair were rampant. Primarily for economic and religious reasons, many people sought to flee this world for a new one, which was full of promise and far from the cultural, social, economic, and political norms from which they wanted to separate. While the immigrant population was fairly diverse and many different countries set up colonies in America (the English, French, Spanish, and Dutch, especially), England eventually came to control the 13 colonies that would become the United States and thus that country left the most distinctive mark on the emerging nation. Notably, however, England did not restrict immigration to English citizens, thus helping to make America the multicultural place that would come to be one of its hallmarks.

Of course, many immigrants came because there was no realistic hope of escaping poverty in the Old World. If you were born poor, you usually died poor. And your children and children's children could not expect much better, as there was little economic or social mobility in life. In most of Europe, the economic and social classes were so rigidly stratified that the social structure resembled the caste systems found in India and other countries in the nineteenth and early twentieth centuries.

Most immigrants came because they already shared values, beliefs, and worldviews that were typically American and yet were not typical of their home cultures. This is true even today. Most Europeans saw little economic hope for the future and yet these immigrants believed that economic change was possible if they were willing to take risks. Many left all that they had in Europe—land, extended family, business ties, and cultural familiarity—to seek a fresh start in America. They were willing to part with the past and look toward a more prosperous future for themselves and their children. Indeed, many even became indentured servants to those who had already settled in America in order to pay for their passage, so desperate were they to come to the country. (Many also came to America by the coercion of the barrel of a gun, and through the harrowing, nightmarish voyage across the Atlantic known as the Middle Passage. These were the African slaves, who were forcibly brought to America and whose numbers increased during the seventeenth century and ballooned during the eighteenth and nineteenth centuries.)[8]

However, the majority of those who immigrated to America, unfettered by the obligations of servitude, seem to have been from the middle and laboring classes, who risked much in order to try to gain even more in the New World.[9]

Of course, many of the early immigrants believed in the so-called American Dream: that anyone could escape from poverty and oppression and that the future would be better than the past or the present. Economic motivations to migrate to America—where land was free or very cheap and opportunities were many—played a significant role in the choice of many early immigrants to come to America. This is not to say that America evolved into a classless society, however. In fact, class differentiations became quite evident in some parts of early America, particularly the South. However, for many immigrants (especially the earliest settlers of New England), religious motivations played a similarly important role in their decision to come to the New World.

The Religious Dimension

For many early immigrants to America, the disillusionment with their homelands that hastened their immigration was derived from deeply held utopian or antiestablishment religious views. These immigrants included members of religiously and politically persecuted sects in Europe, such as the Calvinists[10] and the Puritans.[11] These sects were religious minorities in Europe who were opposed to the Roman Catholic Church or the official religion of their country. They saw these entrenched versions of Christianity as corrupt and in need of reform. They were often willing to go to jail in defense of their religious beliefs and practices, and therefore, from the European perspective, they were viewed as religious fanatics. When they left to make a home for themselves in the New World, where they could put their religious ideals into practice without the interference of the state, many in Europe were glad to get rid of them and saw the New World as a dumping ground for religious malcontents, much as Australia was later seen as a dumping ground for criminals.

When most people think of Puritanism, they likely recall something along the lines of literary critic H.L. Mencken's definition of the sect: "Puritanism: The haunting fear that someone, somewhere, may be happy." This aspect of Puritanism is perhaps the one that most readily comes to mind when one hears the word *puritanical* in common usage, meaning the quality of zealously enforcing a stricter moral code than is the norm. This aspect of Puritanism has often blurred the line between moralizing admonitions and actual political crusades in American history such as the Prohibition movement, the current debate on school prayer and evolution vs. creationism or intelligent design, and the teaching of the Bible in schools. Usually, Puritanism manifests itself in accepted mores and behaviors rather than political movements. Compared to many parts of Europe from which Puritanism was born, in the U.S. there are greater controls on the sexual content on television and American politicians are expected to be faithful to their spouses. Europeans were amused by the Puritanical public reaction to President Bill Clinton's sexual liaison with a White House intern during the Monica Lewinsky scandal.

Some historians believe that the sexual repression and the denial of physical pleasures that was attributed to seventeenth and eighteenth century Puritanism was greatly exaggerated and often confused with the middle-class restraint and sexual prudishness of Victorianism in the latter two-thirds of the nineteenth century. Victorianism was seen as the opposite of the debauchery that the middle classes associated with European aristocratic behavior. Although this movement was named after England's Queen Victoria, it may have actually been stronger in the United States, where the middle classes were larger and more dominant in society and there was a stronger revulsion against nobility and their perceived sensual excesses. The expression "Victorian" today is usually what most people probably mean when they say "Puritanical"—the Puritans of the seventeenth and eighteenth century were actually a fairly earthy people, who apparently had no problem talking about sex or bodily functions.

Most of the religiously motivated immigrants such as the Calvinists and Puritans imagined themselves as leaving behind a religious wasteland in the Old World for the opportunity to create a religious utopia in the New, as can be seen in the memoir of Edward Johnson, one of the early settlers of Massachusetts:

> When England began to decline in Religion . . . in this very time Christ the glorious King of his Churches, raises an Army out of our English Nation, for freeing his people from their long servitude under usurping Prelacy; and because every corner of England was filled with the fury of malignant adversaries, Christ creates a New England to muster up the first of his Forces in.[12]

Their dismal past, real and perceived, was left behind, as these settlers focused on a brighter future in America, with new opportunities for a better way of life for themselves and their children, a life that would also be more in line with their religious precepts. They were optimists who wanted to create a utopian, more democratic, and peaceful society removed from the rest of the world, where they could put their beliefs into practice and take advantage of opportunities and freedom unavailable to them in the Old World. This sentiment, backed with religious fervor, created an overarching desire among many early immigrants to create John Winthrop's "city upon a hill," a community that would be a beacon for all humanity. This sentiment formed the beginnings of the concept of American exceptionalism, one of the foundational cultural values of the country.

For these settlers, their new society would be a democratic *religious* community on a communal scale. This sentiment, however, and the amalgamation of such communities, in time certainly helped to build the secular democratic character of American politics and public life. The traditional Quaker meetings[13] and gatherings of other Congregationalist groups were intensely democratic and egalitarian. The pastor or minister simply convened the meetings during which any member of the community could speak. Rather than leading the congregation, the pastor simply allowed for repartee similar to the role many Americans would attribute to the chair of a public meeting. Quaker meetings, even today, take place in simple meetingshouses where everyone sits facing each other. Congregants can say whatever comes into their minds and share it with others in the community. These comments might involve biblical admonitions and moral lessons or they could also involve current political or economic issues confronting the local community or the nation. This was surely one of the pillars of the "town hall meetings" that we see during such activities as the presidential primaries across the country.

Individualism, Self-Reliance, and the American Frontier

American exceptionalism is, in a sense, a collective notion of another foundational American cultural value: individualism and self-reliance. This value also is rooted in Calvinist thought, which promoted the idea that an individual could forge a unique, personal relationship with God. This was in contradistinction to the prevailing Roman Catholic ideology of the day, which believed that an individual's relationship with God was mediated through the clergy. Protestantism, and especially the American version of Calvinism and Congregationalism, assumed a direct relationship between each individual and God, while Roman Catholicism held that the clergy played an intermediary role.

Calvinism's individualistic focus was further underlined by the idea of predestination. Calvinists believed that the elect, because they had been chosen by God, would be recognizable by their personal and especially economic well-being. Thus, if an individual was successful economically, it was logical that such a person was a member of the elect. Thus, Calvinism contained within it not only the seeds of individualism, but the motivation for personal economic success. This became actualized through the American cultural value of economic mobility, by which the elect could prove their being chosen, and concomitantly through the capitalist economic system. It also meant that the elect were only the custodians of God's wealth and therefore had an obligation to distribute or share the wealth with others. This was the underlying premise of early American philanthropy in contrast with the collectivist and even socialist assumptions in many parts of Europe in the twentieth century that the state had the responsibility for distributing the wealth of the society. Social welfare in the U.S. was traditionally seen as a matter of the elect, and the local church or community, caring for those who were disadvantaged.

American individualism and self-reliance were further developed by the great extent of territory available in the New World, which allowed settlers to expand ever westward. Early immigrants to America staked out small settlements in the New World, many of which—such as Jamestown and Plymouth—remain famous in American folk mythology. Settlers steadily advanced westward, crisscrossing and making inroads into the continent. The enormous size of the continent led to a great diffusion of population. In 1776, most demographers estimate, at least 95 percent of the country was agricultural, and it was not until 1920 that urban population exceeded rural.[14] During this period, the U.S., had no major cities on the scale of London, Berlin, or Paris. It was estimated that the largest city, Philadelphia, had a population of about 35,000 and New York City had only 18,000 residents. Washington, D.C., was largely uninhabited swampland. In 1790, when the first census was taken, New York City was the largest city and only five cities had populations of more than 10,000.

In the years after America became independent, immigrants steadily flowed into the country. Beginning in the 1830s, immigration soared: 143,000 immigrants arrived in the 1830s, nearly 600,000 in the 1840s, and 1.7 million in the 1850s. These immigrants were usually of peasant stock. They were generally not well educated—most could not read or write in their native language, and many did not know English.

Because of their background, many immigrants found success elusive in the developed Eastern parts of the new country. Immigrants who could not succeed in New York City, Boston, or Philadelphia could save their money to buy a covered wagon and move their families West. As the doors to success closed in Eeastern cities, they remained open in the vast expanses of the West. Many followed the journalist Horace Greeley's famous advice for under- or unemployed urban laborers, "Go West, young man!" This process was facilitated by the Homestead Act of 1862, which allowed a head of a family to acquire land consisting of 160 acres, settle it, and cultivate it for five years. At the end of the five-year-period, the head of the family was granted title to the land.[15] This legislation persuaded many immigrants to migrate to the West, and by 1890 all available federal land had been settled by these pioneers. Of course, this land was originally owned by American Indians and many were moved off of the land to make room for European immigrants.

The American Dream of upward economic and social prosperity, dreamt by the country's first immigrants, was perpetuated by westward expansion. Biographies of frontiersmen like Daniel Boone and Davy Crockett helped to create a mythical and magnetic West that was ripe for settlement by rugged individualists. Much like the original immigrants to America, those who settled the west believed that if success and comfort could not be found in the place where they were born, then they were free to seek out new opportunities by moving westward. But success also required individual initiative and responsibility, and a willingness to give up the past and move toward a better future.

This is the basis of the Turner Thesis.[16] Just as Western expansion was coming to an end, historian Frederick Jackson Turner wrote in 1893 that the West provided a safety valve of sorts for America because it reaffirmed the traditional desire for change and the willingness to take risks, and it provided continuing opportunities to achieve economic success when those opportunities were diminishing on the East Coast. More importantly, it reinforced the values of individual freedom and equality and spared Americans from the violent class conflicts that had plagued Europe. Of course, the end of available land in the West—and thus the end of the frontier—introduced the logical extension of Turner's thesis. If the ability to expand was such an important panacea to potential problems, and such an integral part of American character, what would happen once the frontier was settled? It has been argued that increasing international involvement by America, through trade and otherwise, was an outgrowth of the closing of the frontier.[17]

Americans and their values crossed the vast country with astonishing speed. After the War of 1812, and before the Civil War of 1861–1865, there was rapid urbanization in the East and, at the same time, many newly arriving immigrants migrated across the country. By 1853, the United States claimed territory from Canada to Mexico and the Atlantic to the Pacific. In the 1840s, California was flooded with gold miners who came to make their fortunes in the great Gold Rush. By the time the Civil War began in 1861, nearly the entire continent was the domain of the United States.

There was also a missionary zeal to this movement across the continent. The now-famous term *Manifest Destiny* was first used in 1845, to argue that it was America's right to annex territory, because it was "the fulfillment of our Manifest Destiny to overspread the continent allotted by Providence for the free development of our yearly multiplying millions."[18] This meant that it was God's will that Americans (and their values) expand from sea to sea. Americans differed over whether this was to be achieved violently or nonviolently, by governmental fiat or by the fait accompli of the waves of pioneers. Of course, this religious admonition also meant taking the land from American Indians, who were often viewed as heathens to be converted. It also meant taking land from non-Americans, particularly Mexicans. In many ways, Manifest Destiny became the nineteenth century embodiment of the notions developed during the seventeenth and eighteenth centuries of the "city upon a hill"—the special place of America in the world and its license to spread its values. According to this narrative, because of its unique, exceptional character and mission, America had earned as its birthright (i.e., its Manifest Destiny) as much territory as it saw fit to occupy. The famed antebellum senator Stephen A. Douglas summed up this sentiment aptly in 1854: "You cannot fix bounds to the onward march of this great and growing country. You cannot fetter the limbs of the young giant. He will burst all your chains. He will expand, and grow, and increase, and extend civilization, Christianity, and liberal principles."[19]

Self-Reliance and Independence: Cowboy Values

It matters not how strait the gate, How charged with punishments the scroll, I am the master of my fate: I am the captain of my soul.

—FROM "INVICTUS" BY WILLIAM ERNEST HENLEY

The frontier allowed for the fulfillment of the American Dream when opportunities began to fade on the Atlantic Coast. Pioneers had to take the initiative, buy a covered wagon, and move west. To survive on the frontier, each family had to be very self-reliant and independent. There were wagon trains, but each family had its own wagon. Most families tended to eat alone, and they were highly individualistic. Families sojourned west alone, and they settled on farms that were often

FIGURE 4.1 President Ronald Reagan riding his horse, El Alamein. Photo by Pete Souza, Ronald Reagan Presidential Library, National Archives and Records Administration.[20]

days from their nearest neighbor, thus replanting and reinforcing the spirit of individualism, self-reliance, and independence in the West. These were values that were vital for the survival of these pioneers.

To a large extent, these are *cowboy values*—values of the American Western frontier added on to the old European or Calvinist values. These values strike such resonance in American culture that almost every politician who has campaigned for the presidency in the past century has used a picture of himself or herself wearing a cowboy hat. Lyndon Johnson, Ronald Reagan, George H. W. Bush, and Bill Clinton were all photographed while riding horses and these photographs were proudly distributed by the White House Press Office.

President George W. Bush is routinely photographed wearing cowboy boots in the White House and at official functions.[21] Why do politicians want to dress like cowboys? It is all a matter of symbolism. When we think of a cowboy, we visualize some man out in the Wild West all by himself. Cowboys don't ride in groups. It's just the "lone cowboy"—an individual—on his horse with his bare necessities. He is a man of action who manages to survive without any help from anyone else—a self-made man who is totally self-reliant and independent. The American cowboy is a Calvinist on horseback and personifies some of the most important values in the American society.[22]

Geography Also Matters

Some contemporary scholars have argued that the U.S. has been so economically and politically successful in such a short period of time because Americans have unique and special values that allowed for rapid economic growth and a democratic civic culture.[23] This modern version of the American exceptionalism thesis is really an extension of earlier writers such as Max Weber and David McClelland, who claimed that cultural values are the most important determinants of success.[24] If you deconstruct their positions, they are simply arguing that Anglo-Protestant values matter most of all when it comes to the development of a democratic society with strong economic growth. This argument is often used to justify modern nation-building where it is expected that countries must first change their values and practices before the U.S. will provide economic aid. They must first adopt American or Western

Protestant values and create a more capitalistic monetary system after which the U.S. (and the World Bank) will provide more financial aid. This movement was even stronger after the end of the Cold War, when it was assumed that the Soviet Union collapsed because it did not have these values. However, from the perspective of many countries with newly emerging economies, this is a form of cultural imperialism.

But, is it simply a matter of cultural values? It is worth considering that not only were the people coming to America atypical in terms of their values, beliefs, and worldviews and their optimistic focus on the future, but the land itself was atypical. Compared to Europe, with its much greater population density, multitude of urban centers and clearly defined boundaries and borders, America was a land of indeterminate size and seemingly endless bounty, blessed with abundant natural resources and, importantly, a seemingly inexhaustible supply of the physical space that Europe lacked. There appeared to be unlimited natural resources and there was a very small population.[25] The vastness and availability of land meant that, unlike in Europe, one could always settle on land elsewhere in the country and attempt to find prosperity there. Indeed, a popular sentiment in this environment was that if an immigrant was willing to work hard, he or she could and should be successful. While there was an assumption that everyone had an equal opportunity to succeed, some immigrants came with privileges and advantages—particularly education and wealth—which allowed them to succeed more easily than others. But, given these assumptions, it was easy for some early Calvinists to conclude that if someone did not succeed then they were simply lazy, or even worse, that they were not blessed by God. Cynically, one could say the popular attitude was "Cursed are the poor."

American farmers are often idealized as self-made, self-reliant, rugged individualists, and yet neighbors often came together voluntarily. Barn-raising is a good example; it was never viewed as charity, but rather as a matter of common-sense pragmatism and communal reciprocity. No farmer could build a barn without the help of others. And, if needed in the future, the barn-owner could be expected to willingly reciprocate by giving help to anyone else in need. Barn-raising also brought the community together to share camaraderie, good food, and a sense of civic community. There was no sense that somehow accepting help from others produced some sort of dependency or reliance. A farmer simply could not afford the time-consuming task of building his barn on his own, not while fields had to be plowed and planted during a very specific season of the year. A large farmland required the help of others and a good crop would be shared with all who helped in the farming effort. On the other hand, if a farmer could do all of this without the help of others, he certainly was expected to do it alone.

When thinking about the geography of the New World and its impact on American culture, we should ask ourselves: If these early settlers had landed in Antarctica, would there be an American culture there today? Of course not. Individualists could not survive in such a severe physical environment. It would be absolutely essential to depend and rely upon others for food and shelter rather than being independent and self-reliant. Cooperation with others, rather than individualism, would have been the only way to ensure anyone's survival. Pure Calvinist values and beliefs would have soon been found to be counterproductive in Antarctica and probably would have disappeared within one generation. In North America, however, with its fertile geography and moderate climate, these same values allowed the American settlers to establish a young country and prosper in its physical environment, and thus these values became a central, enduring part of the country's culture.

What if the first settlers were Southern Europeans, such as the Portuguese, the Spanish, or the Italians—would there have been an American culture as we now find it in the United States? It is unlikely, because the Portuguese, Spanish, and Italians were very traditional Roman Catholics, who believed in a strong centralized authority, vested in the Pope in the Vatican or a strong monarch. In direct contrast with Protestant thought, they believed that not everyone was equal, and they created a more hierarchical society, reflecting the complicated church hierarchy of cardinals, archbishops, bishops, etc.[26] In addition, and in contradistinction to Puritan beliefs, there was less of an emphasis on the individual, personal responsibility and a direct relationship with the Almighty without intermediaries. Each member of a Protestant congregation could read and interpret the Bible or speak during a religious service, and pastors simply convened these meetings of worshipers. In the Roman Catholic Church, the mass was celebrated in Latin rather than the vernacular and the Vatican had the ultimate authority to interpret the Bible.

The more centralized and hierarchical perspective of Southern Europeans would have hampered the growth of individualism and egalitarianism to the extreme degree in which it is found in America. Indeed, the colonial societies that were created by the Spanish and the Portuguese in the New World (in Latin America) reflected cultural traits and came to be quite different from American society. A strong federal government within collectivist societies with great distance between the powerful and the powerless was quite common throughout Latin America. Social status and roles were fairly rigidly based upon ancestry or family. It is also important to acknowledge that the mercantilist focus of these colonies, rather than the nascent capitalism of the North American colonies,[27] must have inhibited economic growth within Latin American nations.

What Makes Americans and the U.S. Unique or Exceptional?

A combination of cultural factors (such as cowboy values), historical experiences (the differing nature of colonialism), and geography or natural resources came together in a unique way to create the American national or civic culture and the economic and democratic success of this new nation.

The political philosopher and essayist Thomas Paine argued in his January 1776 pamphlet *Common Sense* that America was not simply an outgrowth of Great Britain, but rather a new land with unlimited opportunity. He blamed the reigning British monarch, George III, for the political and economic oppression that existed in the colony and advocated an immediate declaration of independence and the creation of a new nation where sovereignty belonged to the people, not to a hereditary ruling class. His revolutionary republicanism and anti-statism was incorporated into the American Declaration of Independence. This document announced the dissolution of the colonial relationship and was a resounding populist cry for liberty and egalitarianism, and perhaps most importantly, it asserted the profound respect for individual rights and responsibilities. The Constitution was the collection of laws that created the new nation and codified many of the ideals found in the Declaration of Independence. These documents created the framework for an exceptional and unique *political* relationship among citizens of the U.S. and between those citizens and their government.

In 1776, the year of the U.S.'s political independence, Adam Smith wrote his famous *Wealth of Nations*, which linked republican democracy with *laissez faire* economics. Not only were individual rights to be protected in this new political system, but each individual ought to have the opportunity to succeed economically without interference from the state. Again, individualism was a key component of this new creed, along with a belief that the government should be determined by the people and it should not interfere in a free market economic system. The adoption of Smith's credo of capitalism (which resonated with certain preexisting Calvinist cultural values of early Americans) helped to create an exceptional and unique *economic* relationship among citizens of the U.S. and between those citizens and their government.

In the 1830s, Alexis de Tocqueville discovered that a unique kind of democracy had developed in America that was not to be found in Europe, in part due to these unique political and economic relationships. He is often credited with being the first to use the phrase "American Exceptionalism" in his famous book *Democracy in America*.

Many Americans were indeed aware of just how unique their circumstances were. Not only did they live in a country of unprecedented personal freedom, but the economic and political power of the country was beginning to be realized. Yet, what is crucial is that American exceptionalism became not only an *end* (the teleological destiny of American society), but also a *means* (America could act exceptionally in order to achieve its exceptional destiny). This allowed Americans to pursue goals consonant with what they saw as their destiny and values through means that could be inconsonant with these same values. The idea of Manifest Destiny is perhaps the best example of this.

In the 1840s, Jacksonian Democrats used the idea of Manifest Destiny, a variation of American exceptionalism, to justify their annexation of the western parts of the U.S. They combined the Puritan idea of a nation blessed by God (a city upon a hill) with the belief that it was a matter of predestination that the ideals of the nation would spread across the continent. The slogan "Manifest Destiny" was used to mean that it was the will of God that this new nation and its ideals would be spread from the Atlantic to the Pacific Ocean. Yet, the means that they used—aggressive expansionism and often imperialistic militarism—were surely incongruent with the founding values and historical experience of the U.S.

Many scholars would argue that Winthrop and his followers intended their city upon a hill to serve only as an example to others. However, for many Americans it became their mission to "share" and to liberate all those who were politically and economically oppressed. This missionary zeal was not always welcomed and often appeared to be forced onto other nations. For example, after the Spanish-American War (1898), many Cubans, Filipinos, and Puerto Ricans viewed Americans not as liberators but rather as imperialistic occupiers. Almost all Americans believed they would be welcomed with open arms because they were simply trying to free these people from Spanish rule, and at the same time they were sharing American democratic political and economic ideals and practices.[28] This was even worse than political or economic imperialism in the minds of those who were liberated. For many, it amounted to cultural imperialism.

The paradox, then, of American exceptionalism, and to some extent of American national values in general, is that an unusual combination of values at a particular time in human history resulted in the current American political and economic system, which is rather exceptional (and, many have argued, unparalleled) in human history. Yet there has also been at times a missionary-like zeal to spread these values to other places and, sometimes, to other cultures.

There are many American ideals, values, and beliefs that might be admired and even adopted by people of other nations. But, it is important to remember that what is really exceptional is the combination rather than simply a set of unique cultural values. This combination cannot be easily replicated in other nations.

If certain American ideals and practices are valued by people in other countries, they need not be forced upon those people through culturally oppressive public policies or even military force. They will simply take them and modify them, just as Americans have adopted some values and practices of other countries that serve our economic and political purposes. This is a matter of pragmatism, not ideology.

CHAPTER 5

"Don't Just Stand There, Do Something!"

One thing is sure. We have to do something. We have to do the best we know how at the moment . . . if it doesn't turn out right, we can modify it as we go along.

—FRANKLIN D. ROOSEVELT

As AN IMMIGRANT TO AMERICA AT THE AGE OF 12, Andrew Carnegie arrived in a country that was already filled with immigrant dreams and, often, more complicated realities. Armed with a desire to learn and work hard, he started as a telegraph messenger. He advanced through the telegraph company ranks, and eventually set off on his own to build a steel empire that made him one of the richest men on the planet. The story of his life is one of the most dramatic illustrations of the American Dream of going from rags to riches. Stories such as Carnegie's have been told time and time again in America. Yet, from where exactly did this American Dream come?

According to the so-called "Protestant work ethic,"[1] if an individual was allowed political and economic freedom, he or she would work hard and consequently be rewarded by God with prosperity. Not only would the economy grow through the sum of individual efforts, but everyone would also become part of a civic culture in which the community of informed and moral citizens would make decisions with good minds and hearts. The value placed on work, and the religious and moral sanctioning of it, was an important element in placing a premium on industriousness and commitment to one's job, values that are still strong in America. Moreover, it is easy to see how such an ethic, with its emphasis on individual economic action and self-interest could be a boon toward the creation of a capitalist system.

The Calvinism embraced by the early English settlers in the Massachusetts Bay Colony (the Pilgrims) emphasized the rights and responsibility of the individual to participate in the affairs of the community, fostering participatory democracy in the country. About 150 years later, this became the foundation upon which the British philosopher and economist Adam Smith wrote *The Wealth of Nations* in 1776—the year of the birth of the United States.[2] Smith was a Scottish Calvinist whose ideas of a *laissez faire* and liberal free market system where government ought not to interfere in the economy were a logical consequence of Calvinism's tenets of individual responsibility and hard work. The adoption and development of capitalism further helped to enshrine the values of individualism, hard work, economic mobility, and equal opportunity in American culture.

The combination of this economic and political philosophy is broadly called "liberalism" in the United States.[3] In contrast with earlier political philosophies based upon the hereditary status and absolute rule of monarchs with a state religion, liberalism asserted that there should be limitations on the powers of government, the nation would be ruled by laws rather than men, and there would be protection of individual rights such as freedom of speech and freedom of religion.

"Just Do It!"

The early Protestant work ethic brought with it an emphasis on *doing*. Even today, a common American saying is "Don't just stand there, do something." And, many Americans wear T-shirts with the very popular Nike slogan on them—"Just Do It!"

Europeans might claim that this is a problem with Americans—they act without thinking. America is often perceived as a country of thoughtless, action-driven cowboys. Americans turn this around and respond to this accusation by saying, "That's the problem with you

Europeans. You just talk, talk, talk. You don't do anything until it's too late." We perceive—or misperceive—each other through the lens of our own cultural value systems and mutual stereotypes.

Doing, action, and change are all basic American values associated with productivity, individual action, and self-reliance, and can be contrasted with the values of many non-Western cultures. Doing results in progress and, theoretically, a steady income; it can make one wealthy, a part of the economically elect. Inaction, on the other hand, results in mediocrity.

When they first meet, Americans often identify themselves by telling others what they do. "Hello. I'm Mike Jones and I'm an engineer with General Motors. What do you do?" The implication is that people who are not working, or not *doing* anything, really don't have an identity. Unfortunately, this is often true: When we stop doing, or working, the perceived value of our life decreases and our self-esteem is diminished. Many organizations in the United States have no mandatory retirement age, whereas in Japan many employees are required to retire at age 55. In Italy, the average retirement age is 57.[4] Professors at most American universities can teach until they die if they are deemed competent and engage in no behavior that could be interpreted as evidence of moral turpitude.

The standard vacation in the United States is two weeks per year, and many beginning employees must work for a few years before they earn their full two-week paid vacation. By contrast, in Europe most employees are guaranteed a four- to six-week paid vacation in their first year of employment. Many American companies also have the policy of "use it or lose it." That is, if you do not take your two-week vacation this year, you cannot transfer it to next year and take a four-week vacation. Tens of thousands of Americans actually lose their vacations every year because they simply cannot decide when they should leave work because their schedule is too full, the right time cannot be found, or they are afraid that work will simply pile up if they leave. A recent study found that on average, Americans have about 16 vacation days a year, but almost 40 percent did not plan to use all of their vacation days. Only about 15 percent of Americans planned to take a vacation of two weeks or longer.[5]

Even when we go on vacation, when we return to the office, the first question that coworkers ask is, "What did you do?" You really can't respond by saying that you sat in front of the television drinking beer. Rather, a productive American is expected to say he fixed the roof, took a course, caught up on his reading, or went on a trip. You are supposed to *do something* that appears to be productive even when you are supposed to be relaxing.

Even when we die, we are often identified in the heading of our newspaper obituary by what we *did*—"John Smith, lawyer." Family information and relationships are usually listed at the very end of the obituary. Seldom does an obituary notice have a heading or an opening sentence stating "John Smith, father" or "John Smith, husband," which were surely much more important to John Smith than being a lawyer. If we haven't really done much in life, the notice might read, "John Smith, lifelong resident."[6] Until very recently, the obituaries of many married women who had never worked were simply identified as "wife of" their husband.

Doing is often equated with clarity, decisiveness, leadership and masculinity. Little girls will often say that their best friend is the person whom they *share* the most secrets with, while little boys will say their best friend is another boy whom they *do* the most with. President George W. Bush told reporters, "I don't do nuance." Doing has a military terseness and decisiveness about it. "We do deserts, not mountains," Colin Powell said of the American intervention in Bosnia during the Clinton administration. And, Secretary of Defense Donald Rumsfeld declared in the summer of 2003, "I don't do quagmires."

No politician running for office would say to the American people, "Elect me and I'll keep everything the way it is." They all claim that they will *change* things and *do* something. In fact, in 1994, when Speaker of the House Newt Gingrich was running for reelection to Congress he developed a "Contract with America," a document that other Republicans signed listing all the things they would do if elected to the House or the Senate. Even during the Great Depression, President Franklin Roosevelt is said to have told his Cabinet, "Above all, try something." We expect our leaders not just to do something, but also to change things. This also reflects our focus on the future.

There are very few statues in Washington of poets, artists, composers, or philosophers. The most common statue is a man on horseback, usually a soldier going into battle—a "man of action." It is our belief that everyone is born equal, rolls up his or her sleeves, and manages to succeed and earn status in life by *hard work and action*, but not by writing poetry, painting pictures, composing music, or "philosophizing." This is not what Americans mean by doing. By contrast, in Europe the most common statues are of poets, artists, and even philosophers.

Indeed, there is often a stigma against artistic and intellectual pursuits in America. Other than those making it big in Hollywood or New York, actors, writers, and visual artists are often pejoratively described as "starving artists" by many Americans. The implication is that real Americans do things—things that put food on the table— while nonproductive artists starve. Indeed, federal funding for the arts is very low in the U.S., especially when compared to other prosperous nations. This is because justifying taxes for art's sake has never been an easy sell for politicians championing the image of the doing, productive American.

There has never been a sense of fatalism amongst the American people. Not only do most expect the future to get better but they also believe that they can control their own destiny. Ralph Waldo Emerson said, "If the single man plant himself indomitably on his instincts and there abide, the huge world will come around to him," and many Americans live by these words. A 2006 survey by the Center for American Values in Public Life found that 72 percent of Americans believed that their personal success was in their own control, rather than at the mercy of outside forces.[7] A Pew Research Center poll in 2007 returned similar results, with about two-thirds of respondents disagreeing with the statement "hard work offers little guarantee of success."[8]

Our high valuation of doing extends to a political stigma against intellectualism. No politician in the United States would ever campaign using the academic title *Doctor*. The first time an academic title of *Doctor* was commonly used for a politician was probably for Secretary of State Henry Kissinger. He was often referred to as *Doctor* Kissinger. He wasn't born in the United States, however, and he was never elected to public office.[9] In the past decade, many presidential cabinet members have had academic doctorates—Dr. Madeline Albright, Dr. Donna Shalala, and Dr. Condoleezza Rice—and yet they seldom use these titles. Interestingly, these examples are all females. The president or his press secretary would often use the title to describe these cabinet members as if to demonstrate that they were indeed well-qualified to serve as members of his cabinet. This anti-intellectualism in the political sphere extends to most of public life. The one exception to the use of academic degrees is medical doctors; they save people's lives—they *do* something.

To Do and To Be Cultures

In many traditional, so-called non-Western cultures, there is a greater value placed upon who you *are* than what you do. *Being* is more important than *doing*.[10] A traditional rural Mexican might greet you by saying, "Hello. I'm Manuel Gil, the son of Jesus Gil, from Cholula." The primary source of his identity is who he is. It is ascribed or given by birth rather than earned. Status is based upon family and heritage, not what he does as an individual.

Of course, the differences between "doing" and "being" types of cultures are really a matter of degree. While the mainstream American culture could be placed toward one end of a continuum where "doing" is important, we might place some very traditional, non-Western cultures on the other end, where "being" is important. There are a great many gradations in between these two extremes. In fact, it may be that Northern Germans are much more doing-oriented than the average mainstream American, while people from rural Mississippi may be more being-oriented than people living, for example, in Mexico City.

If we take the list of typical American values and contrast them with those of many non-Western cultures, the following chart results (see Figure 6.1 on the following page). Note the bar at the top of the chart, which reflects that this really is a continuum with various combinations. Clearly, the common values of some cultures would place them more on the *to do* side and others on the *to be* side. Northern Germans might fall on the far left (*to do*) while rural Kenyans could be placed on the far right (*to be*) side. Urban Americans could be placed on the left but not as far left as Northern Germans, and Greeks might be on the right but not as far to the right as Kenyans.

In addition, urban young people in many countries would fall on the *to do* side while rural, older people even in the United States might end up on the *to be* end. Some scholars would argue that the *to do* values are typically masculine in the United States while the *to be* values

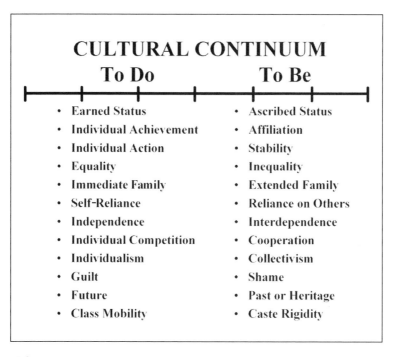

FIGURE 5.1 Contrasting Values: To Do/To Be

are feminine. According to sociolinguist Deborah Tannen,[11] men often are very direct and enjoy debate and verbal confrontation. Women are often reluctant to directly disagree with someone in public discourse and will often phrase their comments with such conditional phrases as, "It is possible to see the situation in this way."

National sports often provide important insights into such contrasting values between *to do* and *to be* cultures. For example, American football is quite different from soccer, which is the most popular international sport. American football is very aggressive, and is often compared to warfare. The ball is only moved forward, and a good game is one in which a team scores many touchdowns. If both teams score only a few points or if there is a tie, the fans are usually very disappointed. In fact, ties are no longer allowed in professional football—teams play in overtime until they score enough points to beat their opponent.

Soccer is much less aggressive. In American football, players tackle and block each other, causing many serious injuries, while soccer players are not allowed to rough each other up and there are fewer injured players. Soccer is more indirect and the ball is moved both backward and forward. Most of the time is spent kicking the ball backward or laterally instead of toward the goal and a great deal of time is devoted to lining the ball up for a good shot rather than actually shooting at the goal. While the purpose of soccer is to win, a tie is okay, especially if it is against a much better team.

Soccer is a collectivistic team sport. Fans usually cheer for the team as a whole, rather than for an individual player—unless he or she is absolutely extraordinary. While American football is certainly a team sport, fans usually refer to a good game by talking about the *individual* player who made the touchdown, the kicker who made a field goal or the quarterback who threw a great pass.

It would be fun to contrast sports in many different cultures and relate them to their national values. The sport that seems to be growing in popularity worldwide that may soon rival both football and soccer is basketball. It is a team sport where the ball moves in all directions, there is not supposed to be contact between players, and it relies heavily on teamwork rather than individual players. It may be that basketball is so popular because it truly is global from a cultural perspective. It involves values that fall in the middle of our continuum between the *to do* and the *to be* world.

Individualism, Earned Status, and Self-Reliance

In the 1970s, the Dutch organizational researcher Geert Hofstede conducted an initial field survey of over 116,000 IBM employees across 40 countries, using four dimensions of culture. He later expanded the study to include more than 60 different countries.[12] His four dimensions were Power Distance, Uncertainty Avoidance, Individualism, and Masculinity. In the 1990s he added a fifth dimension, Long-Term Orientation. Countries that were classified high in individualism tended to have people who were self-reliant and were motivated to succeed in their endeavors as individuals rather than members of teams or groups.[13] Collectivism is the opposite of individualism because people in these cultures view themselves as members of families, teams, groups, or tribes. The United States was rated at the top of the individualism scale, while China was rated near the bottom.

When scholars and politicians mention American exceptionalism[14] they are usually praising the traditional national cultural value placed on individualism. Success is the sweetest when it is *individual* success, and Americans have usually resisted any public policies that appear to be handouts or attempts to take away the rights and responsibilities of the individual over his or her own life.

Because of the great emphasis placed on independence, self-reliance, and individual achievement in America, when an American fails in personal or economic endeavors, he or she feels individually responsible. One often feels guilty for not trying harder, for not being more competitive with others, or for failing to take advantage of an opportunity. A basic American cultural belief is that one ought to *earn status* in the United States based upon what one does. This can be traced back to the old Calvinist belief in individual achievement, which has since been reinforced by capitalism and liberalism. Who your parents are or where you come from should have little to do with your status. To a great extent, most Americans believe that the United States is a classless society.[15] Regardless of what class or social strata you were born into, if you are willing to work hard, you can easily raise yourself. Of course, the opposite is also true. If you fail, it's your own fault.

Both success and failure ought to rest on the shoulders of the individual. No politician would ever say, "Vote for me because of my family and the important people I know." Most try to paint a picture of themselves as someone like Abraham Lincoln, born in a log cabin in the wilderness—the self-made man who arose from poverty and succeeded only by his own self-determination and hard work. On May 21, 2001, President George W. Bush gave the commencement address at Yale University where he told graduates, "And to you 'C' students, you too can be president of the United States." The point he was trying to make is that he was just an ordinary or average American who made it through his own efforts—a self-made man. Of course, being a member of the Bush family surely helped him get admitted to Yale and he is obviously very intelligent. He was also using a rhetorical style that Americans highly regard—a prominent figure who begins his address with the use of both humor and self-deprecation to show that he can joke about himself. Even more, the comment conveyed the subtle message of anti-intellectualism.

American heroes have traditionally accomplished whatever they did in life through their own individual efforts. Daniel Boone, Davy Crocket, Rambo—these are the bold men who exemplify the American spirit of success through their own dramatic individual action. They all are ordinary, relatively uneducated men who met challenges in life by themselves with little help from others. Rambo is an *action* hero, just like Batman or Spiderman. Superman is not only an action hero, he fights for justice and "the American way."

It is significant that all of these examples are male. Not only are soldiers on horseback the most common statues in Washington, D.C., all of them are male except for a statue of Joan of Arc (Jeanne d'Arc).[16] In his research on cultural dimensions, Hofstede found that Japan was rated the highest in "masculinity," which means that male and female roles are quite distinct and male assertiveness is highly valued. Americans were also rated fairly high on the masculine end of his scale.[17] The United States was ranked at 62 compared with a world average of 50. Scandinavian countries usually fell highest of all countries on the feminine end of his scale. There are many more female members of government in Scandinavian countries than in most other countries. This also explains why Hillary Clinton's presidential effort is so significant and controversial in the United States.

Because of the value placed on individual action and responsibility, some Americans even feel that government programs like unemployment benefits and housing assistance are indulgent and unnecessary because they place responsibility for the individual on the collective body of Americans—and they remove the onus of personal improvement from the individual. In a culture that places a high value on individualism and self-reliance, some people find these types of programs discordant with American values. About one-third of Americans believe that it is not the government's responsibility to take care of those who cannot take care of themselves. And, almost 70 percent of Americans feel that the poor have become overly dependent upon government assistance programs rather than upon themselves.[18]

Many Americans perceive those who are unemployed and living off of government assistance ("on welfare") as loafers who refuse to work. However, most would much rather have jobs than to take what they perceive as a "hand out" from the government. Just like most other Americans, they value self-reliance and independence and, if they are able to work, most opt to have jobs. Many actually refuse any type of assistance because they view it as an indication of personal weakness and feel *guilty*. They feel solely responsible or blame themselves for their failure and sometimes believe that perhaps they should have moved to another city to find work or achieved a higher level of education or training. Even recently unemployed people often suffer from pathological guilt and depression. Alcoholism, divorce, and even suicide increases dramatically when one is unemployed. However, they may have lost their jobs as a result of a downturn in the economy, outsourcing, or the invention of new technology.

In many *to be* cultures, if someone loses his or her job, there are family members and friends to turn to for psychological, social and even economic support. While the failure to retain a job may cause some feelings of shame or loss of face—a sense that one has "let others down"—the burden is not placed only on the shoulders of the individual. Support will come from others if needed, including the community or even the government, and there is a greater belief that fate determines what happens to us because no individual can have total control over his or her destiny.

In many traditional, rural, non-Western cultures, children learn that relationships or affiliations are more important than what one achieves as an individual. In fact, achievement for the sake of family or friends is what is important. Stable, harmonious long-term friendships are highly valued, and people want to depend upon and rely upon others. Cooperation, rather than competition, is admired and rewarded at home and in the workplace. In America, however, an emphasis on individualism has even come to pervade social life, and appears to be increasing over time. The average number of "close confidants" that the average American has is only two—which itself is a drop from an average of three 20 years ago.[19] Harvard professor Robert Putnam has asserted that Americans eat dinner together 40 percent less frequently and go to 60 percent fewer picnics today than 40 years ago, helping to atomize the cultural fabric of the nation to some degree.[20] This may be a logical outgrowth of a highly individualistic culture.

The *to do* values affect the way in which Americans conduct business meetings and negotiate. They tend to get down to business in a meeting much more quickly than in cultures where relationships are important. In many traditional, rural cultures, time must be allowed to get acquainted with others and to determine their status before beginning to discuss business. After relationships have developed through informal conversations, then business can begin. Some Americans think that Africans or Mexicans are wasting time when they socialize before discussing business. On the other hand, Africans and Mexicans sometimes perceive Americans as impersonal, cold, pushy, and always in a hurry to conduct business before developing relationships.

Americans think that all meetings take place to get something done, not just to develop rapport or relationships. At the very first meeting, we often ask people to identify themselves. This is often done rather formally—"Let's go around the room and everyone can tell us who you are." Of course, most identify themselves by what they do and their organization. Not only is this too formal, it is too direct for many *to be* people. After people have informally revealed who they are—their family, experience, status, and so on—the first meeting can begin and a leader may be selected based upon this information.

In meetings, Americans are often perceived as aggressive, rude, and abrasive. When asked how a non-American reaches these conclusions, the answer is sometimes "Because the American said 'no.'" In many non-Western cultures, because of the emphasis on relationships, "no" is simply too direct and disrupts the social harmony. Instead of saying "no," people would rather respond by saying "It is difficult," "Perhaps," or even "God willing." Indirectness is often highly valued and viewed as being polite in *to be* cultures, especially if the message is negative. For Americans, this circuitousness arouses suspicion and comes across as being deceptive. Moreover, many Asians tend to say "yes" when they don't really mean yes. They simply want to maintain the social harmony and avoid conflict. It really should be understood as, "yes, go on" or "I understand what you're saying," but not as "yes, I agree with you." It's a polite "yes."

When a meeting ends, it is not uncommon for the leader to lead a discussion about an "action plan." Something should get done during the meeting and the group needs to consider what will be done in the future. Of course, this requires planning, scheduling, and looking ahead.

Action, Change, and a Focus on the Future

The desire for change was common among early immigrants and that desire remains strong in most Americans even today. Change is an important value for Americans and it usually means being flexible and willing to give up the old to try something new. Most immigrants come to the United States because they want change. If they were content with their situation at home, why would they leave? They come to start their lives anew, free of political or religious oppression. Or they come to raise themselves from poverty by taking advantage of the resources and opportunities that exist in America and to create a better life for themselves and their children. Most want the freedom to succeed based upon what they did, not who they are.

The value placed on continual change is sometimes seen as evidence of the superficiality, materialism, and crass commercialism of American society. For Americans, nothing is lasting. They are never satisfied and want a new automobile, a bigger television set, the newest computer or cell phone, and at least 27 different varieties of ice cream. The desire for change and something new is interrelated with the traditional American focus on the future and the willingness to try new things and take risks. This focus has led to a vast array of technological advancements and the continual expansion of the overall American economy. Benjamin Franklin is as well known and admired for his inventions (bifocals, the lightning rod, a wood stove) as much as he is for his record as a founding statesman, diplomat, and publisher. Research and development is a major part of the budget of every American company, and it also is a major task of most American universities.

A national willingness to change has also allowed the United States to avoid social, political, and economic disasters. It would be a very different country today without such dramatic changes as the abolition of slavery, giving women the right to vote, moving the voting age to 18, and manufacturing smaller, more gas-efficient automobiles when faced with Japanese competition and a gasoline shortage. Because

Americans have historically been open to change, the country has often been able to correct its course and proceed in a more efficient and economical manner—or as former President Bill Clinton put it, "to form a more perfect union."

This proclivity toward change carries with it a focus on the future, which is another important American cultural value. Americans tend to focus on the future and disconnect it from the past. We hold the optimistic belief that the future will always be better than the past. In fact, we believe that the past does not have to influence what happens in the future. A completely new beginning is always possible. Immigrants leave their past behind and begin anew, and Americans are constantly moving on to a better tomorrow. Nearly 20 percent of all Americans change their residence in any one year, and the average American moves 14 times in his or her lifetime—often to start over and take advantage of new opportunities. If you can't find work in one city, move to another. It is your responsibility to do something about your unemployment. In 1981, we had fairly high unemployment rate in Detroit. A federal government official was asked at a press conference, "What will the administration do about unemployment in Detroit?" To paraphrase his answer, it was, "If people are unemployed in Detroit, let them move to Texas." In other words, this is the responsibility of the individual, not the responsibility of the federal government. It is difficult to imagine a federal government official in Berlin telling people that if you are unemployed in Berlin, move to Frankfurt.

The typical immigrant family was the immediate or the nuclear family—the husband, wife, and children, but not the grandparents, aunts and uncles, cousins, or distant relatives. This is true even today: the typical American family is still the immediate family; the nearest relatives typically live more than 200 miles away.[21] When a family in Paris or London goes on vacation, they often leave the city to get away from their relatives. On the other hand, Americans load their kids into the car and drive around the country to meet their relatives. This typically small family allows Americans to break away from their roots and take advantage of opportunities that may arise elsewhere, just as the early immigrants broke their ties with their extended families in their homelands to pursue a new future.

In many *to be* cultures there is a strong emphasis placed on tradition and the past. This is true of many European countries also.

People tend to live in the same city or neighborhood as their parents and it would be almost impossible for a politician to tell them, "Forget the past and focus on the future. Move to another city." However, in various surveys of American teenagers, we find that they lack a strong understanding of history. For example, a 2006 study commissioned by the Department of Education found that just 47 percent of high school seniors performed at a basic level.[22] What is important to most Americans is the future, not the past.

Politicians tend to emphasize optimism, change, and a brighter future. Franklin Roosevelt was admired for being cheerful and optimistic in the midst of the Great Depression and World War II—an image he purposely projected. Photographs usually showed him with a broad smile, and no official photographs were published showing him sitting in his wheelchair; that was considered to be too depressing an image. He suffered great pain from polio, but most Americans did not realize that he was paralyzed from the waist down and could not walk.

On the other hand, President Jimmy Carter was attacked for being too pessimistic. During the oil crisis of the 1970s, when Americans lined up for blocks in their automobiles to fill their gas tanks, he appeared on national television to encourage Americans to turn down their thermostats in their homes to save energy. Toward the end of his term of office, Iranians took over the American embassy for 444 days and held American diplomats hostage. Carter was perceived as passive and castigated for not doing anything about the Iranian Embassy takeover, although he did attempt to rescue the hostages and failed. He was also portrayed as too negative and accused of talking about a national malaise. He claims he never used this phrase, but the accusation was that he was too focused on the past and present, and it appeared to too many that he lacked the vision to see a better future.

The Willingness to Take Risks

Another important characteristic of the American people is their *willingness to take risks*. A psychologist at the University of Wisconsin has described this as the T personality type. This personality type describes high risk-takers—people who enjoy jumping out of airplanes with parachutes, climbing mountains, driving race cars, and so on. According to Professor Frank Farley, the United States has the greatest percentage of risk-takers in the world.[23]

Americans admire people who take risks.[24] Popular television shows like *American Idol, The Amazing Race,* and *Fear Factor* all depict people taking audacious risks, to the delight of audiences across the country. Americans are big gamblers; legalized gambling in the United States is an $80 billion industry, and all but eight states run lotteries. There seems to be an imbedded cultural assumption that people who never try anything never grow or change. Furthermore, we hold the belief that we learn as much or more from failure as we do from success. The early immigrants to America were high risk-takers as are many of today's most successful politicians and businesspeople.

Perhaps the greatest growth in the American economy in the past two decades has been in Silicon Valley, California, where many of the modern dot-com electronic communication industries developed. Everyone has heard the tales of young people who started businesses in their garages and quickly became billionaires. Few have heard how many failed. Nevertheless, in Silicon Valley even the failures have an advantage; they are often the first to be hired because of their previous daring and experience. There is a common assumption that the only people who never fail are those who do not take risks. Chances are that very few German managers would ever say, "Let's hire this young woman because she takes risks and she failed." Europeans are generally much more risk-adverse than Americans.

The same is true when it comes to politics. Some of the country's most successful politicians initially ran for public office and failed to get elected. They ran again, and succeeded. President George W. Bush ran for Congress and failed his first time. Thomas Jefferson, Andrew Jackson, and Richard Nixon all ascended to the Presidency after falling short in earlier bids for the office. Abraham Lincoln is another example. He is consistently ranked by historians as one of the very best presidents, and yet he was a loser of sorts. He truly was an ordinary man who was raised in poverty, and he never attended Harvard, Princeton, or Yale. He was self-educated and spent less than one year in formal education. Lincoln was definitely one of the least handsome presidents, he was a manic depressive, he started numerous businesses that failed, and he lost a number of elections. In fact, he was out of office over nine years before he was elected president. And yet he held the country together during the bloody Civil War. Today, he is perhaps the most revered president in American history.

Ulysses S. Grant, one of the most famous and successful Civil War generals, also led a fairly undistinguished life punctuated by business failures and alcoholism prior to his rise to prominence during the War. He is now remembered as one of the country's greatest soldiers. He is enshrined in a huge statue in front of the U.S. Capitol, and his portrait is emblazoned on the $50 bill. In many parts of Europe, if you run for office and fail, it is the end of your political career. In the U.S., it is often just the beginning.

Most Americans (and even many others around the globe) supported President Bush when he used military force to find Osama bin Laden after the attack on 9/11. Both bin Laden and the Taliban claimed they were responsible for the tragic deaths of so many people. Bush really had no alternative; the American people expected him to act. The political kiss of death would have been to do nothing. Under these circumstances, almost any president would have acted militarily.

On the other hand, only history will tell if the overthrow of Saddam Hussein and the occupation and war in Iraq was a reasonable risk. It may turn out to have been an irrational gamble. Individual Americans may enjoy gambling, but they do not expect their leaders to gamble. There is a big difference between risk-taking and gambling when it comes to foreign policy.

Contributing to the Civic Culture: Philanthropy and Volunteerism in America

With success, I have been given great wealth. And with great wealth comes great responsibility to give back to society, to see that those resources are put to work in the best possible way to help those in need.

—BILL GATES

In 1901, Andrew Carnegie sold his steel empire, one of the most prof-itable corporations in world history, to J.P. Morgan for the unimagin-able sum of approximately $447 million (roughly $10 billion in today's dollars). By the time of his death in 1919, Carnegie had given away nearly all of his immense personal fortune, and the remainder of his wealth was donated to philanthropic causes following his demise. With this money, he built over 2,500 free public libraries, in addition to en-dowing multiple foundations for the arts, sciences, and international peace, as well as founding the Carnegie Institute of Technology in Pitts-burgh, which later became Carnegie Mellon University. Carnegie is not alone among fabulously rich Americans who have donated much of their money to philanthropic causes. Among many others, the Rock-efeller family, Bill Gates, Ted Turner, and George Soros all have do-nated millions to charitable ends. Why?

In 1889, Carnegie wrote *The Gospel of Wealth*, which encapsulated his philosophy of giving. "Surplus wealth," he wrote, "is a sacred trust which its possessor is bound to administer in his lifetime for the good of the community." Carnegie believed that the American system, with its emphasis on hard work, individualism, and capitalist opportunity, provided the moral sanction for individual entrepreneurs to generate great personal wealth. Yet he also believed that the civic and moral cul-ture of the country provided a moral mandate for the wealthy to use their accumulated wealth to support philanthropic causes geared to-ward the good of the civic community as a whole.

In a quintessentially American way, Carnegie argued that surplus wealth should not be given as handouts to the poverty-stricken mem-bers of society. Rather, it should be used to endow institutes that would provide the less-privileged with opportunities to better enable themselves to succeed in the American system, chiefly through better training and education. Thus, Carnegie believed that philanthropy should benefit the community as a whole, while also reinforcing core American values such as individualism and industriousness. Carnegie's idea of philanthropy was to willingly provide the tools for advance-ment in society—yet he left the successful application of those tools as the responsibility of the individual. Carnegie's philosophy of giving influenced many of America's greatest philanthropists who came after him; they typically pass on their wealth through institutions that empower and educate individuals rather than as direct handouts to disadvantaged individuals.

Americans with lesser means than Carnegie, and contemporary American billionaires such as Bill Gates and George Soros, also donate a great amount of money to charity. In 2006, Americans set a record for charitable donations, giving nearly 2 percent of the nation's gross domestic product to charity—about a quarter of a trillion dollars, or an average of about $1,800 per family.[25] This sum makes Americans far and away the biggest donors to charity in the world. Regardless of their wealth, Americans donate roughly the same proportion of their income. Compare this to Great Britain, where the poorest 20 percent donate 3 percent of their income and the wealthiest 20 percent only donate 1 percent of their income.[26] And like Carnegie, Americans are more likely to donate to (or, in the case of very wealthy Americans, create) private foundations or organizations that do charitable work, with the mindset that such charities are the most efficient and effective at their work of helping the underprivileged. One could argue that Americans pick their charities much as they might pick their stocks— with an eye toward organizations that are successful, innovative, and that will bring a return on their money, either in capital gains in one instance or in humanitarian advances in the other.[27]

For many Americans, their contributions do not end with money, but continue with *doing*. Many also willingly donate their time to charitable causes. In 2006, more than 60 million Americans—over a quarter of the total population—volunteered, spending a median of 52 hours of their time doing so.[28] Most volunteered for religious organizations, reflecting the religiosity of the country, while a significant portion worked in support of educational/youth service related organizations, echoing the Carnegie ethos.[29] Many of these Americans donated their time to the country's over 1.4 million nonprofit organizations.[30] The nonprofit industry, spurred by the prevalence of charitable donations and volunteering in America, has grown into a huge portion of the economy: A recent estimate noted that nonprofits paid out over 8 percent of salaries and wages in the country.[31]

A rapidly rising number of young Americans are seeking out service opportunities as well. Teach for America, a program that places (usually recent) college graduates in teaching positions in underfunded school districts, had nearly 20,000 applicants in 2006, triple its pool in 2000. In the same year, the Peace Corps accepted its largest group of volunteers—about 8,000—in 30 years. It drew these volunteers from an applicant pool that had risen by more than 20 percent since 2000.[32]

While all this has been happening, however, the American foreign aid budget and the amount of federal money given to the arts has remained relatively small—often much smaller in proportion than similar programs in other wealthy countries. This shows how the actual enactment of civic culture and civic virtue can be found more readily on the local, individual level rather than in the broad national policies of the country. While an American may be against a tax increase to support a larger foreign aid budget, the same American may readily send just as much, if not more, money than the tax would excise to a local or international charity. With this charity and this act of *doing*, Americans hope to do something to combat a social ill and directly better their society.

The Challenge of Capitalism: Balancing American Individualism with Fairness and Moralism

We have discussed how the Protestant work ethic combined with the emphasis on individualism and hard work in America to place the onus of personal success squarely on the shoulders of the individual. Many Americans have worked hard and achieved success. Yet many have not. Just as capitalism handily rewards some, others can become stuck in low-paying jobs or in poor working conditions. In the U.S., extremes of both poor and rich exist, but the government has moved away from Adam Smith's original emphasis on the importance of the *laissez faire* role of the state in a capitalist system. Franklin Roosevelt's New Deal programs are perhaps the most dramatic example of federal involvement in the economy in order to assuage the plight of workers. Even today, the federal government often intervenes in the working of the economy in order to insure certain conditions for workers and set boundaries on the expansion of corporate power.

How did this change, ostensibly so far from the Calvinist ideal, come to pass? The foundation of this dichotomy was built during the late nineteenth and early twentieth century, as industrialization in

America exploded during a period called "The Gilded Age" by Mark Twain because of its emphasis on incredible wealth and flamboyant, conspicuous consumption.

During the Gilded Age the rapid industrialization of the country provided the bridge between the lifestyle of colonial and antebellum Americans—a primarily agrarian, decentralized mode of living, far removed from contemporary America—to the lifestyle that Americans are more accustomed to now, of productivity on a massive scale, of dense urban centers of commerce and population, and of technological proficiency. It was in this transition to the modern, highly industrialized age that the economic potential long seen in America by its citizens and distant admirers began to become reified. America was entering its adolescence—its growth spurt, as it were—and it began to emerge as the nation with the fastest growing population, industry, productive capacity, and wealth.

Industrial competition during this age was cutthroat and often quite unregulated. In some senses, it was as though capitalism and the Protestant work ethic had run amok and both had been taken to their logical extremes. Competition was fierce and the ideal of maximum productivity became gospel among industrialists. Companies grew and grew, until many became behemoths, creating monopolies or near-monopolies (known as trusts) in many industries. Labor-saving machines were developed and they were employed as frequently as possible to reduce the number of laborers, often immigrants, needed. In addition, those laborers who were hired often worked in terrible conditions and for hours on end at the lowest acceptable wages. When they finished their long hours in the factory, many returned to their urban homes to live in squalid conditions.

Industrialization, and the deep class divisions between owners and workers that it helped to foster, threatened America's democratic heritage and impulse with an oligarchic specter. Theodore Roosevelt described this period as "A riot of individualistic materialism, under which complete freedom for the individual . . . turned out in practice to mean the freedom for the strong to wrong the weak. . . . The power of the mighty industrial overlords . . . had increased with giant strides, while the methods of controlling them . . . through the Government, remained archaic and therefore practically impotent."[33] Yet, the core American cultural values of equality and of individual rights chafed at these threats and provided a full-throated, if not entirely successful, response to the negative currents of industrialization.

Many Americans who had come out on the short end of the industrial movement, along with many others from the non-laboring (and particularly middle) class, sought reform in American society in order to save it from the corrupt and overwrought capitalist dystopia that it threatened to become during the Gilded Age. They pursued a number of causes intended to right the course of the American ship and to restore the values of individual opportunity, equality, and individual rights to the center of American life.

These Americans became the components of what was known as the Progressive movement, a loosely defined, loosely grouped collection of reform movements that sought—in an echo of their Puritan forebears' desire for a religious purification of society—to restore the morality and inherent exceptionalism of America by balancing its unbridled economic potential with a more just and egalitarian social order. Indeed, the religious dimension of the Progressive movement should not be underestimated. In the words of historian Robert Crunden:

> At its core [Progressivism] was religious, an attempt by Americans to restore the proper balances among Protestant moral values, capitalistic competition, and democratic processes, which the expansion of business in the Gilded Age seemed to have changed in alarming ways. Having lost the religious faith of their ancestors, progressive leaders still wanted religious values to dominate political and economic life; they wanted better and fairer competition; and they wanted every citizen to participate in the polity . . . they agreed on the need to remoralize society.[34]

Through hard-fought battles with industrialists, leaders of the Progressive labor movement were able to extract better wages, better working conditions, and shorter hours for workers. Unionization and strikes were keys to the success of the labor movement. American labor strikes were often dramatic, and not infrequently violent. Importantly, they raised the specter of outright class conflict and provided impetus for movements toward equality, or at least toward increased respect for the workers' individual rights, buoyed by the general cultural value of egalitarianism.

As the ranks of the urban poor grew with mass immigration and industrialization, the abjectness of their quality of life outside the workplace became apparent to many. Much of this attention was due to muckraking journalists, a hallmark of the Progressive age, who, using the burgeoning mouthpieces of the mass media, exposed the shameful underbelly of the America of the late nineteenth century. The term *muckraker* was coined by Theodore Roosevelt, who likened these journalists to the man, depicted in John Bunyan's *Pilgrim's Progress*, with a "Muck-rake in his hand" who raked up filth rather than gaze upon more splendid things.[35] Muckrakers published shocking and dramatic exposés of corporate, governmental, or institutional inadequacies and corruption, in the hope of raising a public outcry and subsequent change. One of the most dramatic (and brave) examples of this style of journalism was the work of Nellie Bly, who feigned insanity in order to be committed to the infamous Women's Lunatic Asylum on Blackwell's Island in New York City. She published her harrowing experiences there in a book, *Ten Days in a Mad-House* (1887), which caused a public outcry, a grand jury investigation, and a major increase in funding to the Department of Public Charities and Corrections.[36]

Whereas many early Americans had earned plaudits through their efforts to extol the young country, a premium was placed in the late nineteenth century on those who exposed the ills of American society in the hopes of reforming it. Although it may superficially seem unpatriotic, this movement was in fact quite in tune with certain American cultural values, particularly the Calvinist ethos of self-improvement. The Progressive's attitude toward the plight of the poor did clash with parts of America's cultural heritage, however. The Protestant work ethic of self-reliance and individualism, as well as the capitalist impulse to spend money only on things that promised a direct return on the investment, had historically precluded state or federal efforts of public assistance. This changed in the late nineteenth century. Many religious organizations emerged to ease the plight of the urban poor, and reform was enacted in a number of state organizations designed for the poor. This is very different from the European ideal of socialism or a strong federal social welfare system. Here it was left to the community.[37] These reforms helped to set a precedent for the wider-ranging state welfare system set up during the Great Depression.

The American cultural values of equality, individual rights and egalitarianism played out in the Progressive movement through electoral efforts as well. During the post–Civil War era, and particularly the Progressive Age, the women's suffrage movement gained steam. Susan B. Anthony, along with other women's leaders such as Elizabeth Cady Stanton and Carrie Chapman Catt, led a long and contentious struggle to gain suffrage for women, and they presented their struggle as an effort to insure the extension and maintenance of American values among all inhabitants of the country. Through their efforts and those of many others, women were finally given the right to vote with the ratification of the Nineteenth Amendment to the Constitution in 1920.

The moralizing aspect of America's early Puritan settlers was recalled in another Progressive reform movement—Prohibition and the temperance movement. Moralizing temperance movements, which sought to ban alcoholic beverages, gained momentum during the 1840s and 1850s, primarily through the activism of religious groups. The movement even spawned a political party, the Prohibition Party, which was founded in 1869 and is still active today (though it is now well beyond the pale of mainstream politics), making it the third longest-surviving political party in the country after the Republican and Democratic parties. (In another interesting bit of historical trivia, America's first female mayor, Susanna Salter, was elected on the Prohibition Party's ticket in 1887 in Argonia, Kansas.)

The political quest to eliminate personal sin, present in the country since its first settlers, reemerged dramatically with the ratification of the Eighteenth Amendment to the Constitution in 1919, which, along with the Volstead Act, prohibited the "manufacture, sale, or transportation of intoxicating liquors." However, the temperance movement's success also became its downfall. Prohibition brought with it social malaise, including a booming black market for alcohol and the involvement of organized crime and corrupt government officials in its distribution. This eventually led to ratification of the Twenty-First Amendment in 1933, which effectively repealed the Eighteenth Amendment and the Volstead Act. The American body politic, as concerned with morality as ever, decided that one sin was better than the many that proliferated due to the banning of alcohol.

The Great Depression and the Legacy of Progressivism

When the Great Depression hit America in 1929, decimating the economy and creating spiraling unemployment and poverty among American workers, the legacy of Progressivism stepped in through the person of Franklin Roosevelt and the enactment of the New Deal. Roosevelt, the quintessential Progressive president, eschewed critics who argued that government assistance to workers would belie the American tradition of individualism and hammered out an arsenal of programs intended to combat the Depression.

Upon his election to the presidency in 1932, Roosevelt attempted to create more efficiency in business, finance, and government, and created numerous programs and agencies intended to support American workers and reemploy as many as possible. Without the legacy of Progressivism, the precedent for such reforms would have been lacking, and their passage (while still controversial at the time) would have been more difficult, if not impossible. The New Deal achieved a fair amount of success in combating the Great Depression, although the Depression was not conclusively defeated until the onset of the Second World War.

Today, government-run social programs in America are often referred to as being part of the legacy of the New Deal. Yet we could more accurately say that they are a part of the legacy of Progressivism. It is through the Progressive spirit—in which the historical American cultural values of individualism and self-reliance are tempered by the values of equality, liberty, and moralism—that we find a more modern, and perhaps more humane, version of the American Dream. In this dream, the doors of opportunity are still open to all and success is within each individual's grasp. However, should some people encounter more difficulties than others in their pursuit of the dream, Progressive institutions ideally help to protect them from falling victim to the negative side of the dream.

Hard work, individualism, self-determination, equality, doing—taken together these values create a heady elixir that most Americans drink deeply, resulting in a stalwart belief that all Americans can achieve whatever they want through a combination of these values. It is one of the most enduring traits of Americans and one of the most enticing things about America. And yet, these values could only be perpetuated in a land where they could be reinforced by what appeared to be unlimited opportunities, unlimited natural resources, and a continually growing economy.

During a crisis of effectiveness, when extreme *laissez faire* capitalism led to corruption, avarice, and oppression of the working classes or when the economy nearly collapsed during the Great Depression, these values have been modified. They are still strong and their legitimacy has held the country together during these crises of effectiveness. Americans may be idealists but they are also a pragmatic people who are willing to try new solutions to problems. The United States is certainly not a purely capitalistic society because there are times when the government had to provide programs to redistribute wealth and opportunity and to protect those who have suffered from catastrophic illness, unemployment, natural disasters, and so on. "Entitlements" such as social security and Medicare are supported by both liberals and conservatives although they may differ on the scope and size of these government programs.

Most Americans probably would place themselves somewhere between the extremes of libertarianism, with its belief in almost no government, no taxes, and no involvement in international organizations, and socialism. Nevertheless, compared to most European counties and other countries around the globe, the U.S. is probably the most capitalistic and the least socialistic because of the belief most have in traditional American national cultural values.

CHAPTER 6

American Civic Culture

There is a time in every man's education when he arrives at the conviction that envy is ignorance; that imitation is suicide; that he must take himself for better or worse as his portion; that though the wide universe is full of good, no kernel of nourishing corn can come to him but through his toil bestowed on the plot of ground which is given to him to till.

—RALPH WALDO EMERSON

THE UNITED STATES IS A NATION OF IMMIGRANTS, with wave after wave of people coming from around the world to escape political, economic, and religious oppression. They longed to escape from a world of war and persecution and they sought opportunities to begin anew to provide a better way of life for themselves and their children, to live in peace and security and to practice their religions.

The earliest waves fled their homelands to create a more peaceful and secure society that was insulated and isolated from the rest of the world. They also came because they believed they were going to live in a New World where there would be greater opportunities to prosper. Even today, most immigrants come because they believe that the

American Dream will become a reality and the future will hold unlimited opportunities to move out of poverty and hopelessness. The first settlers referred to America as "the New World." But, it has also been known as "the land of opportunity" for those who were willing to take advantage of the natural resources and a continually expanding economy.

Many immigrants also leave their homelands because they share many of the values and beliefs that are embedded in the American social, economic, and political fabric, such as individual freedom, egalitarianism, and democracy. They believe that the future will get better, and that through hard work and moral behavior one can advance up the economic ladder, with each new generation improving upon the situation of their parents. This requires taking advantage of all the opportunities available in the new land and becoming an active member of the civic culture. Fortunately, their values and beliefs are often rewarded and reinforced by the abundance of natural resources, educational opportunities, and low unemployment, even today.

Nativists were very much afraid that immigrants coming might not share all of the traditional American national cultural values and beliefs and shed aspects of their home culture to fit into the dominant (cookie-cutter) culture. Thus, public schools developed courses to teach civic education. All children, but especially immigrant children, were taught values and beliefs held by Americans that promoted democracy and allowed them to fully participate in the political and economic system as adults. These "Civics Courses" also explained how the government functioned, the role of the Constitution and the idea of a nation of laws, and the importance of protecting civil liberties. The public education system provided the knowledge and skills for Americans not only to participate in the civic culture, but also to perpetuate it.

Even immigrants who came here as young adults were often drawn to the United Stated because of the opportunities they believed existed that would allow them to reach whatever goals they aspired to reach. They may not have gone through the public education system, and yet they still shared the values we attribute to the American civic culture, which were reinforced by the political, social, economic, and physical environment. A superb example of this process is Governor Arnold Schwarzenegger of California, who came as an immigrant from Austria with the expectation of having new opportunities to move up the class ladder. Although he may have once had difficulty pronouncing the name of the state he now governs, he is truly a typical American in terms of his civic values and beliefs.

The Foundations of American Democracy and the Balance of Power

Democracy and economic growth are interrelated in the minds of most Americans. You cannot have one without the other. Calvinism assumed a direct relationship between the individual and God and emphasized the power of each person to advance economically, based upon such values as hard work and frugality. While the idea of predestination was central to Calvinism, the individual also had to act and take responsibility for carrying out God's intentions. The World War II saying "God is my co-pilot" succinctly sums up this belief.[1] Each individual has some control over what happens in his or her life. It is not simply a matter of Fate.

This set of religious beliefs fit nicely with *laissez faire* capitalism as described by Adam Smith in *The Wealth of Nations*. Hard work, individualism, and egalitarianism would lead to economic mobility, Smith said; the government should not interfere in the workings of the nation's economy. This philosophy meshed well with the underlying set of principles of American liberalism—protection of individual civil liberties; the balance of power between local and federal government; the checks and balances between the executive, legislative and judicial branches of government; and freedom of speech and freedom of the press.

Aristotle's ideal of Athenian democracy assumed that all citizens would have the opportunity to become part of a "learning society" and would be fully informed about issues of governance.[2] His idea of citizenship was a matter of everyone coming together in Athens to decide matters of common concern. This was the core of politics. In fact, the word *political* comes from the Greek word *politikos* which translates as "of, or pertaining to the *polis*." A *polis* was a city or city-state such as Athens, rather than a modern nation-state. The Greeks (and later the Romans) took these concepts, and the broader idea of civic values, seriously: Monumental disputes emerged over the nature of civic values. These often led to serious consequences, the most famous of which was the forced suicide of Socrates. One can easily understand how the rumor spread that the Continental Congress in Philadelphia actually considered Greek for the national language of the United States. It literally was viewed as the language of democracy.

The founders of the United States certainly incorporated Athenian concepts of democracy into such documents as the Articles of Confederation, the Declaration of Independence, and the Constitution. More importantly, a relatively pure version of Athenian democracy was actually practiced in American congregational church meetings and town hall meetings in small towns around the country. The Calvinists originated congregationalism in sixteenth century England and carried their beliefs and practices to America. The Puritans believed that worship should take place in simple assemblies where anyone could speak out on any issue. The assumption was that men and women of good mind and good heart could reason together to solve the problems of the community.

Civic virtues[3] such as prudence, frugality, justice, fairness, honesty and tolerance were believed necessary to create and support a democracy. Until the past few decades, the phrase "civic virtues" was used to describe traditional habits or practices shared by all members of a community. Today, the term *values* has replaced the old Victorian term *virtues*, although some conservative public figures, such as William Bennett, prefer the term *virtue* perhaps because it has an overtone of Victorian middle-class obligation to behave in certain appropriate ways that will insure the civic order. Civic virtues were an important subject not only to Greeks like Socrates and Aristotle, but also to Roman writers like Seneca, Renaissance thinkers like Petrarch, and Enlightenment philosophers like Rousseau.

The American founders viewed themselves as the end point in a direct line of descent from Greco-Roman, Renaissance and Enlightenment thought, all of which placed a heavy emphasis on the importance of civic virtues and inuring them in society. Early American church leaders often preached to their congregants about the importance of living by a moral code, to the benefit of the community. The same church leaders often attempted to enforce these dictums through law. Some of these edicts—now known as "blue laws"—are still on the books today, including ones that limit or prohibit the sale of alcohol or the opening of stores on Sundays.

America's founding fathers also felt that a strong sense of civic duty and virtue was important for all Americans. A young George Washington transcribed a sixteenth-century manuscript of "Rules of Civility and Decent Behavior," replete with maxims concerning one's behavior in a civil society, and containing injunctions such as "Labor to keep alive in your breast that little spark of celestial fire called conscience." The work is often cited as being crucial to the building of Washington's character. Similarly, in his bestselling annual *Poor Richard's Almanack*, Ben Franklin included some of his favorite homespun witticisms, many of which encouraged his readers toward civic virtue, such as: "The idle Man is the Devil's Hireling; whose Livery is Rags, whose Diet and Wages are Famine and Diseases"; "Virtue and a Trade, are a Child's best Portion"; "No longer virtuous, no longer free; is a Maxim as true with regard to a private Person as a Common-wealth"; and "The nearest way to come at glory, is to do that for conscience which we do for glory."

The founding fathers believed not only that civic virtue should be the goal of all citizens, but that the government should be set up in such a way as to encourage the pursuit and reinforcement of civic virtues. This was to be achieved through the involvement of citizens in the governing of the country and making them stakeholders in the strength of the country's civic values. This involvement was manifested not only in voting, but in becoming involved in politics at a local level. There are currently over 87,000 local governments in the United States, including roughly 3,100 counties, 22,000 municipalities, and thousands of townships, school, and other special districts. Each of these governing bodies has its own elected officials, bureaucracy, jurisdiction, and budget, and all are designed to meet the most immediate needs of people such as criminal and civil law enforcement and adjudication, fire and safety protection and codes, licensing, sanitary regulations, public transportation, education, public utilities, and on and on. Thus, thousands upon thousands of Americans hold a publicly elected office or work in the public sector for the good of their community or for the country as a whole.

Moreover, each of these governing bodies is charged in some way with strengthening and furthering American civic culture. Whether it is the school board official who helps to decide what U.S. history textbooks should be read, the city planners who organize a city's Independence Day celebration, or simply the townspeople who come together at a town hall meeting and vote on local issues, all are not simply practicing American civic virtue, but are also preserving and shaping it for the next generation.

In order for all citizens of the country to feel as though they may exercise some political clout, power must be widely diffused throughout the country. Ensuring that this power is in balance, however, was a key concern of the founders and has been a perennially important issue to the country since its beginning. The balancing of power within and between all levels of government goes back to the creation of the the nation and its founding documents.

Before the federal government was created with the signing of the Constitution, each colony was autonomous and had governed itself independently.[4] Similar to the European Union (EU) today, the first step was to create a confederation of states under a treaty of agreement. In the U.S., the Articles of Confederation simply created an alliance among rebel states and stipulated the autonomy of each state. Similarly, in 2007, the EU found that it could not agree on a Constitution for a United States of Europe with Brussels as its capital city. The first step had to be a treaty of confederation before a federation could be formed.

The American confederation's powers were perhaps too dispersed. It had no authority to tax, no executive leader, and it could not regulate commerce. The only way for the former colonies to come together was to create a unified federal government. The federal system created an executive (president) whose powers are checked and balanced by two chambers of Congress (the House and the Senate) and an independent court system (the Supreme Court and lower federal courts). No one branch of federal government has exclusive power. More importantly, the federal government shares sovereignty with the individual states and their local governments. Education, adjudication of crimes, and almost all other public policies in the United States were left up to the local or state government by the founders, rather than the federal government. The federal government was responsible for foreign policy and national security, international commerce, and interstate criminal behavior, until very recently.[5] This division of power between the federal, state, and local levels was intentional because of the reluctance to give the federal government power over the individual, but also over state and local jurisdiction. Between the different branches and levels of government, the power to shape how the country's civic values are defined and practiced is shared. No branch or level of government can monopolize the definition or enforcement of these values.

The U.S. has a decentralized structure of government with power dispersed over many different levels. Congress has the power to make laws, but the president can veto laws. Congress can then, with a two-thirds vote, legislate a law over a presidential veto. The Supreme Court can invalidate acts by both Congress and the president if they are deemed "unconstitutional" according to the interpretation of the Court. Of course, just as New Testament biblical scholars may have various interpretations of the Bible and some may believe it must be taken literally, Supreme Court justices differ in their interpretations of the Constitution. Some, known as strict constructionists, believe that it must be taken literally as the original authors intended. Others, known as loose constructionists, believe that it must be interpreted in the context of a changing society and new technology.

A majoritarian democracy, such as exists in nations with a parliamentary system, is much simpler than the American system of pluralistic democracy, with its multiple centers of power. In a parliamentary system, the dominant party or coalition usually passes legislation proposed by government ministers, and most courts have limited power to invalidate the legislation. Since the 1790s the U.S. has had two major parties and, since the Civil War, they have been the Republican and Democratic Parties. At times third parties appear, but their positions are often absorbed by the two major parties before an election. In a majoritarian parliamentary system, third parties frequently form coalitions after elections.

In addition to the federal government, almost every citizen is governed by a state and a local government—usually a city or county. While there is overlap between jurisdictions, matters that are within state or local borders are generally viewed as the exclusive concerns of state and local government, so long as these laws or practices at the local level do not contradict or violate the Constitution or the laws and treaties of the United States. For example, in the 1970s the federal government agreed to allow the British-French Concorde plane to land at New York's Kennedy Airport. However, in what was referred to as the Battle of Concorde, large protests were held by people from Howard Beach, New York and other parts of southeastern Queens to keep the plane out of Kennedy because of the great amount of noise it generated. Protesters formed motorcades to clog the airport's main roads. The result was that local noise control laws were tightened and rather than 50 flights a day, the Concorde was restricted to only four.

A further example occurred in March of 2007, when citizens in a small Vermont town first discussed fixing local sidewalks and bridges, and then debated and passed a resolution calling on the state's sole Congressman to file articles of impeachment against President Bush. "As a teacher I can't say to my kids that what happens on the national level doesn't affect us at the local level," one supporter of the measure argued. Soon after, four other Vermont towns passed similar measures. Did the advocates of the resolution expect immediate results and the sure impeachment of the president? It's doubtful. However, did they believe in the historical and symbolic—if not always actual—potency of local government? Absolutely.[6]

States and local governments have occasionally enacted legislation independent of, and sometimes quite different from, the federal government's stated policies. For example, California has set aside billions of dollars in funding for stem cell research, while the Bush Administration has adopted an anti–stem cell research policy. And, in opposition to the present administration's abstention from the Kyoto Protocol, over 600 mayors in American cities have signed the Mayors Climate Protection Agreement, pledging to reach Kyoto's targets in their own communities.

However, the federal government has occasionally stepped in to enforce national legal norms and overridden local government. Just as there is a balance of power between the executive, legislative, and judicial branches within the federal government and all state governments, there is also a balance of power between the federal, state, and local governments. At certain times and in regards to certain issues, the state government would have more power than the federal government. Education is a very clear example of this. However, during times of war or national economic crisis, the federal government would have more power. The balance is constantly shifting back and forth but no one level of governance would have absolute power over the others.

When states or cities in the South refused to allow their high schools and colleges to be integrated in the 1950s, the federal government had to step in to enforce federal laws that prohibited discrimination based upon race. When a handful of black students showed up to attend a previously segregated high school in Little Rock, Arkansas, in the fall of 1957, Governor Orval Faubus called out the Arkansas National Guard to surround Little Rock Central High School "to preserve the peace and avert violence" that may be caused by extremists who came to Little Rock "in caravans." Of course, the intent was to prevent black students from entering the high school. President Eisenhower sent the Army to Little Rock to allow the students to enter the high school.

Here was a clear example of a conflict between states' rights and the federal government. In this case, the federal government had to intervene to protect the individual rights of black students to attend school although the schools were controlled by the local school board and the Arkansas National Guard was under the command of the governor. President Eisenhower had to uphold the ruling of the Supreme Court that made discrimination illegal.

Thus, although the federal government can act as the final authority on some civic matters, we can see that state and local governments are afforded a wide swath of power in the American system, allowing them much influence not only over local policy, but also over how civic culture is practiced on a local level. Perhaps the most visible—and, as we have seen, often most controversial—venue for this is in the public school system.

Public Schools and Learning the Civic Culture

I know no safe depository of the ultimate powers of the society but the people themselves; and if we think them not enlightened enough to exercise their control with a wholesome discretion, the remedy is not to take it from them, but to inform their discretion by education.

—THOMAS JEFFERSON

Civic virtues were taught to all Americans, especially immigrant children, in the public education system. In the nineteenth century a sequence of textbooks compiled by Scottish Calvinist William Holmes McGuffey, and entitled *McGuffey's Eclectic Readers*, were used in almost all primary schools. The readers were intended to teach reading skills, but they also instilled the virtues and values that McGuffey believed were essential to maintain civility. The books were filled with religious and patriotic themes. Each reader contained essays, speeches, and stories of people with strong morals, who also displayed honesty, independence, hard work, truth, and strong allegiance to their country. William Bennett, the Secretary of Education under Ronald Reagan, tried to update these readers by creating readers of his own—*The Book of Virtues: A Treasury of Great Moral Stories* and *The Children's Book of Virtues*. As with McGuffey's readers, Bennett's stories and essays celebrate the white, Anglo-Saxon, Protestant ideal. The chapter headings for *The Book of Virtues* include ten basic virtues: self-discipline, compassion, responsibility, friendship, work, courage, perseverance, honesty, loyalty and faith.[7]

Here are some examples of lessons from one of the pages of the old *McGuffey's Readers* (see Fig. 6.1). The first is a lesson on the use of the letter *I* and yet it also contains a moral lesson on the virtue of separating work from play and doing things well.

Another example illustrates how the reader, which was used in almost all public schools, clearly taught lessons about a higher being ("the Lord") and hard work:

All you do, and all you say,
He can see and hear;
When you work and when you play,
Think the Lord is near.
All your joys and griefs he knows,
Sees each smile and tear;
When to him you tell your woes,
Know the Lord will hear.

From *McGuffey's First Eclectic Reader*, p. 60

Of course, *McGuffey's Readers* were not alone in their effort to teach civic virtues to America's children. In 1910, the Boy Scouts of America was founded to promote youth outdoorsmanship. Since its

while   might   time   things
done   right   your   hälves

Work while you work,
*   Play while you play,*
One thing each time,
*   That is the way.*

All that you do,
*   Do with your might,*
Things done by halves,
*   Are not done right.*

FIGURE 6.1   From McGuffey's *First Eclectic Reader*, p. 53.

inception, over 100 million Americans have been members of the organization, including several presidents and all but one of the 12 Americans to walk on the moon. Through outdoor activities boys learned civic virtues essential to good citizenship. (However, what the organization had in mind as an ideal citizen is interesting, when we consider the long history of its exclusion of admitted atheists and homosexuals from the organization.) Every Boy Scout can recite from memory the Scout Oath:

> On my honor I will do my best
> To do my duty to God and my country
> and to obey the Scout Law;
> To help other people at all times;
> To keep myself physically strong,
> mentally awake, and morally straight.

Around 50 million Americans have joined the Boy Scouts' sister organization, the Girl Scouts of America, whose purpose and oath is similar to that of the Boy Scouts:

> On my honor, I will try:
> To serve God and my country,
> To help people at all times,
> And to live by the Girl Scout Law.

Together, these two organizations have helped to carry on the inculcation of civic virtue in American youth throughout the last century.

While these organizations, and *McGuffey's Readers*, supported the conception of a common, national civic culture with certain universal American values, the transmission of this civic culture occurred primarily on a local level and was due to local organizations and policies. The federal government, on the other hand, has rarely gotten involved in the implementation or enforcement of civic culture on a local level. While the conception of civic culture has often been national, its implementation—and precise definition—has commonly been local.

In the early nineteenth century, Horace Mann established the public school system in Massachusetts not only to provide an opportunity for all children to learn together in common schools, but also to acculturate children to the American civic society. He believed that a progressive, democratic, and egalitarian government had a responsibility to educate all of its citizens. These public schools, run by each state and municipality, were especially important to illiterate or poorly educated immigrants who wanted their children to have a proper education. Public schools were where the children would learn English and acquire skills necessary for economic advancement and a better way of life. For the general society, this was where the children would learn how to be good citizens in their new home. Courses such as American History, American Government, and American Civics were required in most public schools.

Even most college undergraduate curricula, until very recently, required students to take a course in American government, politics, and history. In the fall of 2005, the University of Connecticut's Department of Public Policy was contracted by the Intercollegiate Studies Institute to undertake the largest statistically valid survey ever conducted to determine what colleges and universities were teaching their students about America's history and institutions. They found that students who demonstrated greater learning of America's history and institutions were more engaged in citizenship activities such as voting, volunteer community service and political campaigns.[8]

Today, civics courses are often not required in middle or high schools because room has been made in the curriculum for such modern courses as computer technology. Nevertheless, most public schools still find a venue to teach the basics of American citizenship—the Declaration of Independence, the Constitution, the Bill of Rights, writings by the founders of the country, and such core beliefs as the idea of free and open elections, freedom of speech and religion, and equality of citizens before the law.

One such venue is The Pledge of Allegiance. At the turn of the twentieth century the United States was swamped with a wave of immigrants from Southern and Eastern Europe. Not only were children expected to take civics courses, they also had to declare that they were patriots and loyal to the Untied States. To both acculturate and assimilate the immigrant children, starting in 1892, a Pledge to the Flag[9] became a daily routine in America's public schools, and in 1945 it was officially titled The Pledge of Allegiance:

> I pledge allegiance to the Flag
> of the United States of America,
> and to the Republic for which it stands:
> one Nation indivisible,
> With Liberty and Justice for all.
>
> June 14, 1924

In the middle of the Cold War, the United States Congress wanted to make clear that, in contrast to "godless Communism," America was favored by God. Thus, on June 14, 1954 (Flag Day), President Dwight D. Eisenhower approved adding the words "under God."

> I pledge allegiance to the Flag
> Of the United States of America,
> And to the Republic for which it stands:
> One Nation under God, indivisible,
> With Liberty and Justice for all.
>
> June 14, 1954

As he authorized this change he said, "In this way we are reaffirm-ing the transcendence of religious faith in America's heritage and future; in this way we shall constantly strengthen those spiritual weapons which forever will be our country's most powerful resource in peace and war."

The Pledge of Allegiance has often generated debate. For example, the Supreme Court ruled in 1940 that a public school student could be compelled to recite the Pledge. Two Jehovah's Witness school children, 10 and 12 years old, were suspended from school in Minerville, Penn-sylvania, because they refused to say the Pledge of Allegiance and salute the American flag. In their minds, it amounted to saluting a govern-ment that violated their religious beliefs. The Supreme Court ruled that saluting the flag was a means of creating national loyalty and unity.[10] In the 1943 case that reversed this 1940 decision, Justice Jackson of the Supreme Court wrote:

> The very purpose of the Bill of Rights was to withdraw certain sub-jects from the reach of majorities and officials. One's right to wor-ship, life, liberty, and property, to free speech, a free press, freedom of worship and assembly, and other fundamental rights may not be submitted to vote; they depend upon the outcome of no election.[11]

The 1943 Court took the position that it was a violation of indi-vidual liberty to force an individual to give a salute that violated his or her religious beliefs, even if the person belonged to a minority religion and the person was only one child asserting his or her civil rights.

This case illustrates the tension between the importance of reli-gion and the importance of the individual's right to free expression. This conflict—pitting the innate religious character of many Ameri-cans against the sacred belief in the country of protecting the free-dom of the individual—has always been contentious because of the importance placed on each of these values in American culture. It also shows how American cultural values—while often working in tan-dem with one another—can also occasionally clash. With such broad freedoms given to—and held dearly by—Americans, defining the boundaries of these freedoms, if there are any, has often been a har-rowing process. This case also illustrated the tension between local school boards and the federal courts. While education is left up to the local municipality or state, everyone has the right to ask the court sys-tem to guarantee the protection of an individual's constitutional rights. But, issues of educational standards and practices are usually a matter left up to the local government.

Local control of education has led to the teaching of highly divergent curricula across the country. One such divergent area is the teaching of evolution and creationism in public schools. Given the religiosity of Americans in general, it is logical that creationism finds stronger support in the United States than in most countries in the Western world, including all of Europe. Indeed, the place of creationism and evolution in public schools has long been a contentious issue in this country. Several states have passed laws preventing public school teachers from denying that the account of creation given in the Bible is not the literal truth.[12] These laws were later struck down in a higher court, however.

Creationism is often referred to as Intelligent Design in this ongoing educational debate. The assumption is that the superiority of human beings on earth must have been part of a higher power's design and is not simply a matter of a series of biological accidents. Under the umbrella of Intelligent Design an overarching combination of attacks has been launched against scientific methodology in general, which creationists view as philosophical materialism. (Some local school boards take the position that both Darwinian evolutionary theory and creationism should be taught as co-equal explanations of how life began on earth. Teachers and students can then pick whatever view they like.)

The evolution/creationism debate is an issue in which extreme positions have proven to be not only divisive, but detrimental to American cultural life in general. If we take the position that creationism should be taught in schools, then the scientific training of students will suffer and the ingenuity and great scientific aptitude that have been byproducts of American culture will likely suffer. Yet if we deny the intense importance of religion to the country and many of its citizens, we may threaten the steadfast moral consciousness of the national culture that has been similarly important to American culture. When two internal cultural values clash, as they do in this case, it is difficult if not impossible to find a nationally acceptable solution. This is in part why many conflicts of this nature are resolved on a local level yet continue to fester on a national level. The local decision allows the input of as many citizens as possible and the result is as congruent as possible with the localized version of the national culture.

Book banning is another highly contentious issue in local education. Freedom of thought and inquiry are basic tenets of education in the United States, and yet there have been efforts to prevent young people from reading certain books. Some individuals and groups have attempted to ban books from local schools and libraries because they are deemed to be threatening to the local perception of the civic ideal. The belief is that these books will have a corrupting influence upon children and will steer them away from adhering to the dominant civic and moral culture. Books touching on racial or sexual (particularly homosexual) issues, or ones in which violence and profanity appear, are sometimes banned on a local level due to pressure from a town or county's residents. According to the American Library Association, another primary reason for a book to be banned is the accusation that it promotes "the occult or Satanism,"[13] again reflecting the conflict between religion and the rights of the individual—in this case, the right to read whatever one would like.

Some of the most frequently banned books are also some of the most famous and bestselling books in the country. The Harry Potter series is often a target for book banning advocates because of its positive portrayal of witches and witchcraft. Toni Morrison's books, particularly *Beloved*, though cited by *The New York Times* as the best book of the last quarter century,[14] is another frequent target for banning. Bans are also frequently attempted on books such as J.D. Salinger's *Catcher in the Rye*, John Steinbeck's *Of Mice and Men*, Maya Angelou's *I Know Why the Caged Bird Sings*, Harper Lee's *To Kill A Mockingbird*, and Mark Twain's *The Adventures of Huckleberry Finn*.[15]

Again, we find here a conflict between religion and individual rights, with a dichotomy of rationales similar to the creationism/ evolution debate. And again, it is a key feature of the American civic culture that such issues are settled locally. When issues or conflicts are simply too contentious or complicated to be worked out locally, then these especially difficult, divisive issues—such as abortion and immigration—are pushed to the national level for debate and resolution.

Many countries have a national educational policy administered by a federal office. Despite great controversy and opposition, the U.S. Department of Education was created in May of 1980 and it is the smallest cabinet-level department in the federal government. Compared with other countries, there really is little to speak of in terms of a national educational policy in the U.S. Funding for public education usually comes from local property or income taxes and elected municipal or state school boards decide on the curriculum. Moreover, communities prefer to be able to influence what their children learn, rather than feel that bureaucrats in Washington are making this decision for them. Nevertheless, all public schools are open to every child, including undocumented immigrants, and from the very beginning of the country these schools have taught children American virtues. They provide free schooling to everyone and acculturate immigrants to their new land.

While public schools in the U.S. have usually been open to all and have been academically very strong until recently, in many parts of Europe, private schools were usually better than public schools, and they were intended for the very wealthy and upper classes of the society. Furthermore, European schools that were funded by taxes often allowed children to be segregated into their particular religious groups. In the Netherlands, there were Protestant public schools for Protestant children, Catholic public schools for Catholic children, Jewish schools for Jewish children, and more recently, Muslim schools for Muslim children. These groups even had their own hospitals and other social services. On the other hand, universities and colleges were often open to all, but only those who had come from the best private schools made it to the university.

Many of the institutions of higher education in this country are public universities and colleges. Each state has its own system of public universities and colleges, which were created to meet its needs for manpower to maintain a growing state economy.[16] Thus, the University of Wisconsin, for example, as well as other Midwestern institutions of higher education, emphasize agricultural engineering and research, medicine, and law in order to serve the interests of the state. The federal government engages in little oversight or regulatory activity in American universities, in contrast to higher education systems in many other countries. The federal government, however, did have an important hand in the original establishment of the public university system in the country, with the passage of the Morrill Land Grant Act in 1862. This act donated large tracts of federal land to the states for the specific purpose of building universities.[17] Although the federal government acted as an enabler of higher education, it did not become directly involved in it, allowing education in general to remain a local issue. A second Morrill Act in 1890 was aimed at the Southern states, and carried the provision that public universities established under the act must not use race as a factor in admissions decisions, or, as an alternative, that separate universities be created for African-Americans. (This was an early institutionalization of the separate but equal approach to race relations, upheld by the Supreme Court in 1896 in the *Plessy v. Ferguson* decision, and eventually overturned in the landmark *Brown v. the Board of Education* decision of 1954.)

Despite the prevalence of state schools today, the first universities in the country were private. Private universities such as Harvard (1636), Yale (1701), and Princeton (1746) were fashioned after the British idea that a liberal education was designed to produce well-rounded leaders for the entire country, people with a broad background in many areas of knowledge. In these early private universities the British concept of liberal education was combined with the German emphasis on research.[18] Each of these universities was founded by churches and they were to become beacons for the new learning society. Indeed, until within the past 50 years, often only the very elite in the society were accepted into these universities. Despite this, these universities set the standard for the quality and character of higher education in the country and ensured that the industrious pursuit of knowledge was a hallmark of the civic culture.

Growing Up: The Death/Birth Cycle of National Identity

Governance is always a matter of balance and compromise in the United States. There has always been a distrust of an overly powerful central federal government, and the ongoing conflict and balancing of powers between all branches of government makes impulsive governmental action difficult at all levels. This was the clear intention of the founders of the nation who wrote the Constitution and formed the government. During emergencies, such as a threat to the national security, more power is given to the federal government and the executive branch. Once the emergency passes, the other levels and branches of government soon restore the balance. Furthermore, there is continual interpretation and reinterpretation of the laws to decide which branch or level of government has jurisdiction over a public policy.

The same is true for American civic culture. Who defines and communicates it and how they do so is often also a matter of balance, compromise, and continual reinterpretation. Sometimes it is the federal, state or local government that transmits and defines it, and sometimes it is a private citizen like William McGuffey who acts as a primary transmitter of it. Sometimes it is learned in schools, sometimes in groups such as the Boy Scouts, and sometimes even by watching American movies. Yet from all of these widely varying sources, American civic culture retains and passes on the underlying core values of the culture that resonate with all Americans. While we may debate what individual freedom entails, we can all agree that both individual freedoms and the ability to debate them are intrinsic values of American civic culture. While this ongoing balancing act may appear to be chaotic and unpredictable, it is necessary to effectively meet the needs of the nation during times of continual change and to overcome national and international challenges.

Just as an individual must assume new responsibilities and perceive the world in different ways as he or she matures, the country also grows as it resolves various national crises within its borders or with other nations. These shared historical experiences strengthen the national identity of Americans.

Humans need to give up some old ways of thinking, resolving problems, and perceiving themselves and others differently to allow for maturation. While we keep our youthful ideals, they are tempered and seasoned with the harsh realities of life. All Americans can agree that political and civic participation is a key civic virtue of the culture. When we are young, we might wish to run for office. Yet following the difficult experience of running for office, or of losing an election, we may wish to express this virtue differently, perhaps by volunteering at a local homeless shelter or by working in the public sector.

Regardless of how we express them, these ideals and values give us the strength to psychologically withstand enormous crises and to learn from those experiences. For many families, they usually strengthen the familial bonds. Unfortunately, for some individuals and families, severe stress can also be very destructive.

Individuals and nations can weather crises and grow if their foundations are strong. But, this requires introspection, flexibility, and the tolerance of continual change. We may long for the simplicity of an earlier period, and at times we may regress to these earlier ways of thinking. However, most human beings grow, and nations progress as they go through a kind of death/rebirth cycle. The metaphoric "child" dies as the "adolescent" is born. Moving from childhood to adolescence is usually confusing and painful for most humans as we give up childish ways of doing things to adapt more adult ways. The young, single adult "dies" as the husband, wife, father, or mother is "born" with a new identity, new responsibilities, and new ways of solving problems.

The values of the civic culture provide legitimacy to the government when it may not effectively meet the needs of the people or when it is going through a national crisis. Both good and bad experiences strengthen the bonds between members of a family just as shared national experiences—both good and bad—have strengthened the civic culture. The Vietnam War and the civil turmoil of the Civil Rights Movement and the Anti-War Movement in the 1960s and 1970s seemed to tear the country apart, and yet it allowed for enormous growth and change resulting in the end of legal discrimination and greater cooperation between the U.S. and other nations to end the Cold War without using military force.

The United States is on the verge of ending conflicts in Iraq and Afghanistan, an African-American may be elected president, and a great deal of research shows that the American people want the U.S. to be engaged in the world through international negotiation and cooperation rather than through the use of unilateral military force. As we will begin to discuss in the following chapters, after the national identity crisis that followed the end of the Cold War and especially the attacks of 9/11 (what we term America's midlife crisis), we may now be on the cusp of a new era for America, one in which the country, its values, and its national and international character reach a decisive—and new—stage of development and maturity.

Maturity requires responsible behavior and an understanding of our realistic limitations. While we may continue to debate how the values of our civic culture are expressed, we need to retain and embrace our fundamental civic values and ideals to provide direction and guidance as we begin to play a new role in a continually changing world.

CHAPTER 7

Prosperity at Home, Prestige Abroad

Foreign Policy

The American flag has not been planted on foreign soil to acquire more territory, but for humanity's sake.

—WILLIAM MCKINLEY AND TEDDY ROOSEVELT CAMPAIGN
SLOGAN FOR THE 1900 ELECTION

O FTEN, WHEN TRYING TO UNDERSTAND AN INDIVIDUAL'S behavior, we first consider their childhood or formative years. Values and beliefs that are learned informally during these years last a lifetime and shape behavior. Traumatic childhood experiences within the family or in the community are carried into adulthood. Freudian psychoanalysts would even claim that unresolved conflicts between a son and his father are often played out later in life in conflicts with male authority figures that represent the father figure. Feelings toward the father are transferred onto the bearded professor, a policeman, or a tyrannical boss.

We can draw an analogy between the development of an individual's personality and the civic culture of a country.[1] Just as we can consider an individual's personality and his or her identity as a result of child-raising practices and childhood experiences, we can also view a country and the national identity of its people as a result of social, economic, and political factors that shape, and are shaped by, historical events.

If a society is fairly homogeneous, such as a rural community where everyone shares the same religion, language, and child-raising practices, then everyone can be expected to have roughly the same values, beliefs, and worldviews. In an Arabic-speaking Sunni Muslim village most people would share the same external and internal culture as well as a common identity. How they perceive themselves and others depends upon their mutual experiences growing up as Sunni Muslims in this particular community. If during childhood everyone is taught to be afraid of people from a neighboring village, this perception of threat carries into adulthood and shapes the interrelationship between the two villages.

Of course, we need to be mindful of the differences between an individual and a society or nation. We can say a person is paranoid, but it is a stretch of a concept to say that an entire society or nation is paranoid. However, if the nation has frequently been invaded by its neighbors over many generations, it is reasonable to say that their foreign policy is very defensive and based upon an assumption of imminent threat. Thus, the history of a people helps to explain their public policy.

The same is true regarding morality and ethics. We cannot ascribe to the state emotions such as love, hate, and jealousy, which play such a large part in individual morality. An individual may be very moral or ethical, but the leaders of a nation must make decisions that are essential for the survival of an entire country. Can the actions of a nation be judged by the same standards of morals and ethics as applied to an individual? Although we might expect a state to be generous, just, and altruistic, the interests of the nation must come first.[2]

The period from the birth of the nation until the Spanish-American War (1898) and World War I (1914–1918) could be viewed as analogous to an overprotected and *prolonged childhood or the formative years* for an individual if we consider the foreign policy of the United States. While the U.S. was involved with other nations in terms of commerce and certainly sought to extend its control of North America at the expense of Native Americans and Mexicans, its foreign policy was relatively isolationist. It was during this period that the new country viewed itself as almost utopian: an exceptional country built on moral values, innocent, peaceful, and, most importantly, uninvolved in the Machiavellian wars going on in Europe. Of course, Americans fought a bloody, fratricidal Civil War (1861–1865), which tore the nation apart and led to the death of over 600,000 soldiers. But this was a domestic, not an international, conflict. During this struggle, the country began to leave its childhood utopian idealism as it became clear that the perception Americans had of themselves as living in a peaceful, harmonious confederation was naïve. The fact that two increasingly dissimilar societies were emerging in the North and the slave-holding South had been increasingly evident and led to the war. This very painful "identity crisis" helped to solidify the sense that the country was also a unified nation with a federal government operating under a constitutional system of laws.[3]

With the Spanish-American War the United States left its relative peaceful isolation and insulation from the turmoil of the rest of the world and entered into military combat with other nations. The period from the beginning of the Spanish-American War until the end of World War II (1945)[4] can certainly then be regarded as the *adolescence* of the United States. Adolescents leave the warmth and security of the family to enter both friendly and unfriendly relationships with outsiders. This involvement is often very emotionally intense and highly idealistic with unrealistic and naive expectations, and usually very awkward. Sometimes it leads to acceptance, but it often ends up with rejection. At that moment, many adolescents vow to never get involved again, and become mired in apathy or withdrawal. For example, unrequited love can lead to withdrawal and the false security that stems from noninvolvement. However, most of us venture out again, but with the wisdom of experience. We are more realistic in our expectations; we know that there is the possibility of failure and we realize that there is both pain and pleasure in all intense human relationships. While non-involvement is secure and risk-free, it offers no possibility of growth or pleasure.

Total head-over-heels idealistic involvement and total cynical withdrawal from relationships are often characteristic of the ambivalent extremes of adolescents. Of course, during the childhood period, the new country was always commercially involved with the rest of the world because trade, especially agricultural trade, was the only way to bring capital to the New World. Even the earliest British colony at Jamestown in Virginia was a business venture, not exclusively a matter of Europeans fleeing religious persecution. However, when it comes to military involvement and foreign policy, historically the United States has shown something of a pendulum pattern: A period of total—and often military—internationalism, often based upon some kind of crusade or high idealism, is followed by intense foreign policy and military disengagement or isolationism and a focus on internal affairs.

The United States went into the Spanish-American War with the noble and idealistic intention of liberating Puerto Rico, Cuba, and the Philippines from a colonial power, Spain. However, this was followed with a period of overwhelming disillusionment and disappointment when the U.S. was viewed as an imperialist occupier by many in these newly independent nations. Perhaps the most dramatic—and famous—example of adolescent idealism in American foreign policy came when Woodrow Wilson, a devout Presbyterian,[5] led the United States into a major war in Europe—World War I. Our allies in England and France were defending themselves but this was not simply a matter of helping friendly nations or crass national interests. It was depicted as a "war to end all wars" and a "war to make the world safe for democracy."

When the war ended, Wilson tried to extend American constitutionalism and values to the entire world, through the vehicle of the League of Nations. If everyone could just meet and reason together, he asserted, then they would agree to avoid war. There was no way to force nations to agree to be peaceful and even the smallest nation had the same vote as the most powerful. It was a liberal, democratic way to prevent war. Yet, even the United States Senate refused to ratify the Treaty of Versailles and never joined the League of Nations, wary of the open-ended military commitments that membership in the League might entail.

The country's adolescence—and its ability to effectively avoid international commitments—ended with World War II. Wilson's utopian idealism and his belief in some kind of moral legal system to provide security and peace came to an end in the 1930s with the rise of Hitler. The United States was attacked at Pearl Harbor in 1941, Hitler had invaded most of Europe, and our allies were being occupied by Nazi troops. Franklin Roosevelt had to take action and defend his country. This was a matter of realism, not idealism.

Young *adulthood* began with World War II, and the United States could no longer remain withdrawn behind its own borders. Like a young adult who must now get a steady job, pay the bills, and act maturely, the U.S. could no longer shirk its role as a world leader. The Cold War, beginning after the conclusion of the Second World War, demanded continual involvement and a more mature, adult America to handle its challenges. There was no possibility of withdrawal again. But, could the U.S. retain its ideals as it played this new role on the world stage or would it remain imprisoned in adolescent cynical realism?[6]

Before answering that question, and discerning what stage of development America and its foreign policy sits at today, we must look at the origins and course of American foreign policy and its influence on the country.

The First American Foreign Policy: Isolationism, but with Commercial and Moral Expansionism

In popular thought, both in this country and around the world, America is often seen as a nation that is *isolationist* at its heart. According to this narrative, America is occasionally thrust onto the international stage either through moral imperative or the inevitable tide of events, only to withdraw once the crisis has passed. In terms of military and political adventurism, this is indeed true. The U.S. during its childhood period really wanted to be left alone and it did not want to "dirty its hands" in European affairs, especially those involving war. The opposite foreign policy would be what most international relations theorists would call *internationalism*—robust military and political involvement in the international system.

When we look at the country's history, even back to its colonial days, the U.S. in reality has been morally, territorially, and commercially expansionist with only relatively short periods of isolationism in these respects. In these realms of foreign affairs, the U.S. has been an active participant and sternly reacted when any other nations tried to stifle these kinds of international expansionism. However, it was not until the Spanish-American War and World War I that the U.S. enlarged its foreign involvement to include long-lasting, concentrated military action. At this point, it lost its innocence of noninvolvement in the brutal competition between nations. It behaved as many European nations. And, until after World War II, it withdrew from such military recklessness.

What are the cultural values that contributed to this unique foreign policy outlook? One is certainly the liberal tradition that was embedded in the country's founding documents and civic culture. The belief that these values were universal and should be extended to all mankind fueled (or, we could also say, justified) a number of wars and foreign policies undertaken by the nation. The celebration of these values was the Manifest Destiny of the world. The moralizing aspect of this liberal tradition—and the belief that others could be converted to it—also found its origins in the religious roots of the country. It is only a short step from the idea that certain good works and living by a particular moral code are the only paths to personal salvation to extending this to believe that liberal political values are the only path to the political salvation of mankind. The missionary zeal held by so many American religious figures and early settlers was matched by the missionary-like zeal of many of the founders and later American leaders in regard to liberal values and their universality.

American exceptionalism also figures into this discussion, in a double-edged manner. On the one hand, from the first settlers of the country, Americans have believed that they are a people set apart, with a divinely ordained mission to be at the zenith of all countries in the world. In the words of John Quincy Adams, the country's sixth president, America was "destined by God and nature to be the most populous and powerful people ever combined under one social compact."[7] Thus, in this line of thinking, American exceptionalism meant that America should be at the head of all nations, preaching the glories of liberal values and fighting (rhetorically or otherwise) the forces of tyranny.

The flipside of American exceptionalism is the belief that America should or could "go it alone." When the country was young, a key reason for this attitude was so as not to become bogged down in the same potentially destructive political chess matches that many European nations engaged in. America would instead pursue its own interests and not become entangled in unnecessary conflicts. Many early American immigrants from Europe knew the harmful domestic ramifications of such involvements firsthand. In his Farewell Address, typically cited as the founding document of American isolationism, George Washington warned his countrymen:

> The great rule of conduct for us, in regard to domestic nations, is in extending our commercial relations, to have with them as little political connection as possible. Europe has a set of primary interests, which to us have none, or a very remote relation. Hence she must be engaged in frequent controversies the causes of which are essentially foreign to our concerns. Hence, therefore, it must be unwise in us to implicate ourselves, by artificial ties, in the ordinary vicissitudes of her politics, or the ordinary combinations and collisions of her friendships or enmities.

This sentiment was echoed by Thomas Jefferson, who noted that "commerce with all nations, alliance with none, should be our motto."

American political and military isolationism evolved into American *unilateralism* in the international arena. That is, America at times acted isolationist in the sense that it carried out completely unilateral, solo actions in the international arena. While this may not appear isolationist (since it does necessitate involvement on the world stage), what is crucial about this brand of isolationism, which makes it consistent with the younger version of isolationism, is that it is international action *on America's own terms*. Thus, the foreign entanglements that Washington so strongly counseled the nation to eschew would theoretically remain avoidable if America adopted a unilateralist policy, unencumbered by foreign allies and their whims. Moreover, because the U.S. was not in danger of alienating allies by shirking its commitment to some collective foreign policy, the country could also define the terms and length of its own commitment to whatever policy it chose to pursue, foreshortening—or eliminating—any indefinite entanglements. (This was seen in Vietnam and is currently being seen in Iraq.) While America did not have the power to act completely unilaterally during the earlier part of its history, it can be argued that once it attained such power, the country's unilateralism provided a new kind of isolationism, albeit one much different from what Washington may have intended.[8]

Through a brief survey of American foreign policy, we can trace how this evolution occurred, and where it may be headed in the future.

Early Foreign Policy: Commerce and Pirates

Early post-independence America followed an internationally isolationist stance, while at the same time its domestic posture was undeniably expansionist. Early Americans pushed back Native-American Indians through a combination of disease, warfare, and exploitive treaties. During the course of the nineteenth century, Native Americans saw their lands dwindle further and further, and the beginning of the establishment of Indian reservations in the 1850s and 1860s cemented the Indians' status as the victims of a burgeoning sense of Manifest Destiny and the settlers' expansionist urges.

Internationally speaking, the oceans on either side of North America allowed the young country to be securely isolated and insulated from the rest of the world. During the colonial period, Americans became involved in larger international conflicts, such as the French and Indian War, by virtue of their association with the British Empire. Naturally, this isolation was broken during the Revolutionary War, which started to some degree because Americans felt that Britain was hampering their ability to expand economically[9] and was not allowing them to expand their political voice in London (thus the famous complaint of "taxation without representation"). Yet, following the war, America focused more on domestic expansion than international involvement, encouraged by its cloistered position on the world map. This geographic isolation was reinforced politically by America's early leaders. Patrick Henry worried that the new country might aspire to become a "great and mighty empire" rather than keep its focus on "liberty . . . [which is] the primary object."[10] American foreign policy went through a prolonged, protected childhood; ideals and reality were the same during the colonial period. American ideals were not buffeted by the winters of adversity. Thus, when the country later went into the world it was with enormous, unrealistic idealism.

In 1785, the ruler of the city-state of Algiers took two American ships hostage, asking for $60,000 in ransom for the return of their crews. After some debate, the U.S. government decided to pay the fee, and for the next 15 years, the United States paid tribute to the Barbary states (in modern day Algeria, Libya, and Tunisia) to insure their sailors' safe passage on the seas and to retrieve the Americans intermittently taken hostage by Barbary pirates. This tribute equaled nearly 20 percent of total American revenue in 1800.[11] Thomas Jefferson, long opposed to the nation's payment of tribute, refused to continue payment when he became president in 1801, setting off a war between the U.S. and the Barbary states from which the U.S. emerged victorious.[12] Jefferson suggested that Americans must be willing to go to war to ensure what he called "freedom of the seas." As a farmer, he also realized that the only way the economy of this emerging nation could grow was by exporting its agricultural products to Europe, underlining the importance of keeping the seas open to American ships.[13]

While the United States has had—and continues to have—many protective tariffs, unimpeded commerce and the freedom to ship goods on the high seas are still viewed as basic tenets of American foreign policy. In 1987 and 1988, why was the United States involved in the Persian Gulf with military force during the Iran-Iraq war? The official explanation of the United States Department of State was to ensure "freedom of the seas," which in 1987 and 1988 remained just as crucial to the commercial interests of the U.S. as they had been in 1815.[14]

The War of 1812 also was fought for reasons relating to America's lack of patience with foreign powers who threatened its ability to expand commercially or territorially. In this case, the power turned out to be Britain. During its war with France, Britain prohibited American commercial expansion by blockading ports through which supplies could be procured by the Napoleonic forces. Britain also adopted a policy of seizing American sailors from vessels at sea and impressing them into service in the Royal Navy. From the American perspective, there was also a territorial *casus belli* in the form of British support of Indian militarism against Americans, which retarded the American ability to expand westward into Indian lands in North America. America suffered some military defeats during the war—notably the capture of Washington, D.C., and the burning of the White House, as well as a failed attempt to invade Canada, a little remembered, but significant manifestation of the American drive for territorial expansion on the continent. Nevertheless, the U.S. was able to fight the British to a stalemate, which resulted in the Treaty of Ghent of 1815 and the end of both the impressment of American seamen and the British blockade of ports.[15]

There were two significant additional outcomes from the War of 1812. First, during the course of the war, the United States was able to rout many of its Indian antagonists, thus paving the way for greater Western expansion following the war. Secondly, the war resulted in an upsurge of American confidence and nationalism. Not only had America stood up to Britain once again in what many thought of as a "second war of independence," but the Americans, under future president Andrew Jackson, had trounced the British in a battle at New Orleans. Many chose to see the war as a legitimization and evidence of American power. In this interpretation, America was on the course that many of its earliest citizens and founding fathers had foreseen: It was a country whose legitimacy had now been doubly assured, and it was on the fast track to prosperity and power on a scale scarcely imaginable. Thus, the War of 1812 provided concrete support for American exceptionalism, while clearing the way for further territorial expansion and the spread of Americans, their values, and the zealous pursuit of their Manifest Destiny in the frontier.

The Monroe Doctrine: "Just Leave Us Alone!"

Many adolescents just want to be left alone. But they also want to venture out and grow. American isolationism in the early years was also a matter of *non-interventionism*: the U.S. would remain neutral in European conflicts and Europe ought to stay out of the American sphere of influence, the Western Hemisphere. An example of non-intervention in European issues occurred in the 1820s when the Greeks sought to become independent from the Ottoman Empire. Both Turks and Greeks sought the support of the United States. Congress debated what stand to take and finally concluded that it was a European matter and that the United States would maintain a policy of non-involvement and non-alignment. It would take no side in European conflicts. This was quite similar to the foreign policy of nonalignment held by many emerging Third World nations during the Cold War.

James Monroe, the fifth president of the young country, made this a matter of stated U.S. foreign policy. He proclaimed to Europeans in

1823 that the United States "should consider any attempt on their part to extend their system to any portion of this hemisphere as dangerous to our peace and safety." This was later termed the Monroe Doctrine. It became an ingrained foreign policy position of the U.S. that America would stay out of the affairs of Europe and the Europeans should stay out of the Western Hemisphere. The young nation thereby tried to insulate the entire Western Hemisphere from direct European influence. Most importantly, this reflected the American desire to avoid wallowing in the muck of international conflict beyond American borders.

A strict interpretation of the doctrine has often been tested, and at other times has been subject to glaring violations. For example, the Doctrine was clearly violated during the 1982 Falkland/Malvinas Islands War between Argentina and Britain. President Reagan shared intelligence information with the British and sided with them against Argentina. Furthermore, Reagan declared United States support for Britain and imposed economic sanctions against Argentina.

As adolescent America attempted to isolate itself during the nineteenth century from the conflicts taking place in Europe, it turned its attention to domestic affairs, which, in turn, impacted American foreign policy when it came to the issue of the settling of the country. Americans perceived themselves as peaceful people who wanted to be left alone, but they also wanted to expand and grow in terms of contiguous territory and economics. As Americans continued to move westward, and as immigration to America picked up during the 1800s, American territorial ambitions grew and the fever of Manifest Destiny impacted its foreign policy. Some of these expansionist urges were satisfied through the purchase of territory and via negotiations, such as the Louisiana Purchase and the Adams-Onís Treaty, which resulted in U.S. control of Florida. Other expansions came through dramatic negotiations over territory with other countries, such as the settlement of the border of the Oregon Country with Britain.

It should be noted that this desire to expand was not universal, nor was it without ulterior motives. In fact, the desire of Southern slaveholding states to expand the number of slaveholding states (by the acquisition of new territory and the subsequent admission of new slave-holding states to the country) for economic and political gain was an important catalyst of this expansionist tendency.

The Mexican-American War of 1846–1848 was noteworthy for its ramifications vis á vis American notions of Manifest Destiny and territorial expansion. Though the reasons for the war were complex, the direct *casus belli* was the annexation by the U.S. of the Republic of Texas, a breakaway state carved from Mexican territory and populated by American settlers. The declaration of war did not come without opposition. Charging that the war would serve as a boon for slavery, a number of Congressmen voted against it, including a former president (John Quincy Adams) and a future president (Abraham Lincoln). Abolitionists were also strongly against the war. One of the most famous of their number, Henry Thoreau, was jailed for his refusal to pay taxes in support of the war, prompting him to write his famous essay, *Civil Disobedience.*

Though the war was hard fought and costly—more than 13,000 U.S. soldiers and 25,000 Mexican soldiers perished—the United States proved to be the decisive winner. The U.S. obtained undisputed control of Texas, and also received California, Utah, Nevada and parts of Colorado, New Mexico, Wyoming and Arizona (roughly 500,000 square miles), territory throughout which American settlers would soon spread, mobilized by Manifest Destiny and in search of new opportunities for prosperity and economic mobility. The war was also seen by some as a means by which America could spread democracy and liberty. Yet this energized American nationalism and expansionism was tempered by the issues that grew out of the new territory that the war brought: The debate about if (or how) slavery would expand into the new territories eventually tore the country asunder in a bloody civil war. As Ulysses S. Grant wrote, "The Southern rebellion was largely the outgrowth of the Mexican war. Nations, like individuals, are punished for their transgressions. We got our punishment in the most sanguinary and expensive war of modern times."[16]

An Adolescent Identity Crisis: Internationalism or a Return to Domestic Innocence?

Following the Civil War, American foreign ambitions expanded along with American industry. Much of this was due to a desire to secure foreign markets for American goods, which were being pumped out of factories at the fastest rate in human history. As it had been prior to the Civil War, much of American foreign policy was still market-driven and economically catalyzed. This more mundane and utilitarian motivation was backed up by the American tradition of Manifest Destiny—the boundaries of that destiny expanded whenever it was politically, economically, or ideologically convenient. This was all compounded with the general spirit among the industrialized Western great powers of the Kiplingesque "white man's burden": to colonize, civilize, and control non-Western territories.

The latter part of the nineteenth century and beginning of the twentieth century proved to be a period of adolescent-like total involvement in the world beyond the Western Hemisphere followed by pangs of remorse and even guilt, followed by a desire to totally withdraw behind the two oceans. As America had matured and ranged further out into the world and community of nations, the country discovered that the repercussions of its involvement were more severe. In the early twentieth century, America tried to translate its unique domestic values into international norms, attempting to bring its idealism and values into common international currency. As we shall see, the results of this effort had a decisive effect on the course of American foreign policy to the present day.

"A new consciousness seems to have come upon us—the consciousness of strength—and with it a new appetite," wrote a *Washington Post* editorial in the late 1890s. "The taste of Empire," it continued, "is in the mouth of the people as the taste of blood in the jungle."[17] Having met with little resistance in its expansion thus far, and as American industry, population, and self-confidence all blossomed, Americans continued to look for new opportunities to expand the nation's influence and its markets, as well as to legitimize its pretensions as a world power by acquiring overseas territories, much like the storied colonial empires of Europe.

One outlet for these desires was Cuba, then a Spanish colony. A Cuban rebellion against Spanish rule in 1895 aroused U.S. business interests, which had long coveted Cuban markets, as well as American idealism. The war was seen by its many supporters as a perfect conflict—"a splendid little war," in the words of John Hay. It would liberate Cuba from a despotic European overlord in the interests of democracy, while at the same time opening up the island to U.S.

commercial interests. Although the American people believed that this was a war of liberation, there were surely some leaders who saw this war as an opportunity for the U.S. to snag the remnants of Spain's colonies and become a bonafide international power.

Americans finally left their childhood isolationism from world affairs with the hundred-day Spanish-American War. This was justified with the idealistic goal of freeing the Philippines, Puerto Rico, and Cuba from the evil Spanish. It was the white man's burden to liberate these "little brown brothers" (in Kipling's words) from European colonialism and oppression. The war was justified and presented to the public as good against evil, led by President William McKinley, who told reporters that God told him to occupy the Philippines.

McKinley, the twenty-fifth president, was a very fundamentalist Methodist who tended to believe that the United States ought to help spread Christianity and American values to the rest of the world. In his first Inaugural Address on March 4, 1897, he said, "Our faith teaches that there is no safer reliance than upon the God of our fathers, who has so singularly favored the American people in every national trial, and who will not forsake us so long as we obey His commandments and walk humbly in His footsteps."

In 1898, hostilities began between the two countries, with the U.S. routing the Spanish forces. The two countries signed the Treaty of Paris in December, with Spain ceding to the U.S. many of its colonial possessions, including Puerto Rico, Guam, and the Philippines. The ratification of the treaty met many opponents in the U.S. Senate, however, because some of its members were less enthusiastic than other Americans about acquiring the beginnings of an empire and leaving behind the nation's international semi-isolation.

But, the result was unrequited love. Americans were viewed by the populations of their new possessions as occupiers as much as liberators. The retention of an overseas empire required the enforcement of the country's control over it, and in the Philippines this proved neither easy nor morally unambiguous. And, the mood in the U.S. swung back toward withdrawal into the innocence of isolationism and away from military adventurism. McKinley supported the war for a mixture of reasons, though ones deeply rooted in American cultural values. His support of the war and the American acquisition of empire stemmed from a conviction in American exceptionalism and his Puritanical belief that the ends of the war were part of God's preordained plan for humanity. Defending the decision to retain the Philippines, and over-looking the fact that most of these new American subjects were already Christians, McKinley said, "I went down on my knees and prayed Almighty God for light and guidance. . . . And one night later it came to me this way. . . . There was nothing left for us to do but to take them all and to educate the Filippinos and uplift and civilize and Christian-ize them."[18]

Soon after American troops landed in the Philippines, fighting broke out between Filippinos trying to establish their independence and Americans trying to establish their control. After years of fighting and the deaths of thousands of Americans and tens (if not hundreds) of thousands of Filipinos, American control was asserted over the ter-ritory. Yet, this conflict stirred the forces of anti-imperialists at home. Mark Twain summed up the feelings of this segment of the population, writing, "I thought we should act as their protector—not try to get them under our heel. But now—why, we have got into a mess, a quag-mire from which each fresh step renders the difficulty of extrication im-mensely greater. I'm sure I wish I could see what we were getting out of it, and all it means to us as a nation."[19]

American eagerness to charge onto the world stage was some-what daunted by the difficulties encountered in the Philippine War. In 1900, McKinley campaigned on promises of "Prosperity at home, Prestige abroad," with "Commerce" and "Civilization" his adminis-tration's guiding lights. Another campaign poster proclaimed that "The American flag has not been planted in foreign soil to acquire more territory, but for humanity's sake," thus distancing American motiva-tions for acquiring territory from the crass, and associating them with American exceptionalism and the spread of American values. Spurned in its attempt to emulate the colonial empires of its European peers, the U.S. sought to tone down its rhetoric of expansionism and refrained from embarking on forays onto the international stage as dramatic (and violent) as in the Spanish-American War.

When McKinley was assassinated in 1901, following his re-election on this platform, Theodore Roosevelt, a hero of the Spanish-American War, ascended to the presidency. Roosevelt continued McKinley's internationalist outlook. In December 1904, Roosevelt attempted to provide the U.S. with theoretical backing for increased

FIGURE 7.1   "Prosperity at Home, Prestige Abroad," a McKinley/Roosevelt Campaign Poster from the 1900 election.

FIGURE 7.2 "The American flag has not been planted in foreign soil to acquire more territory but for humanity's sake," a McKinley/Roosevelt Campaign Poster from the 1900 election.

involvement in Latin America, based upon the Monroe Doctrine. In what has been called the Roosevelt Corollary to the Doctrine, he declared: "Chronic wrongdoing . . . may in America, as elsewhere, ultimately require intervention by some civilized nation, and in the Western Hemisphere the adherence of the United States to the Monroe Doctrine may force the United States, however reluctantly, in flagrant cases of such wrongdoing or impotence to the exercise of an international police power." Acting on this justification, the U.S. became involved in the affairs of the Dominican Republic, Haiti, Nicaragua, and Honduras over the next 10 years.

However, America's sometimes hesitant involvement on the international stage was soon overshadowed by the outbreak of World War I in 1914. As the war engulfed Europe and swallowed scores of thousands of its citizens, the United States under President Woodrow Wilson sought to maintain its neutrality, and the president urged Americans to be "impartial in thought as well as in action." Wilson shared the disillusionment with the Spanish-American War and the relative isolationism that followed. And yet he also had a strong liberal belief in American constitutionalism. If a war resulted in the creation of some organization that was based upon American ideals, then the war was actually a just war.

The U.S. engaged in military conflict with the Barbary pirates, with Mexico over acquiring Texas, and the Spanish-American War. Wilson also sent ships to Tampico in 1914 and won the approval of the Senate to use military force, because he believed that during the Mexican Civil War, the U.S. had been insulted when American sailors in Tampico were briefly detained.[20] He also thought that the politicians vying for power in Mexico were often immoral. Nevertheless, military involvement with or against major European powers had heretofore been successfully and purposefully avoided, other than the War of 1812.[21] Accordingly, the desire to keep out of the destructive European war was strong, and the country maintained its commerce with all parties involved in the war. Wilson won reelection in 1916, campaigning in part on his record in keeping the country out of the war. Yet, German attacks on American ships, despite repeated warnings by Wilson, combined with the Zimmerman Telegram scandal, in which Germany proposed an alliance with Mexico to attack the U.S., to draw the U.S. irrevocably into the war.

The war quickly took on a melodramatic cast, with the Germans depicted as the evil foil to the forces of good—America and its allies. Wilson established the Committee on Public Information, a propagandistic organ of the government that commissioned movies such as *The Kaiser: Beast of Berlin* and *The Claws of the Hun*. The Committee also encouraged changes in nomenclature, such as using "Liberty Sandwich" instead of hamburger and "Liberty cabbage" instead of sauerkraut. Civil liberties were also curtailed through laws such as the Espionage Act.

The war came to a close relatively shortly following American involvement in it. The U.S. entered the war in April of 1917, and the war ended in November of the following year. The most important aspect of the war for American purposes, however, is what happened after the guns quieted and the post-war settlement negotiations began. Wilson, a latter-day Calvinist who believed himself to be a member of the elect and divinely chosen to lead,[22] came to the peace conference in Paris determined to apply American ideals to international affairs and to solidify the ascendancy of America in the world, an ascendancy that had been gaining more and more speed and power as the decades passed.

It was at this juncture that Wilson and his supporters believed that America would pass from its adolescence into its adulthood as a leader of the nations. Indeed, the American army—which had jumped from a prewar size of 200,000 to a postwar force of 4,000,000—already reflected this contemplated expansion. Wilson was something of an amateur, however, when it came to international politics. He once remarked to friends in 1913 that, because of his shortcomings in this arena, "It would be an irony of fate if my administration had to deal chiefly with foreign affairs."[23] And, the United States was something of an amateur when it came to complex dealings with established global powers on the international stage.

Perhaps inevitably, it all came crashing down and Wilson's idealistic dream shattered. Wilson encapsulated his hopes in his Fourteen Points, which he presented to Congress in January 1918, and carried with him to Paris as the basis for a peace settlement. The Fourteen Points reflected an application of progressive American cultural values to international affairs, and contained among them stipulations for free trade and freedom of the seas (i.e., capitalism), decolonization, and national self-determination, and a proposal for the creation of the League of Nations, an international multilateral body charged with maintaining international peace.

The Fourteen Points were viewed with apprehension by many in America, who shrank from such deep foreign entanglements, and by many in Europe, where it was felt that Wilson's plan lacked the quality of *realpolitik* necessary to functionality and usefulness. Critics in Congress, such as Henry Cabot Lodge, echoed these concerns. Wilson, blind to these concerns and increasingly ill due to a series of strokes, refused to compromise, eschewing the realist and pragmatic—though less inspirational—approach of the Europeans and Lodge and his supporters in favor of his own unbridled, though perhaps more traditionally American, idealism. (Wilson once said, "Sometimes people call me an idealist. Well, that is the way I know I am an American.")

The Spanish-American War and World War I were the first military adventures overseas that involved other nations and alliances. But, shortly after this period of military adventurism and political idealism, the U.S. withdrew behind its own shores. During the interwar period of 1918–1941, the foreign policy of the U.S. was "fortress America": build a strong defense, pay attention to domestic concerns, but stay out of foreign military involvement.[24]

Ultimately, America did not join the League of Nations, which itself was replaced following the Second World War by the United Nations. When its somewhat youthful and characteristic idealism was spurned by the realities of international politics, the United States turned inward. Like a jilted adolescent, the U.S. again withdrew to the security of home. But the nation's youthful innocence and untested virtues of non-involvement were forever lost. The United States had bloodied its hands in an international war without sufficient idealistic or material remuneration to justify its involvement.

This isolationist approach was vindicated in the 1920 presidential election, which sent Warren Harding to the presidency by an unprecedented margin of victory. Harding had campaigned on a "return to normalcy," by leaving behind the international stage and retiring to the domestic arena. In a campaign speech in Boston, he said,

> America's present need is not heroics, but healing; not nostrums, but normalcy; not revolution, but restoration; not agitation, but adjustment; not surgery, but serenity; not the dramatic, but the dispassionate; not experiment, but equipoise; not submergence in internationality, but sustainment in triumphant nationality. . . . If we can prove a representative popular government under which a citizenship seeks what it may do for the government rather than what the government may do for individuals, we shall do more to make democracy safe for the world than all armed conflict ever recorded.

Thus, America returned to its position as the city upon a hill—exceptional, yes, but also voluntarily far removed from the rest of the world.

In the 1920s and 1930s, America reveled in its isolation. Immigration quotas were imposed, emblematic of U.S. desire to cut itself off from the rest of the world. In 1922, the U.S. set limits on the buildup of its navy. In 1929, an idealistic U.S. Congress ratified the Kellogg-Briand Pact, which effectively rendered warfare illegal. A near war with Mexico in the mid-1920s over commercial interests was averted when the pacifistic and isolationist U.S. public put such pressure on the government that it resolved to settle the dispute via diplomacy rather than arms. In 1930, Secretary of State Henry Stimson went so far as to repudiate the Roosevelt Corollary. In 1934, despite shouldering the territory with difficult economic conditions, the U.S. passed an act promising the Philippines independence in 12 years. In general, a sense of developing a "Fortress America" pervaded—a fortress constructed on paper, via international agreements and diplomacy, and bolstered both by America's geographic isolation and public sentiment, which would forestall any bloody, disappointing involvements with the world.

The stock market crash and subsequent onset of the Great Depression rocked America to its core and jolted it from its complacency. While the domestic result of this shock was the New Deal, the international manifestation of this ultimately was American involvement in another world war.

Young Adulthood: World War II and the Cold War

As the drums of war began to sound in the mid-1930s, America clung to its neutrality. Military confrontations between China and Japan escalated in July 1937, American civilians were killed, and a U.S. patrol ship was sunk, purportedly accidentally, by Japan in December. Nevertheless, 70 percent of Americans preferred removing the country's official and unofficial presence from China rather than escalating the situation.[25] This was a marked contrast, one would say, from the 1964 Tonkin Gulf incident and the road to war in Vietnam, or the sinking of the *Maine* preceding the Spanish-American War.

Between 1935 and 1939, the U.S. Congress passed a series of Neutrality Acts designed to prevent America from becoming involved in a broader war through the back door of commercial interests (as it appeared to many had happened in World War I) by restricting war-related types of commerce with belligerent nations. Further reflecting the zealous isolationist spirit of the time, the Act of 1937 somewhat nonsensically prohibited U.S. citizens from even traveling on the ships of belligerents.

As the German war machine steamrolled through Europe, sweeping through declaredly neutral nations, the U.S. began to edge toward the same initial posture as it adopted during the First World War: attempting to wield economic weapons rather than guns and bombs. A series of laws were passed in the late 1930s and early 1940s that were particularly favorable to the Western democracies such as England and France. These allowed the U.S. to supply belligerents with arms. In an effort to forestall Japanese belligerency in the Far East, the U.S. did not embrace military confrontation, but rather imposed embargoes on materials essential to the Japanese war effort and encouraged America's allies to do the same, presenting a deep challenge to the industrial foundations of Japanese expansionism. These embargoes were met with a 96 percent approval among the American public.[26] Although America was increasingly transparent in its aid for the Allied powers, roughly 80 percent of Americans still desired neutrality.[27] Finally, on a calm morning in Hawaii, America's desire for military neutrality was shattered, and its long-postponed adulthood finally began.

When 2,400 Americans died during the Japanese attack on Pearl Harbor on December 7, 1941, there was no way the United States could remain neutral. The American people expected their leader to be a man of action and to respond with immediate and overwhelming force. Roosevelt obliged this sentiment, and war was declared by Congress the next day.

This war was a matter of protecting the United States and defeating other nations that had attacked Americans on their own soil. The attack on Pearl Harbor was a clear act of military aggression. Franklin Roosevelt did not tell the American people that this war was fought to extend American values or ideals. It was not a war to free colonies or to make the world safe for democracy. It was not sold to the American people with great utopian ideals and illusions. In turn, Americans were not disillusioned at the end of the war as they had been after the Spanish-American War and World War I.

The United States was defending itself not only against Japan, but also against Hitler's Nazis and Mussolini's Black Shirts. There were realistic, pragmatic reasons to fight this war. The intentions of the adversaries were very clear from the American perspective. Japan had attacked without warning. Hitler really was an evil, anti-Semitic, genocidal maniac who was intent upon world domination. And Mussolini was supporting Hitler with his own brand of fascism.

World War I was perhaps an accident that occurred at a time when European world powers were particularly paranoid, and they attacked each other in preemptive strikes. Miscommunication caused an incident (the assassination of Archduke Ferdinand) to spiral into a world war. The motive for aggression was fear. Idealists would say that had they communicated better, perhaps through some sort of world forum, World War I might have been prevented. This was the primary rationale that Wilson gave for the creation of the League of Nations. World War II was very different because only force could have stopped Hitler.

For those who came of age during the World War II era, this war is often described as the "Great War" and Tom Brokaw even wrote a book in 2000 describing Americans of this era as *The Greatest Generation*. Unfortunately, members of this "greatest generation" who later became leaders, such as Ronald Reagan, have seen nearly every international conflict after World War II as some kind of repeat of the Great War. The lesson they learned was to have a strong military with a willingness to use it, and to view international negotiation and diplomacy as somehow comparable to British Prime Minister Neville Chamberlain's 1938 meeting with Hitler in Munich.

The motive for aggression by Hitler in World War II was raw hegemonic drive. In fact, communication between Chamberlain and Hitler actually encouraged Hitler and made the situation worse. This is the primary reason that the United Nations has a Security Council of major powers who can come together to sanction the use of force when it is necessary to insure the collective security of all nations. There was no such body in the League of Nations.

Even before World War II ended, it was clear that the United States could never withdraw militarily from the world again. While many Americans did not want to join the UN and some nostalgically longed to regress to the innocence of isolationism of the childhood era, there could be no adolescent withdrawal behind the shores of a secure homeland. Even before American atomic bombs were dropped on Nagasaki and Hiroshima, the Soviet Union was expanding across the borders of nations that were devastated by World War II. The Cold War began well before Japan, Germany, and Italy surrendered, and within a few years the United States was involved in a war in Korea, followed by another war in Vietnam.

American adolescence was filled with growing pains, ambivalence, and periods of arrogant overconfidence followed by great insecurity, disillusionment and fear. However, a new national identity was developing that retained many of the ideals and values of the past tempered by the reality that the United States could not withdraw from the world. The question was no longer "Should the country withdraw from the world" but rather "When and how should it be involved?"

At the end of World War II, the U.S. realized that it was the only country that could counterbalance the weight of the Soviet Union. If America remained isolationist in the face of this expansionist global power, it not only risked becoming isolated in a sea of communist countries, it also risked forfeiting its global economic and political heft. Therefore, the country had to shoulder the responsibilities of a mature adulthood and abandon its youthful isolationist tendencies and mercurial involvement in world affairs. Not only was the U.S. fully involved in forming the United Nations and participating in all of its endeavors to maintain peace and promote the common welfare of all nations, it also joined military alliances such as NATO to protect member states from armed aggression. It seemed that isolationism and unilateralism had come to an end and the U.S. was willing to participate as an adult in the international system.

The early adulthood of the U.S. ran until the fall of the USSR in 1991. Thereafter, the U.S. had a sort of midlife crisis: Should it return to the idealistic isolationism of past periods, or should it increase its involvement in world affairs? What were its global interests and how should they be pursued? We will explore these questions at length in the final chapter of this book.

CHAPTER 8

What Holds America Together Also Tears It Apart

If we cannot now end our differences, at least we can make the world safe for diversity.

—JOHN F. KENNEDY[1]

*I*N SUCH A DIVERSE SOCIETY, in which extreme individualism is a primary cultural value, what holds the United States together? How can Americans maintain a harmonious and cohesive society if each person is only trying to maximize his or her own personal gain in competition with everyone else? Given the enormous diversity, why doesn't the country just break into distinct and conflicting ethnic, religious, social or economic groups? This is the dire warning of nativists such as Patrick Buchanan and Samuel Huntington. They define "multiculturalism" as separatism in which each group will create its own way of life that is not only a contrast to the dominant culture, but even worse, in conflict with mainstream America.

Immigrants left their loved ones and risked their lives to come to the New World because they valued the opportunity and freedom they had to excel as individuals. There was little chance that they could advance economically in their homelands and create a better way of life for their children. In America they could begin life anew if they gave up their past—sometimes including their family and the heritage home country—and ventured into the uncertain future. It really was a death/rebirth cycle of sorts. *Individual freedom* was the common value that pulled these immigrants to America and is shared by almost everyone regardless of the region in which they live or their ethnic and racial background. It ties the country together. However, if this value is carried to its extreme, it can also lead to extreme individual competition and alienation that could possibly tear the country apart.

Why haven't we become a nation of individualists where the family unit and the civic culture become nonexistent—a fear that Francis Fukuyama expressed when he wrote *The End of History*? In fact, Fukuyama was so concerned about extreme individualism and the disintegration of the family and community that he wrote *The Great Disruption*,[2] warning Americans and Northern Europeans that when we carry our liberal capitalist ideas too far, they become self-destructive.[3]

Another author who has expressed concern about the impact of excessive individualism on a democratic society is Robert D. Putnam, who wrote the book *Bowling Alone: America's Declining Social Capital*.[4] He found that over the past 20 years Americans have ceased joining social organizations in the large numbers they once did, and that many have become very skeptical and cynical about their government. He notes lower voter turnout, decreased attendance at public meetings, and less involvement in political parties. He uses bowling as a metaphor for this pattern. While the number of people who bowl has increased in the last 20 years, the number of people who bowl in leagues has decreased. Because they bowl alone, these Americans do not participate in social interaction and civic discussions that might once have occurred in a league environment. Putnam attributes this to the impact of individualistic modern communications and entertainment technology such as television and the Internet, which take the place of face-to-face human interaction.

Values that we share as Americans and that are inherent to the American character also can produce very strong and emotional conflicts. While most Americans value individualism, they also believe that it is necessary to participate in the civic culture and help others in our community. While we love individual freedom, we accept that we must sacrifice some freedoms to provide for the common order and protect the freedom of others. Smokers cannot smoke wherever they want if their smoke interferes with the freedom of nonsmokers to breathe fresh air. International visitors are often amazed by the many street signs telling Americans when and where they may park, how far they can park from an intersection or fire hydrant, and where pedestrians may cross the street. These overt rules and restrictions are the only way to guarantee some predictability of behavior in a society of such diversity.

Over the years, Americans have somehow balanced individualism and individual freedom with the respect for differences, cooperation with others, and a civic order that has grown out of political and legal change. The tension between these apparently opposing values has at times led to conflict, but it also has led to very creative ways of resolving these contradictions. When the country moves to an extreme version of one of these basic values, it seems to develop a counterbalancing value or force that somehow integrates and reconciles the differences. This, in turn, has created an even stronger sense of national unity.

For Americans, multiculturalism and diversity are not the same as separatism or assimilation; rather they are a unique form of national cultural synergy in which the whole is greater than the sum of the parts. The richness and beauty of the American mosaic or tapestry is based upon the contrasting colors and textures. If you remove one piece from the mosaic or one thread from the tapestry, you diminish it. In other parts of the world, immigrant citizens often must give up their individual and cultural differences to assimilate to the dominant culture. This was true of the United States until the mid-1960s. Today, it is not an either-or question. One can keep these differences and still be a true American.

The diversity of national, ethnic, and racial identities leads to great productivity and creativity in our multicultural society. An American can hold various identities at the same time and need not choose only one. We can be hyphenated Americans: Irish-Americans, Catholic-Americans, or gay-Americans, or any combination such as a gay, Irish-Catholic American. But these differences also create enormous tensions within the heterogeneous society and have in the past erupted into violence between groups.

The issue in the United States is not that differences are obstacles to overcome, but rather how the individual and the society use these differences to enhance productivity and creativity. Research has shown that the more diverse a group is, the better their collective productivity, efficiency, and decision-making often is.[5] Therefore, diversity is a strength, not a weakness, and it actually holds us together. This was true of the initial Dutch colony in Harlem, which was incredibly diverse in terms of religions and nationalities. This colony initially struggled to create an environment in which these differences could flourish. But, once this delicate balance was found, the little colony grew into arguably the world's most creative and productive city: New York City.

From the very beginning of the nation, there has been continual movement between values that unite and divide. This has led to creative tension and oftentimes a creative balance. The United States moved from diversion (individualism, diverse religions and races, even the confederation of states) to conversion (one nation with shared values, experiences, language, etc—and a federation with a constitution). But, in a somewhat dialectical pattern, the continual tension between the extremes of diversion and conversion, individualism and collectivism, led to some sort of synthesis or cultural synergy. It seems contradictory, but there really is some sort of union of opposites: not an either/ or but rather *both*. The hyphenated American—Italian-American, African-American, Jewish-American, Muslim-American—illustrates this. This is truly unique and distinguishes the U.S. from almost all other nations. In the creation and success of its tapestry, America really *is* a very exceptional nation.

Numerous things unite and divide Americans. However, freedom, equality, and the recognition of each other's diversity are crucial values to ensuring that our divisions do not run too deep. Yet throughout our history, Americans have oscillated in how well we practice these values. In this chapter, we will examine these values and their implications for the national character of the U.S., particularly after 9/11.

Individual Rights: Guns, Abortion, the Death Penalty, and Euthanasia

One day in 1788, while serving as ambassador to France, Thomas Jefferson opened a letter from James Madison, then a member of the

Continental Congress. "Wherever the real power in Government lies," Madison wrote, "there is the danger of oppression. In our Government, the real power lies in the majority of the Community, and the invasion of private rights is chiefly to be apprehended, not from acts of government contrary to the sense of its constituents, but from acts in which the Government is the mere instrument of the major number of Constituents." Madison knew that Jefferson was a receptive audience for such words. "A bill of rights," Jefferson had written to Madison the year before, "is what the people are entitled to against every government on earth, general or particular, and what no just government should refuse, or rest on inference." These two founding fathers of the country helped secure the addition of the Bill of Rights to the Constitution, a victory for the many Americans who yearned for their rights to be enumerated and protected, rather than ignored or trampled upon, as they had felt them to be under the British or in their native countries.

These rights were not enumerated in the Articles of Confederation, the young country's guiding document until the passage of the Constitution. The Articles were a treaty between individual and separate states, somewhat similar to the current situation with the EU Only after the Articles of Confederation were signed did the various states realize that they needed a central authority to provide for a common currency and trade, to conduct foreign affairs (something the EU does not have) and to protect citizens from external threats. But, the powers of the central authority created by the new Constitution were in conflict with—or at least could be interpreted to conflict with—basic individual rights. The Constitution defined the areas in which the central government had authority. It failed to directly delineate areas in which it did not have authority. Many feared that what remained unstated also could be interpreted as powers belonging to the central government.

The founding fathers felt it was incumbent upon them to immediately add amendments to the Constitution that spelled out the rights that every citizen retains. The first 10 amendments to the Constitution—now known as the Bill of Rights—clearly enumerated and protected Americans' individual rights. Furthermore, the Bill of Rights also said explicitly that anything *not* specifically mentioned in the document as being a right or duty of the federal government was to be regarded as a right or duty retained by the separate states and individuals.

The creation of a constrained federal authority was intended to guarantee the protection of individual rights. The early settlers did not want kings, queens, or popes who could define the laws and liberties of the people according to their whims, as had happened in the Old World. The founders of the country had a healthy distrust of an overly powerful central authority and they purposefully invested the states and local governments with a significant amount of jurisdiction. The majority of the founders believed that the local community, rather than the federal government, should deal with common interests that impacted the everyday life of the citizen, a belief, when enshrined into law, that distinguished the United States from many other countries, and harkens all the way back to the town hall and church meetings of the early settlements.

Yet once these rights were clearly established in the law (and indeed before they were established), they were debated hotly. And they continue to be reinterpreted and argued over to this day. Americans' strong sense of individualism shudders at any attempt whatsoever to put limitations on what many view as their sanctified, God-given, individual rights, whether that is the right to own a gun (Second Amendment), the right to say whatever comes to their mind (First Amendment), or their right to a fair trial (Seventh Amendment).

During times when security or safety has been a paramount concern for Americans, such as during times of war, individual liberties have been sacrificed or put aside to strengthen the power of the government to provide protection and order. However, competing with this value most frequently is the moralistic Puritanical echo in American culture that seeks to define what is good along the lines of what is the best moral choice. The only thing that may trump, or challenge, individual rights, is a moral imperative to do otherwise, often believed to be from a higher source. We have seen this since the colonial era Salem Witch Trials—when individuals' rights to privacy and freedom were trampled in the cascading, irrational, moral crusade against witchcraft. And we have seen this quite recently, with the acrimonious debate over gay marriage, as the individual's right to marry whomever he or she wishes is confronted with a moralizing, Puritanical drive for the government to define the moral character and form of marriage. Americans are united in their desire to protect their individual rights, yet divided in their enthusiasm for the consequences of certain rights that they enjoy.

What are some examples of how the American emphasis on individual rights both unites and divides the country? One such issue, gun control, is a very volatile political issue. The framers of the Constitution, it is argued, were afraid of an overly invasive government that would take away the individual citizen's right to bear arms. While some argue that every American has an individual right to carry a gun, others want to control that right with restrictions on the purchase of guns and regulations on their use. Opponents of gun control recall heroic images of early American citizen-soldiers banding together to oust their British masters and of contemporary citizens defending themselves from criminals with their own guns. It also calls to mind romantic images of Americans pushing West with gun in hand to defend their homestead and kill their dinner.[6] They also feel that the Constitution guarantees citizens the right to bear arms, and that gun control laws impinge upon this freedom.

These sentiments were epitomized perfectly when the well-known actor Charlton Heston, then-chairman of the National Rifle Association (NRA), addressed an NRA convention in 2001. Heston declared to his audience, "You are of the same lineage as the farmers who stood at Concord Bridge," an early Revolutionary War battle. He then grasped a rifle used in that war and raised it over his head, proclaiming, "I have only five words for you: from my cold, dead hands."

On the other side of the debate, supporters of gun control also mold their position in a characteristically American way. Echoing traditionally powerful moral arguments, many feel that it is the community's duty to protect public safety by regulating the behavior of those who abuse guns. While few advocates of gun control support banning the ownership of all guns by all people, many believe that taking the most dangerous guns—those that have little practical use for hunting or defensive purposes—off of the streets will enhance the country's ability to uphold the pledge of protecting the life, liberty, and property of its citizens as enumerated in the Fifth Amendment.

In most of Europe, there are strong gun control laws because there is a belief that the government should control firearms, except for those that are legally licensed and allowed for hunting or sportsmanship. In most major cities of the United States, the majority also believe that there ought to be restrictions on guns because hunting is probably not as popular as in rural areas, and with a high concentration of people, the incidence of gun violence appears to be more common. There is also greater fear of youth gang activity and gun violence harming innocent bystanders.[7] Although many cities and states have these laws, one can almost always easily travel to another city or state where the laws are very lax. Most gun control advocates simply want some restrictions on who may buy a gun, based upon age, criminal record, and mental well-being. They also think that the only guns that should be available for purchase are those that can be used for hunting or individual self-defense.

Those who oppose gun control often exaggerate the impact of any restrictions, and they use fear of the government to bolster their position. Hunters and sportsmen are told that "They'll break down doors and confiscate all the guns" if restrictions are legislated into law. Who are "they"? The federal government. Again, we see the conflict between individual or states' rights and the need for public safety with an overlay of fear of an overly powerful central authority.

The tension between these two positions, and the hysterics that they are capable of, was aptly summed up by Bill Clinton during the signing ceremony for the 1993 Brady Bill, a gun control law. Clinton remarked, "I come from a state where half the folks have hunting and fishing licenses. I can still remember the first day when I was a little boy out in the country putting a can on top of a fencepost and shooting a .22 at it. . . . This is part of the culture of a big part of America. . . . We have taken this important part of the life of millions of Americans and turned it into an instrument of maintaining madness. It is crazy."[8]

The friction between inherent American cultural values is also quite striking in perhaps the other most controversial individual rights issue in America, abortion. We can see these basic cultural values embedded in the slogans of the pro- and anti-abortion camps. While those supporting abortion proclaim that they are "Pro-Choice," referencing notions of egalitarian democracy and the idea that all citizens have a right to decide what is best for themselves (emphasizing their individualism), opponents of abortion trumpet their own slogan, "Pro-Life." We can actually find the cultural antecedent for this slogan in the

Declaration of Independence, when all are given the "unalienable rights" of life, liberty, and the pursuit of happiness. This argument was used during the *Roe v. Wade* case, when the attorney for Wade argued that the Fifth Amendment in the Bill of Rights—"No person shall be deprived of life, liberty, or property, without due process of law"—precluded legalizing abortion.

This is much more complicated than simply protecting a "person's" life. For example, what is a "person"? Some pro-life advocates would argue that the moment an egg and sperm unite, a human life (a person) exists, while pro-choice advocates might take the position that only when the fetus can survive outside the womb does a real human being exist. In the third trimester of pregnancy, many pro-choice supporters oppose abortion. In cases of rape, incest, or to save a mother's life, both pro-life and pro-abortion proponents could agree that abortion is acceptable. Most Americans probably fall somewhere between the extreme positions of pro-life and pro-choice advocates. The debate also boils down to how far the right of privacy extends, as each camp argues whether abortion is a private matter for a woman or a matter of public policy and law.

Religious sentiments weigh heavily upon the abortion debate. Religious Americans are much more likely to be pro-life than the more secular, and some religious groups—such as Catholics and Mormons—are on record as being strongly against abortion. These same religious groups also play an important part in the debate over stem cell research, where the religious question of when life begins comes into conflict with the ethical complications of making illegal a potential avenue of research that could lead to cures of several diseases.

Religion—and individual rights—also play a role in the debate over capital punishment in America. About two-thirds of Americans have supported the death penalty over the last 30 years.[9] Most advocates of the penalty support it because they believe that it acts as a deterrent for criminals, saves the state the costs of imprisoning them for life, and, chiefly, because it is appropriate to the crime—an eye for an eye.[10] Yet despite this, 12 states do not have a death penalty, and debate against it can be strong.

Opponents of the death penalty argue that it is a form of "cruel and unusual punishment," from which individuals are protected by the Bill of Rights. Moreover, the state should not be allowed to take someone's life—to engage in some form of legalized killing. With the modern use of DNA evidence, dozens and perhaps hundreds of convicted criminals have been found innocent and released from prison. How many innocent people may have been executed by the state?

How do religious voters come down on the issue? As in the case of abortion, some are impelled by religion to come down on the side of pro-life. An American who attends church weekly or nearly every week is more likely to be against the death penalty than one who never attends church, and practicing Protestants and Catholics are more likely to oppose the death penalty than non-practicing.[11] Conversely, some churches in America, such as the Southern Baptists, support the death penalty. Mormons hold a neutral position on it. And assuredly, many religious Americans support the death penalty because it follows the Biblical injunction of an eye for an eye.

Euthanasia—the right to terminate one's own life when faced with a terminal and debilitating illness or to get assistance from a doctor in doing so—is another contentious debate in America that pits morality, religion, and individual rights against one another. While General Social Surveys show that about two-thirds of Americans believe in the right to end one's life because of an incurable disease,[12] it is legal in only one state, Oregon. Interestingly, while most respondents felt that having an incurable disease was reason enough to end one's life, virtually no Americans—less than 10 percent—felt that bankruptcy or dishonoring one's family were sufficient cause to end one's life. While proponents of the right to terminate one's life point to individual rights in support of their argument, opponents frequently counter with religious arguments (suicide is immoral, etc.). Indeed, studies have shown that Americans who consider themselves more religious are more likely to oppose one's right to end his or her own life than those who consider themselves less religious.[13]

This debate played out dramatically on American TV screens in early 2005, when the Terri Schiavo case dominated the news. Schiavo, a woman who had suffered brain damage and was deemed to have been in a persistent vegetative state since 2000, became the symbol of the difficulties and emotionalism tied to this larger debate. When Schiavo's husband sought to remove her feeding tube and thus let her die, her parents made every effort to keep her alive. Her parents and husband fought through the legal system over who—if anyone—had the right to definitively take her off, or leave her on, life support. When her husband received a court order allowing him to remove the feeding tube, the Florida state legislature went into an emergency session and passed "Terri's Law," which gave Governor Jeb Bush the authority to order that she be kept on life support. The State Supreme Court then struck down the hastily passed law as unconstitutional.

Quickly the U.S. Congress intervened, going to extraordinary measures to keep Schiavo alive, including issuing a subpoena for Schiavo to testify before Congress. While she clearly was not in a capacity to do so, being under subpoena gave her federal protection, which made it a federal crime to prevent her from giving her testimony—necessitating her return to life support. President Bush flew back to Washington from his vacation in Texas to sign new measures into effect in the middle of the night, which transferred the case to the federal courts. However, these measures were to no avail, as federal courts denied appeals to keep her on life support, and Schiavo was allowed to die soon after. Although a majority of Americans believed that Schiavo had a right to die, many religious Americans of all political stripes, from Jesse Jackson to the Christian right, believed that Schiavo should be kept alive, illustrating both the acrimonious nature of the debate and how the issue united groups that were otherwise at opposite extremes in their views.

Separation of Church and State

Issues such as abortion, the death penalty, and euthanasia have divided Americans because for many, they are religious issues. There are many ways in which religion—which has divided Americans immeasurably throughout the country's history—also unites them. During a crisis such as the Civil War, religion brought the country together. Martin Luther King and other religious leaders brought the country together when it was trying to overcome centuries of racial discrimination.

Immigrants have brought countless different religions to the shores of America—and others have been created here—and religious diversity is still very extensive. A common belief in the existence of God, coupled with a belief that religion is important in our lives, brings us together, and these two beliefs have brought Americans together since the inception of the country. Alexis de Tocqueville made note of this during his travels in the young country, writing that:

> Upon my arrival in the United States, the religious aspect of the country was the first thing that struck my attention; and the longer I stayed there the more did I perceive the great political consequences resulting from this state of things, to which I was unaccustomed. In France I had almost always seen the spirit of religion and the spirit of freedom pursuing courses diametrically opposed to each other; but in America I found that they were intimately united, and that they reigned in common over the same country.[14]

De Tocqueville made this observation in the 1830s, yet a foreign visitor to the U.S. today might say much the same thing. Americans are certainly among the most religious people in the industrialized world. Nearly 60 percent of Americans claim that religion plays a very important role in their lives; this is roughly double the percentage of people in Canada, the U.K., Italy, and Korea who feel this way, and about triple the percentage of Germans. In Russia, France, the Czech Republic, and Japan, the percentages are in the teens.[15] At least 90 percent of all Americans claim they believe in God while only 1 percent would describe themselves as atheists.[16] Furthermore, a greater percentage of American Christians attend church services every Sunday than in any other country in the world. More than half of American Christians attend Sunday services nearly every week, if not every week.[17] Roughly 80 percent of Americans call prayer an important part of their daily lives *and* state that they never doubt the existence of God.[18] Many are religious literalists as well—more Americans believe in creationism than citizens in any country in Europe.[19]

At least 75 percent of all Americans call themselves Christian. About half categorize themselves as Protestants and about 25 percent are Roman Catholics. Less than 2 percent are Jews and about 1 percent are Muslim.[20] Even those who do not identity themselves as Protestants more often than not act like Protestants and share such traditional Calvinist values as individualism and a healthy dislike for overly centralized authority. Although Calvinists (strictly speaking Presbyterians in the United States) are less than 5 percent of the population, most Americans act like Calvinists and Calvinism has influenced all religions in America. Evangelical, or born-again, Christians represent a large proportion of the population, and their emphasis on personal experiences of salvation also recalls Calvinism. The percentage of American Catholics who practice birth control is roughly the same as Protestants. Many American Catholics believe that priests ought to be able to marry and nuns should be able to perform the same religious ceremonies as priests. Finally, they contribute much less money to the Vatican than European Catholics.

The founding fathers acknowledged the importance of religion in America but they did not want to establish a national religion. They understood how kings had used religion to oppress people and therefore they wanted a secular state. Furthermore, they knew how religious conflicts had divided Europe and led to wars lasting hundreds of years. They believed that a national church would divide Americans rather than unite them. Many supported the view of Roger Williams, the religious dissident who founded the state of Rhode Island. Williams wrote that there needed to be a *"wall of separation* between the garden of the church and the wilderness of the world."

This was congruent with the Calvinist tradition that emphasized an individual's direct relationship with God without any interference by other people or any institution. Individuals, rather than the state, mandated the nature of their relationship with God. In an 1808 letter, Thomas Jefferson reflected on how a secular nation conformed with American traditions of individualism and had helped the country avoid any divisions along religious lines. He wrote, "We have experienced the quiet as well as the comfort which results from leaving every one to profess freely and openly those principles of religion which are the inductions of his own reason and the serious convictions of his own inquiries." Government should not interfere in religious practices or become an intermediary between the individual and his or her deity. In the words of Jefferson, "Religion is a subject on which I have ever been most scrupulously reserved, I have considered it as a matter between every man and his Maker, in which no other, and far less the public, had a right to intermeddle."

Many Americans would also claim that it is more than a "separation of church and state" or government, but that there also should be a separation of politics and religion. Nevertheless, religion and politics have always been mixed together, and among our most contentious political issues are those that are, in fact, religious in nature—abortion, stem cell research, and the rights of homosexuals to marry. In the 1990s and 2000s, these wedge issues were often among the most important issues for fundamentalist Christians. These religious and political issues created great emotional division among Americans. But, religion and politics also brought the country together to heal the wounds of the Civil War in the 1860s and, a century later, to overcome racism during the Civil Rights Movement.

Indeed, the country has always struggled with determining the desirable amount of cross-pollination between the spheres of religion and politics, and this balance has continued to evolve over time. For example, while many associate Thanksgiving with football games and eating as much turkey, cranberry sauce and pumpkin pie as humanly possible, the holiday in fact had deep religious undertones in its inception and early practice. Many also apply another layer of mythology to the Thanksgiving story, recalling it as a moment of cooperation and camaraderie between whites and Native Americans, marking one of the short blips in the American national consciousness in which Native Americans make an appearance, and a positive one at that.

For the Pilgrims, who are popularly credited with the inception of the holiday, the day was a religious celebration—a giving of thanks to God for looking favorably upon their enterprise. In this spirit, George Washington began a presidential tradition of issuing Thanksgiving proclamations in 1789, with an address that would have sent the American Civil Liberties Union into a frenzy: "Whereas it is the duty of all Nations to acknowledge the providence of almighty God, to obey his will, to be grateful for his benefits, and humbly to implore his protection and favor. . . . I do recommend and assign Thursday the 26th day of November next to be devoted by the People of these States to the service of that great and glorious Being, who is the beneficent Author of all the good that was, that is, or that will be—That we may then all unite in rendering unto him our sincere and humble thanks." Thomas Jefferson, mortified by such a union of religion and government, refused to make Thanksgiving proclamations during his presidency, and from 1816–1861 no proclamations were made.

Thanksgiving has become secularized over the years; for example, in contrast to President Washington, in his 2006 Thanksgiving proclamation, George W. Bush—widely viewed as one of America's most ostensibly religious recent presidents—only mentioned God twice, both times in passing. Yet, the holiday's religious origins provide a window onto the sometimes hazy line between religion and politics.

We can identify several other intersections between religion and politics in the U.S. One such instance is the Great Seal of the United States, used to authenticate government documents and ubiquitous via its position on the dollar bill. The reverse of the Seal features the Eye of Providence—an eye, symbolizing God, encased by a triangle (recalling the Trinity)—hovering atop a pyramid with 13 layers (one for each original state), topped by the Latin phrase *Annuit Coeptis*, meaning "He [God] favors our undertakings." The phrase *Deo Favente* (by the grace of God) was originally included in the seal. *Annuit Coeptis* took its place because the phrase was 13 letters long, recalling the number of original states. Below the pyramid sits the phrase *Novus Ordo Seclorum*, meaning "New Order of the Ages," a nod to American exceptionalism and the city upon a hill motif. The origin of both phrases can be found in Virgil, the Roman poet who wrote the *Aeneid*, the founding myth of the Romans—a myth and an exceptional people that many Americans have identified with from the founding of the nation to the present.

Benjamin Franklin, John Adams, and Thomas Jefferson had designed another (ultimately rejected) version of the Great Seal that was even more religious in its imagery, depicting Americans as the new Chosen People and inheritors of the mantle of the ancient Israelites. Circumscribed by the motto "Rebellion to Tyrants Is Obedience to God," the reverse side of the seal depicted Moses and the Israelites on the shores of the Red Sea, as the sea closes in on Pharaoh and his soldiers. (It is also interesting to note that the Seal of the short-lived Confederate States of America also contained a divinely inspired motto: *Deo Vindice*, "Under God, Our Vindicator.")

Of course, the national motto, "In God We Trust," is another case in point. A final example of the frequently blurred line between religion and politics is the tradition of Red Mass, during which the justices of the Supreme Court, Congresspeople, and high government officials (often including the president) attend a mass together to pray for guidance prior to the convening of the Court in October.

Yet, despite these blurrings of the line between church and state, the founders' fear of nationalized religion—and the discord and strife that they feared were concomitant—have not materialized. While

Americans often argue over the place and influence of religion in the public and political spheres—from debates about school prayer and the teaching of evolution and creationism in schools to quarrels over whether the Ten Commandments can be placed in courthouses—de Tocqueville's perception of America as a land where the "spirit of religion" and the "spirit of freedom" co-reigned has proven accurate.

While Americans can become divided over issues concerning the role of religion in the country, religion has been an important unifying factor as well. In the country's earliest history, it gave its settlers and its citizens unity of purpose—to create a city upon a hill and a pluralistic moral utopia. Throughout the country's history, churches, synagogues and mosques have played important roles in bringing together community members for social, cultural, political, and other purposes. Today, religion remains the country's most prevalent associational membership.[21] And, religion has helped to inculcate and nurture the sense of "chosenness" that, as we have seen, is crucial to American culture.

Egalitarianism

Just as each American ought to have individual religious, economic, or political freedom, the early Protestants would also claim that all are "equal in the eyes of God." This value placed on *equality or egalitarianism* was embedded in the economic, legal, and political belief system where everyone is supposed to have "an equal opportunity" to move up the class ladder, each person should be treated the same in the "eyes of the law" and every citizen's vote should count, regardless of race, class, or gender. In practice, it took hundreds of years before all Americans were treated as equal and guaranteed this freedom, but, as Americans often say, "this is a work in progress" and we have come a long way towards implementing this value.

The reluctance of Americans to use titles is a result of the value placed upon equality. European immigrants left their ancestry overseas and began in the New World without titles. In fact, during the colonial period, people often addressed each other as "Citizen"— Citizen Thomas Jefferson, Citizen Benjamin Franklin, or Citizen George Washington. In many countries some kind of title or respect is often used in everyday conversation, especially with older people. Although they may have just met for the first time, within a few minutes it is common today for Americans to simply use first names when talking with each other—Manolo, Jim, Alia, or Mary—regardless of age, gender, rank, or position.

The President of the United States is referred to as "Mister (or Madame) President," just as a typical American is usually called Mister Jones or Mister Lopez. Very often the president is addressed by only his first and last name without any title of respect: Jimmy Carter or Ronald Reagan. American ambassadors cannot be called "Your Excellency." The proper address for an American Ambassador is simply "Mister Ambassador" or "Madame Ambassador." In the nineteenth century, the Department of State forbade American ambassadors from wearing the ribbons and feathers that other ambassadors wore at formal events. The regulation stipulated that they had to wear a "simple black suit, like any ordinary American."[22] Of course, an American ambassador is *not* like any ordinary American. An ambassador represents the president overseas and has very special privileges and responsibilities.

Egalitarianism simply means that each individual ought to be treated equally in the society. No one should have an unfair advantage because of their family background, education, income, race, gender, or religion. "Equality" doesn't mean "the same as." This was often the unspoken position of so-called white "liberals" in the 1960s: "there are no differences between white and black people; given an equal opportunity, they would be just like us." Of course, black Americans wanted an equal opportunity to be well-educated, find good jobs, or win elections to public office. But they were also very proud of their differences. A slogan for the black identity movement was "Black Is Beautiful."

There are genuine biological differences between men and women, cultural differences between Mexican-Americans and Euro-Americans, and religious differences between Muslims and Buddhists. It is almost cruel to take the position that even those born in poverty, in crime-ridden neighborhoods and broken families, have as equal an opportunity to achieve as someone born into a wealthy family who attends one of the best private schools. There are great differences in opportunity and circumstance and some people have more privilege, power, and authority than others. Why don't Americans recognize these differences?

This confusion between egalitarianism and sameness often leads to frustration for people from other cultures where differences are acknowledged and even valued. International students are often perplexed when they hear an undergraduate or graduate student address a professor by his or her first name. This is often perceived as an indication of bad manners and disrespect, but even worse, it may create a suspicion that the student and professor may have some sort of intimate relationship. This seems the only logical explanation for the professor allowing the student to be so informal. Some international students (and even some Americans from the rural South) find it almost impossible to avoid using the title Doctor or Professor. They may use the first name instead of the surname to communicate friendship. Just as some people will refer to their priest as Father Don or Father Bill, there are international students who will only be casual enough to address a favorite professor as Doctor Gary or Professor Jim. The host of a very popular television show—who is also a psychologist— is warmly referred to as Dr. Phil.

American business cards are often without a clear indication of position or rank. Complicated or verbose academic titles are seldom if ever used on business cards. In comparison, until recently most Japanese business cards showed the person's position within the organization, rank, and even academic title.[23] This informality is also found in the workplace where an American subordinate might use the first name of a superior. In some companies, everyone is addressed by the first name—Sue, Mike, Fred. In most of Latin American, this would be seen as rude and too familiar, and it would imply a lack of hierarchy and respect for authority.[24] Latin American workers do not want to call their boss Manolo, as if the supervisor is a close friend and of equal rank. The employee knows that Manolo can fire him.

Members of both major American political parties often label their opponents as elitists and then paint a picture of themselves and their followers as so-called "average Joes."[25] Elitism is the polar opposite of egalitarianism. Although Republicans controlled both houses of Congress and the White House in 2000, and many members of the Supreme Court shared most legal positions held by Republicans, the party still portrayed itself as a small group of average Americans fighting against a large, very powerful left-wing Democratic Party populated by sophisticated, rich, liberal, cosmopolitan elitists.[26] In the 2004 presidential election, much was made of Senator John Kerry's supposed elitism and President George W. Bush's average Joe quality.

Kerry actually grew up in a fairly average middle-class family and was a Vietnam War hero. However, he spoke French and his wife could speak at least five or six languages, and he was photographed windsurfing—a sport that was portrayed as an "upper-class" activity. Bush came from one of the elite families of America (the bluest of the "blue bloods"), went to the most exclusive preparatory schools, and although he was a member of the National Guard, he never served in Vietnam. His image was one of a cowboy driving himself in a pick-up truck on his small "ranch" in Texas. He often joked that he had trouble speaking English and his Spanish was fairly rudimentary.

Polls were commissioned to explore this dichotomous image of Kerry and Bush, with Bush coming out on top in response to the question of who respondents would rather have a beer with. He also won a poll that asked which candidate came off as more of a "real person."[27] The point, however, is not that Bush won, but that the egalitarianism/elitism discrepancy is so important in America that such polls were even commissioned.

Equality has been a shared value that holds America together. The class differences of Europe have never been part of the American tradition where being a "classless" society is viewed as a virtue. It seems that everyone wants to be average or equal. If one is a member of a higher economic class, it is considered crass to display your wealth unless you are a somewhat "superficial" athlete, movie star, popular singer, or television celebrity. Nevertheless, egalitarianism is an ideal or goal rather than an undeniable reality. The gap between the rich and the poor is wider today than it has been in over 60 years and racism and discrimination also tore this country apart in the 1960s and 1970s.

The Impact of Fear on Freedom and Equality in America

Fear has had a dramatic impact on American society since 9/11. People are insecure, anxious, and afraid of a plethora of real and potential threats—terrorism, anthrax, snipers, natural disasters, and even computer viruses. Some of these fears are greatly exaggerated and even irrational. But it makes little difference if these threats are realistic or not because the reactions are the same.

During times of threat, people think differently and perceive the world differently than when they are secure and unthreatened. They long for simple explanations for complex and ambiguous anxieties, and their group membership provides psychological security, making the in-group/out-group distinction more important. Nothing creates a better sense of "we" than to have a good "they" out in the world, especially when "they" seem to be threatening us. This may explain the rise of anti-immigrant sentiment in the United States, even toward Mexicans, who were obviously not in the planes that were used as missiles on 9/11.[28]

Since 9/11, policy changes that are very new to America have been enacted. Unprecedented powers are being granted to the federal government; new security agencies are being created that are very nontraditional. Protecting the individual rights of citizens against an overly powerful federal government has always been a paramount virtue and practice in the American political and civic culture. But, a virtue is really not a virtue until it has been tested in the real world. We can be very chaste when living in a convent or monastery, where there are few temptations. We can be very humble when we have little power or wealth. We are not consumed by fear, selfishness, greed, or envy when we are secure and have plenty. During these times everyone can be very kind, empathetic, and generous. And, when the country is secure and prosperous, we can be very tolerant of dissonant opinions and protect the civil rights of everyone. Now is not that time.

Our virtues are now being tested. The safety and security provided for over 200 years by the geographic insulation of two oceans was undermined by hijacked planes commandeered by suicidal and homicidal terrorists from halfway around the globe. With the passage of the Patriot Act on October 26, 2001, civil liberties have been challenged. Fear of external and internal threats have shaken the resolve Americans have in protecting the rights of all citizens.

While such civic virtues or values as individual liberty and civil rights are strongly adhered to during times of peace and security, they are often compromised during times of threat and insecurity. During the Civil War, Abraham Lincoln suspended the writ of *habeas corpus*,[29] and during World War II over 120,000 Japanese-Americans were arrested and interned in camps in California. Civil liberties and individual rights were also compromised during World War I, when the Espionage and Sedition Acts imprisoned those who dissented from the war effort. But, in most past cases, once the immediate threat waned, the old traditional civic virtues were restored.

Shortly after 9/11, a new federal agency was created to provide "homeland security." The word *homeland* itself is very non-American when it is applied to the power and authority of the federal government. Domestic matters have usually been the political purview of the state or municipal government, not the federal government. The British have a "*Home* Office" and a "*Home* Secretary." In the United States, the family and local community have traditionally provided safety and security for the American people. For example, the National Guard is a military force controlled by the state, not the federal government.

There is a ranking of needs for most human beings and this ranking is not necessarily fixed; this may be equally true for nations as well. Psychologist Abraham Maslow has written extensively about a "hierarchy of needs."[30] "Lower-order needs" must be satisfied, he says, before we can be concerned with the satisfaction of "higher-order needs." For example, people are not concerned about their civil rights or the nature of their government until their physiological need for food and water are met. Security and safety are much lower-order needs than civil rights or liberty.[31] As fear wanes and a sense of general safety rises in America, many citizens' tolerance for the potential abridgement of civil rights declines rapidly. As (and if) these trends continue, history tells us that we can expect a reinvigoration of civil rights protections and a marginalization, if not the outright disappearance, of the Department of Homeland Security.[32]

A Return to Normalcy?

There are reasons to believe that this is only a temporary period of stress and fear that Americans are going through, and there may be a return to the normalcy of the past, including traditional American national cultural values. Less than a quarter of Americans feel that "life has not returned to the way it was before the [9/11] attacks."[33] Still, there are Americans who were arrested by the federal government following 9/11, charged with aiding terrorists, and who have not yet had access to lawyers or been formally tried. These cases are working their way through the legal system. Many civil libertarians and lawyers argue that they cannot be denied their right to due process and a speedy trial. Just as President Lincoln's suspension of *habeas corpus* was viewed as a violation of the Constitution when the Civil War ended and civil liberties were restored, there is reason to believe that the legal system will eventually restore the rights of all to a fair and speedy trial. On the other hand, if the so-called war against terrorism continues for many decades or there are even more horrendous attacks against Americans, the changes that have taken place in the American political and social system may become more permanent.

The Patriot Act is not permanent and must be renewed by Congress. While many in the Bush Administration would like to make all the provisions of the Act permanent, and some administration members even seek to expand the authority of the federal government further, this is unlikely to happen unless the American people and Congress are convinced that the country is in ongoing danger. Those parts of the Act that give the federal government the authority to violate the civil liberties of Americans will probably soon be stricken from the law by Congress.

It is quite possible also that the judicial branch of government will rule that some of the provisions of the Patriot Act are unconstitutional—especially the parts of the Act that give the federal government the power to inspect citizens' medical records, to determine what books they have read, or to record their personal communications without a court order signed by a judge. These all can be viewed as violations of the right to privacy and the protection against unreasonable searches, which are both guaranteed by the Constitution.

Some Americans may believe that in a national emergency, the security of the nation and the prevention of terrorist attacks supersedes individual civil rights and also allows the federal government to ignore due process. Just after 9/11, a majority of Americans supported the sacrifice of some civil liberties in order to fight terrorism. Yet today this has completely changed: A majority now does not believe that the erosion of civil liberties is necessary to fight terrorism.[34] We suspect that most Americans long to return to the traditional

American virtues of tolerance for various viewpoints, democratic debate, and respect and protection of individual rights and liberties. If we do not return to these rights, then the terrorists have indeed won the war and proven that we are really quite an *unexceptional* people.

CHAPTER 9

A National Midlife Crisis?

Where Do We Go from Here?

HUMAN BEINGS GO THROUGH STAGES OF PSYCHOLOGICAL and social growth, and as we move from one stage to another we frequently experience some form of stress. As we give up an immature identity and grow into a more adequate way of dealing with the demands of a complex world, we go through a traumatic period when we are disoriented and long for the simplicity and clarity of the past. We all have gone through a death-rebirth cycle in which the child dies and the adolescent is born. In most religions this crisis is institutionalized in a puberty ritual or rite of passage, the point in time when the community agrees that childhood ends and adolescence begins. This might be a Confirmation ceremony for Catholics or a bar mitzvah for Jews. In turn, the adolescent dies and the young adult is born; eventually we leave home and perhaps marry, and so on, in some sort of linear progression.

The transition period during which we give up one identity and take on another is filled with threat, confusion, disorientation, and doubt. During adolescence, we can no longer assume the carefree identity of a child as we assume new responsibilities. When we behave badly it reflects on our family and community. Most adolescents would very much like to return to the innocence of childhood, the lack of responsibility and the protection provided by our parents. Yet within a few years, the child identity must finally die to allow for the birth of a young adult.

There are many identity crises we go through and they seem to occur about every seven years—childhood to adolescence, adolescence to young adulthood, adulthood to middle age, and so on.[1] Often there are months or years of uncertainty as we give up an inadequate way of solving problems and dealing with others and take on a new and more mature problem-solving system and set of relationships. Change events such as leaving home to go to college or moving to another city for a job, getting married, having our first child, reaching the age of 40, or first experiencing the aches and pains of old age are often remembered as turning points in our lives. Although these events are both pleasant and painful, they are also psychologically stressful as we move from one identity to another.

When does adolescence end and young adulthood begin? It depends upon the individual and the culture. Because the United States is so heterogeneous, there is no agreed-upon age. When someone becomes 18 years old, they can vote and serve in the military but they cannot drink alcohol. At the age of 26, most automobile insurance rates go down because it is assumed that young adults have fewer accidents. And, there is no agreed-upon age for marriage, but it seems to be getting later with each generation.

Adulthood often begins with the end of formal education and securing a job or perhaps joining the military. During young adulthood there is economic and social uncertainty but ideally this turns into years of economic stability, increased responsibility for oneself and others, independence and self-reliance, and planning for the future. One is often considered a mature adult when he or she leaves home and perhaps gets married and has children. When we buy a home we own property and have adult financial responsibilities.

After decades of security, Americans go through another stressful period when they are not sure if they have experienced or accomplished all they wanted to in life. They have engaged in delayed gratification as they focused on the future of owning their home, raising their children, and developing a successful career. We begin to accept our own mortality and realize that we will hand over our wealth (if we have any) to our children. We are no longer young in body or spirit. We don't want to give up the adventures of youth and yet we are not ready to accept the reality that we are getting old.

At this time, many American men regress to their adolescence and buy the sports car they always wanted as teenagers. They might dye their graying hair and some even have affairs with younger women as a way of recapturing the amorous adventures and challenges of their lost adolescence. Often this is triggered by some trauma such as losing a job, turning 50 years old, going through a divorce, or grieving the death of a loved one.

People from other cultures might not agree that there are identifiable crisis periods that humans must go through as they mature, and it may be that the idiosyncratic behavior described above applies to only a minority of Americans. Still, it offers an interesting way to extend our comparison of the growth of a national identity and a civic culture in the United States. Just as individuals go through developmental stages and experience various identity crises, the image that people share of their country and its role in the international system must change and grow.

The Growth of a Nation: An Isomorphic Model

When we compare the growth of an individual to the growth of a nation, we are using an isomorphic model or historical sociology. Just as we can examine the development of a person's personality beginning with childhood, we can examine the development of the national identity of a people beginning with the formative years. Of course, this is only a model and we must be cautious when comparing individuals with groups, societies, or entire nations. Individuals may be moral, ethical, self-righteous, and motivated by pride, fear, or perhaps hatred. We cannot easily attribute these characteristics to groups. But, this approach does allow us to consider the development of a nation and how the people perceive their country and the rest of the world.

The national identity of a people grows and develops as a result of unique shared historical experiences and natural resources. While there are individual, ethnic, racial, and regional differences, most Americans share common national values and beliefs, which are continually reinforced in schools and the mass media. As we interact with the rest of the world, we become even more aware of our national culture, and our national identity usually becomes even more important to us. Just as individuals mature, over time the American national identity has changed, and there are stages of growth and crises we have gone through that have altered our worldview and national image.

We can clearly see that the pre–Spanish-American War period was analogous to the state of an overprotected child whose worldview is naive utopianism. This prolonged childhood and its contemporaneous idealism was perpetuated by the nation's incredible economic success and its isolation and insulation from the rest of the world. The continual economic growth and political stability of this very young nation was considered as evidence that somehow the United States was an exceptional country with exceptional people.

Just as children go through the emotional turmoil and ambivalence of adolescence with its conflicting bouts of overconfidence and fear as they socialize with others outside the warm protection and love of their family, in much the same way the United States entered onto the world stage oscillating between periods of total involvement followed by a relative withdrawal. National adolescence ended and early adulthood began with the prolonged involvement of the United States in the world during World War II and the Cold War. The U.S. could no longer withdraw behind the two oceans.

A national crisis can increase patriotism and strengthen a people's resolve to stand by traditional civic values, but it can also move the country in new and unexpected directions. World War II gave Americans a deep and broad sense of national unity, and for two or three decades, traditional American "can-do" optimism soared. Throughout this period, there was a strongly held belief—despite many national and international crises—that Americans could achieve great things. Men and women with enormous talent and vision gave us the United Nations, the Marshall Plan, NATO, the G.I. Bill, the interstate highway program, the Peace Corps, the space program, the Civil Rights Act, and much more. Like a young adult finding a secure job and a stable family life, the country was settling into success—and routine success at that.

During the 1950s, schools and the military were finally integrated following hundreds of years of racial segregation and discrimination. In the late 1960s, massive civil demonstrations and riots against racism and the Vietnam War, and the assassinations of leaders such as John Kennedy, Martin Luther King, Malcolm X, and Bobby Kennedy seemed to rip apart the social fabric of America, and yet these events also led to affirmative action programs that dramatically increased opportunities for minorities to get jobs and enter colleges and universities. Although this was the era of the Cold War and the atomic bomb—along with the Korean War and the Vietnam War—which put Americans in continual or potential military conflict, it also led to the increased use of diplomacy and increased American involvement in international organizations.

However, adults under stress can regress to an earlier immature behavior that once provided security. There have been times of regression to early eras of oppression and extremism, simplistic utopianism and jingoism throughout American history. With the end of the Cold War, many nostalgically wanted to withdraw into a pre–Cold War era of isolation from international alliances and their potential obligation to fight wars.

Yet overall the pattern has been one of growth and progression into a more mature country with forward-looking and optimistic idealism, but grounded in practical or pragmatic reality. The United States has been militarily and culturally arrogant and aggressive, as well as overconfident in its own success, but in the past few decades, especially since the Vietnam War and 9/11, this appears to have been tempered somewhat by greater humility and a profound understanding among many Americans that we are interrelated and interdependent with countries and cultures around the globe.

We could describe the period from the end of the Vietnam War (1965–1975) and the end of the Cold War (1991) up until September 11, 2001, as a period of fairly mature adulthood. The Vietnam War was the first war the U.S. "lost" and it was the most expensive and long-lasting in American history. Nevertheless, the U.S. remained on the world scene politically, economically, and militarily. It developed alliances to control nuclear armaments and it participated in numerous international forums and organizations to foster better care of the environment, to control the spread of diseases such as AIDS, and to bring war criminals to trial in the World Court.

During the 1990s, President Clinton led the U.S. into military action in the war in Bosnia-Herzegovina, commonly known as the Bosnian War (1992–1995), but this was in response to what the U.S. viewed as genocide. The U.S., as a member of NATO, led Operation Deliberate Force in 1995. The war was brought to an end with the signing of an agreement in Dayton, Ohio, on December 21, 1995, known as the Dayton Agreement.

However, in 2000, President Bush was reluctant to support Clinton's internationalism. He viewed the U.S. involvement in the Bosnian War as "nation building" and this involvement in the world was not in the national interests of the U.S. Bush refused to sign the Kyoto Accords to control global warming, he withdrew the U.S. from the antiballistic missile treaty with Russia, he would not allow the U.S. to join the International Criminal Court, and he threatened to withhold money from the U.N. Furthermore, with the attack on the U.S. on 9/11 and the 2003 Iraq War,[2] he developed a new policy of unilateral pre-emptive military strikes against an enemy and declared that there was an "Axis of Evil" between Iran, Iraq, and North Korea that threatened the U.S. and world peace. This was a return to the earlier, less mature behavior of the U.S. during its early years—its childhood and early adolescence. These actions recalled the U.S. of the Mexican-American War and of the Monroe Doctrine, not the more recent (and more mature) U.S. of the Marshall Plan and NATO.

Carrying forward our analogy between the development of an individual and the nation, the U.S. was beginning a midlife crisis even before 9/11. Many Americans supported Bush's withdrawal from international agreements and alliances. They were uncertain as to whether they wanted to continue their full involvement in the world. Indeed, after the end of the Cold War, there was a sense of drift. The country was extraordinarily successful and an economic and military juggernaut. Although it was far from a primary concern, some wondered how America's international role in the world could be defined as it grew into a powerful, mature member of a less bellicose international community. With the attack on 9/11, there was no way the president could withdraw completely from the international community, but his involvement was primarily one of unilaterialism and the use of military force rather than the international negotiation that the U.S. had increasingly practiced as it aged.

How 9/11 Changed the United States

With the end of the Cold War, it seemed that the United States was finally entering its golden era of adulthood. The victory over communism and the Soviet threat convinced many that the superiority of American ideals and its way of life had been affirmed by history. There was no need to prove its strength; America was both economically and militarily the strongest nation in the international system. There appeared to be no rivals. Like a successful young adult, the country seemed to be coasting toward the success that it had always envisioned for itself.

This self-confidence was destroyed by the terrorist attacks on September 11, 2001. It seemed that just as the country was ready to settle into the benign role of a mature citizen in the world community, we instead entered a new transition period or midlife crisis. It no longer seemed certain that our self-confidence and security were guaranteed or indeed even justified. Confusion and mistrust reigned. Our fears and anxieties led to the creation of the new Department of Homeland Security and the Patriot Act.

Has the trauma of 9/11 produced enormous national self-doubt with a concurrent desire to return to the childhood innocence of the past? Do we still see ourselves today as being special compared to other nations, and will this perception continue into the future? Our traditional national values and beliefs have proven to be very resilient and have been firmly held throughout the history of the United States. But, have these national civic values and beliefs survived the tragedy of 9/11 and will they be retained in the future?

Just as the United States could land men on the moon, there has been a pervasive optimistic belief that this country could solve any national or international problem. A "can-do" spirit characterizes the American people, and yet the United States has not been able to win the war in Iraq, a war that has now lasted longer than World War II. The Chinese and Indian economies have soared at rates at least double that of the United States in the past decade, while Americans seem unable to solve problems of poverty as the gap between the rich and the poor has grown wider than it has been in over 60 years. With the arrival of Hurricane Katrina in 2006, the world watched as the poverty-stricken citizens of New Orleans were trapped in the flooding because they had no transportation. And, it was very clear to everyone that the poverty in New Orleans was related to race: The citizens who were swimming to rescuers or trapped in stadiums were by and large African-Americans. Poverty and racism are still intertwined in the United States. While the majority of poor Americans are white, people of color are much more likely to fall below the poverty level. Still, this can-do spirit meant that 9/11 and its aftermath were just another problem for the U.S. to tackle. Yet, the manner in which this problem was tackled has meant a return to earlier behaviors and practices of the country, which is indicative of some sort of national midlife crisis.

In many ways, the evolution of United States foreign policy does indeed parallel the growth of an individual from childhood to adolescence to early adulthood. But, to carry this analogy further, we must admit that individuals *not only progress, but also regress*. A perfectly mature adult, in a difficult situation, can often lose control and revert to an earlier way of dealing with the world. Some actually throw tantrums just as they did when they were five or six years old.

Since the attacks on the United States on September 11, 2001, the country has in many ways returned to the simplifications of its past. However, it may well be that this is not really some kind of regression, but rather is merely a reassertion of an ongoing pattern of response to the rest of the world. That is, the overwhelming fear and confusion of having over 3,000 civilians killed by foreign terrorists may have made Americans even more receptive to a traditional melodramatic national image of good and evil, good guys and bad guys. As with any individual under stress, there is a nostalgic desire to return to a perceived past when life was simple and unambiguous—a time when there were very clear distinctions between right and wrong, and our own family provided a safe haven from the threats of the outside world. Contemporary insecurities have recently caused Americans to accept simple answers to the many complex problems and ambiguities of the world.

There is also a present desire in the nation to find some country or persons upon which to vent and displace our anger. Just as individuals who are going through a traumatic and stressful life event will often long for the simplicity and security of childhood, a country experiencing the fear and insecurity of war will often return to the national images of its past. Faced with a difficult, hard to define crisis (much like a midlife crisis), the U.S. couldn't buy a sports car to make itself feel better. However, the country needed to address what was perceived as an existential threat with concrete actions—with the "can-do" spirit. Yet, this desire for action can be rash and misdirected.

In their hurt and anger, individuals will sometimes irrationally lash out at any apparent enemy, and the people of a country also often want to strike out at any enemy who seems to be a threat. A year after the attacks of 9/11, over 60 percent of Americans believed that "we should get even" with anyone who crosses the U.S.—a 20 percent increase over a pre-9/11 poll asking the same question.[3] Rather than accepting the tragic reality and uncertainties of a dangerous world where there are no clearly defined good guys and bad guys, we perhaps have regressed to an earlier worldview. In many ways, the reaction of the American government is very traditional: We resorted to a dualistic, black-and-white, unambiguous and melodramatic worldview.

On September 12, 2001, while the remains of the World Trade Center were still smoldering, President George W. Bush addressed the nation and gave a very clear view of what was to come throughout the remainder of his presidency: "This will be a monumental struggle of good versus evil." The president often uses cowboy metaphors and sensational, melodramatic, and dualistic imagery—"the Axis of Evil" being perhaps the most well known. Peter Singer found that from the time Bush took office until June 2003, he spoke about "evil" in nearly one-third of his speeches. Perhaps even more interestingly, Singer found that Bush used the word as a noun much more frequently than as an adjective—meaning that the president sees evil as a Manichean force, a "thing" rather than a quality.[4]

Evil is a religious word. In many languages, it translates into "demonic" or "satanic" and demons or Satan are the polar opposites and opponents of the "good people" of God. This oversimplified and melodramatic imagery allows for no ambiguities and no gray area between what is black and what is white. Most importantly, it follows logically that there can be no compromise with absolute evil. The goal then becomes the total destruction of the enemy, who is not just a foe of America because of some political or economic conflict. The evil opponent threatens all of humanity. This harkens back to a time when Ronald Reagan called the Soviet Union the Evil Empire, which by implication was naturally opposed by the good, democratic, and benevolent United States.

Somewhat like a prize fighter, George W. Bush has urged members of the Iraqi insurgency to "bring 'em on." Immediately after the World Trade Center towers were destroyed, he even used the word *crusade* to describe the war between the United States and terrorists, invoking images of a righteous, religious struggle. He no longer speaks of crusades, and even many of the cowboy phrases are seldom heard now, but the word *evil* is still very much a part of his rhetoric.

Immediately after the 9/11 attack, most of Europe and the rest of the world sympathized and empathized with the American people. Having fought wars on their own soil with large numbers of civilian casualties, they understood the senseless loss of life that the United States had experienced. They were quite willing to support efforts to stamp out terrorism. Many thought the United States would lead an international effort to finally eliminate this scourge worldwide. Rather than soliciting and accepting the support of the international community, however, the United States decided to return to the self-reliance of the past, when it could disengage from the world at will.

The same sense of ingratitude and rejection that Americans felt after the Spanish-American War and World War I may have been felt by many other countries as the United States charged ahead without much support from other nations. The dualistic U.S. foreign policy position of "You're with us or against us" eliminated any possibility of finding gradations of support among nations. Even before 9/11, the United States had been moving toward a unilateralist policy and was withdrawing from—or refusing to join in—many international agreements regarding nuclear disarmament, preserving the environment, and adjudicating war criminals. And, in the eyes of many countries, the United States seemed to be rejecting and weakening the United Nations, the international organization that it had helped to found after World War II to preserve peace.

Many people, inside the U.S. and out, have wondered whether the combination of withdrawal from international agreements and negotiations, coupled with unilaterist militarism, is a permanent change in America's international behavior and foreign policy. Many European journalists and politicians criticize America's foreign policy as overly simplified, bullying, and narrow-minded—prone to confrontation rather than compromise. As China's economic and military power slowly rises across the Pacific, there is a growing fear that if U.S. foreign policy continues to display these behaviors, much of the world will become bystanders to another tense, bipolar stand-off between two superpowers, reminiscent of the Cold War.

However, we believe that this dangerous future will be avoided, and that the immediate foreign policy consequences and behaviors wrought by 9/11 will not be permanent. In fact, they are quite contrary to the general attitudes of most Americans. These attitudes were reflected in the outcomes of the 2006 midterm elections, which rejected many of Bush's policies. These same attitudes in the general electorate will likely be further driven home in the 2008 elections. Indeed, we believe that these attitudes, as they come to the forefront more and more, will allow America to pass through its midlife crisis, and move comfortably—and perhaps more humbly—toward a dignified and secure maturity.

Ironically, when it comes to national policy, the American people may be more sophisticated, mature, and progressive than many of their political leaders. They do not want to withdraw from the world; they favor international involvement and international organizations; and they would like to use diplomacy and negotiation rather than military force. While the majority of them want to end the war in Iraq, they are not sure how this can be done effectively and with the least amount of harm to the U.S. and Iraq. Some conservative politicians would call this position one of "cut and run" or defeat, but it is not an "either-or" situation of either victory or defeat. It is unclear what "victory" means but it is clear that Americans will no longer support a war that appears to many a matter of occupation rather than liberation.

Many Americans believe that it is not in America's national interest to remain in the middle of a foreign civil war and continue to incur enormous national expense in terms of dollars and human lives. They are unsure as to how the U.S. will militarily disengage from the Iraq War, but it is clear that they want American troops to return home. This was also the situation in the late 1960s and early 1970s when it came to the Vietnam War. The majority of Americans were united in the firm belief that the war must end, but there was a great deal of uncertainty as to how that might be done.[5] However, when the Vietnam War ended the U.S. remained fully involved in international affairs, it expanded its involvement in international organizations, and today the U.S. has given Vietnam a "most favored" nation status.

At times in the past, Americans have longed to return to some sort of isolationism from the international arena following a costly military engagement, and yet just the opposite seems to be true today. This is a remarkable indication of a more mature and realistic attitude among our citizens toward the U.S. role in the world community. As a nation, we have come to realize that it is impossible to disengage from the international system of nations. Nearly 9 in 10 Americans now believe that it is best for the U.S. to be active in international affairs. Despite the war in Iraq, frustrations with Iran and North Korea, economic tensions with China, and palpable American unpopularity around much of the world, this number has barely declined since 2003. If this number was "soft"—i.e., if Americans did not feel strongly about it, we would expect this number to drop precipitously given all of these frustrations—we would expect Americans to want to distance themselves from the world behind their two oceans. Yet the numbers have not declined, showing that Americans are willing global citizens.[6]

Similarly, in 2002 the Chicago Council on Foreign Affairs found—for the first time since it began polling in 1974—that a foreign policy issue (terrorism) was cited as the largest problem facing the country. In that same year it found that 41 percent of the problems that Americans mentioned as facing the nation were related to foreign affairs. Certainly people in other countries might find this percentage to be fairly low in light of the impact the United States has on the rest of the world. However, one must bear in mind that in 1998, this number was just 7 percent.[7] The trend continues today: The number of Americans who take an active interest in foreign affairs news has increased markedly over the last several years, and is statistically greater than the respective numbers of Chinese, South Koreans, and Indians who follow foreign affairs.[8]

Americans as a whole are also moving toward a multilateral rather than unilateral global posture, even if this posture has not yet "trickled up" to the upper echelons of government. In 2007, the lowest percentage ever of respondents in the 20 years of Pew Values Surveys indicated that they agreed with the statement "The best way to ensure peace is through military strength."[9] There is strong support for many multilateral treaties and organizations. Seventy percent of Americans support joining the Kyoto agreement. Nearly 90 percent support the Nuclear Test Ban Treaty. Over 70 percent support U.S. participation in the International Criminal Court. And more than 60 percent support making more decisions with the support of the United Nations, even if the decision reached is not the same position advocated by the U.S.[10] The dichotomy between the people and the government of the U.S., which we discussed in the Introduction, is real. Yet, just as someone going through a midlife crisis must eventually make their actions appropriate with their age in order to pass through the crisis, the U.S. government must better reflect the majority sentiments of its people in order to pass through its own midlife crisis.

We referred earlier to a poll which reported that after 9/11, more than 6 in 10 Americans believed that the U.S. should "get even" with countries that attempt to take advantage of us. Today, only 40 percent believe that getting even is desirable, a percentage that is the lowest in 20 years. Nearly 6 in 10 now *disagree*, apparently eschewing the traditional American tendency to see events—particularly foreign affairs—in black-and-white, good versus evil, action/reaction binaries, and apparently adopting a new openness to accepting and examining the gray areas in international affairs.[11] The disastrous experience of the Iraq War—perhaps born out of a misplaced desire to get even with those who threaten America—may have taught the country that reverting to a childish behavior of seeing things as good or evil—with no in-between—reaps poor, unexpected, and complicated results.

In the next decade, political leaders who focus on the future and share these more progressive, internationalist views are likely to win the support of the American people. While fear may have motivated the either/or, dualistic, melodramatic national mindset after 9/11, it appears that Americans are returning to their traditional optimism and that they seek leaders who will restore the moral confidence of the American people.

Immediately after the Vietnam War, many conservative politicians spoke of the "Vietnam Syndrome," referring to Americans' reluctance to get involved in another war. This reluctance was never really a result of Vietnam. Before every war, Americans have fiercely debated the wisdom of military action. This reluctance to go to war was voiced very clearly by Abraham Lincoln when he opposed the war with Mexico, arguing that the nation was being led to war by a president who simply wanted to expand American territory. The motive, he said, was not defensive, but a matter of hegemony.

If there has been a regular oscillation between international involvement and a tendency to withdraw behind the two oceans, for this nation that oscillation has probably ended with the Iraq War. The United States is politically, economically, and militarily interconnected with the rest of the world, and it is now impossible to maintain a policy of non-involvement in international affairs—or to conduct a foreign policy based on unilateral militarism. The public opinion polls clearly show that somehow the national image held by most Americans has indeed become more sophisticated; the country expects its leaders to be actively involved in the world.

The American Tapestry: Regression or Progression?

Fear has had a profound impact on American society since 9/11. Fear of terrorism convinced Congress to sacrifice individual rights for the sake of security, thereby giving the Executive Branch the power to gather information on citizens that before 9/11 could only be obtained with a court order. Individual privacy and the protection of civil liberties were compromised to protect the country from external threat. This appeared to be a step backwards to other historical periods.

This regression to earlier eras of fear seems to be reversing itself. Congress is questioning the excesses of the Department of Justice and it has modified many parts of the original Patriot Act that clearly violated the Constitutional protection of civil liberties. It has also taken back some of its authority to protect privacy and to control information-gathering. Court cases are moving through the judicial system, challenging the violations of civil liberties by the federal government under the act.

Fear also provoked Congress to give the president enormous powers to conduct a war[12] and to engage in interrogations of enemy combatants that some would argue were violations of various international agreements outlawing torture. Members of Congress and numerous courts are questioning the authority of the president to ignore international agreements regarding the treatment of prisoners.

The immigration debate has taken on a new aspect: How can we prevent terrorists from crossing American borders? Regressive xenophobia has dominated much of the debate regarding illegal and even legal immigrants. But, as the memory of 9/11 has receded, border control has returned to a focus more on how to control the numbers of undocumented Mexican laborers rather than Muslim militants coming into the country. Those who fear a flood of illegal Mexican immigrants would like to build a wall between the U.S. and Mexico, but it is unlikely that such a wall could be built along the entire border in the near future and the cost could amount to billions of dollars. In addition, the way to control illegal immigration is to increase the number of visas to allow people to legally immigrate. Some even joke that if the U.S. builds an 11-foot-high wall, and there are no additional visas, then many Mexicans will have 12-foot-high ladders.

Immediately following 9/11, there were incidents when citizens who were perceived as Arab or Muslim were harassed, attacked, or even arrested and accused of being terrorists. Mosques and Islamic schools were vandalized. These incidents were relatively few, however, and immediately after the attacks of 9/11 President Bush appeared at the Islamic Center in Washington and spoke to the nation to assure Americans that this was not a war against Islam or Arabs. There have not been the same kinds of organized governmental racist overreactions toward Arabs or Muslims following 9/11 as those that occurred during World War II when over 120,000 Japanese-Americans were transported to internment camps in California.

Many great powers grew strong by the absorption of cultural contributions from other nations, including the talents of their immigrants. Tolerance of religious practices and different customs not only made immigrants feel welcome, but also encouraged them to contribute their unique human resources. Very often these nations declined when their leaders stopped embracing diversity and started repressing those who were different in the name of extreme nationalism, racial purity, or religious orthodoxy.[13] For a moment after 9/11, it appeared that Americans would demonize immigrants and lean toward intolerance and a xenophobic backlash. Some pundits and writers began to attribute America's success to Anglo-Protestant virtues alone and ignored the fact that many of the technological advances and the continually expanding economy were clearly a partial result of immigrants, many of whom were not Anglo-Protestants. The backlash was very mild and soon died out.

Indeed, diversity in America has progressed since 9/11. Even before 9/11, Senator Joseph Lieberman, a Jew, was a Democratic candidate for vice president in the 2000 presidential election. Hillary Clinton, a woman, and Barack Obama, an African-American, hotly contested the Democratic Party's presidential nomination in 2008. Other candidates included a Mexican-American (Governor Bill Richardson) and a Mormon (Governor Mitt Romney). And during the campaign season there was surprisingly little discussion in the country about whether or not "America was ready" for a minority president. What this says about diversity in America is quite important. In 2007, only 5 percent of Americans said that they would not vote for a candidate because he or she was black. Contrast this with 50 years earlier, when more than half of Americans said they would not vote for an African-American candidate. A similar trend can be seen in attitudes toward women: 70 years ago, only 3 in 10 Americans would have even considered voting for a female candidate. In 2007, 9 in 10 Americans would consider voting for a female candidate.[14]

Overall, race relations in the country are improving. A majority of Americans, and a majority of African-Americans, feel that race relations in the country are good or very good.[15] There has never been higher acceptance of interracial dating, long one of the most contentious aspects of race relations in America. Today, over 80 percent of Americans support interracial dating; just 20 years ago less than half did. And this number is likely to increase: Ninety-four percent of America's youngest generation (Generation Y, representing people born from 1977 onwards) support interracial dating.[16]

This is not to say that race relations are completely harmonious and need no further attention or improvement. The nativist undertones in the current immigration debate are worth noting, although they have been a recurring feature of nearly every American debate on immigration. Moreover, a majority of African-Americans are dissatisfied about how they are treated in society.[17] Incidents of racial injustice and brutality such as the Rodney King beating in 1991, the Diallo shooting in 1999[18], and the specter of racial profiling, among other things, continually remind Americans that improving race relations is a constant duty, and one that is commensurate with the most basic ideals of the country.

Minorities have been disproportionately impacted by the increasing disparities between the rich and the poor, as we saw in August 2005 when Hurricane Katrina devastated New Orleans. In the past decade, the gap between the rich and the poor has grown wider than at any time in over 60 years, and people of color are at least twice as likely as white people to be below the poverty level. Furthermore, it is more difficult today to move from poverty to the middle class than it was 60 years ago. A number of recent studies have shown that upward mobility in the United States is lower than in other industrial countries. One study found that mobility between generations—people doing better or worse than their parents—is less in America than in Denmark, Finland, Canada, Sweden, Germany, and France.[19]

Poor people—especially African-Americans—disproportionately fill jail cells.[20] And, the educational opportunities for poor people are often much fewer than those available to wealthy citizens.[21] While this might appear to be a regression to the racism of the past, it is unlikely that we will continue to ignore these problems of race and poverty for much longer. This gap has come to the attention of politicians such as former Senator John Edwards, who ran for the Democratic presidential nomination in 2004 and 2008, and it is imbedded in the currently pressing issue of providing better health care for all Americans.

Egalitarianism, fairness, and the belief that everyone should have an opportunity to succeed if he or she is a good law-abiding citizen who is willing to work hard—these are very basic American values. The idea of inflexible social and economic classes with no upward mobility has never been a part of the American civic culture. While racism has certainly existed throughout American history, since the Civil Rights Act of 1964 the country has dramatically changed, and it is now abhorrent to the majority of our citizens to consider people of color as somehow destined to mistreatment by the justice system, greater poverty, inferior education, and poor health care.

While Senator Edwards did not win the Democratic nomination to run for the presidency in 2004 or 2008, the chances are very high that his attacks on poverty, his appeal to fairness, and his aggressive health care proposals will become a part of the Democratic platform of 2008 and will lead to reform in public policy for the next decade.

Religion in America: Increasing Secularism?

Despite what some have claimed, the Constitution did not establish the United States of America as a Christian nation.[22] The phrase "in the year of our Lord 1787" is the sole mention of God in the Constitution. A secular state and religious liberty, with respect for all religions, are basic tenets of the American creed. The founders genuinely believed that all men are created equal—even when it comes to religious faith, which they considered to be a part of the national tapestry rather than the entirety of it.

Fundamentalist Christians seemed to permeate many institutions in the United States in the last several years. This has happened before in American history, for example during the McKinley era when religious fundamentalism was prevalent in politics. President Reagan had the strong support of evangelical Christians and became a spokesperson for many of their causes. During the Presidential debates in 2000, President George W. Bush claimed that Jesus was the philosopher who most influenced his life, and he appointed Supreme Court judges who appeared to support fundamentalist Christian social causes.

Religion has always been important for Americans, with over 90 percent of Americans claiming to believe in God, while only about 60 percent of Britons, French, and Germans say the same.[23] In America, politics and religion have always been intertwined in ways that no longer exist in most of Europe, where there has been a dramatic increase of secularism and atheism. On the other hand, in the U.S., various polls show that a Muslim or a homosexual has a better chance of being elected president than an acknowledged atheist.

Nevertheless, rather than regressing to the McKinley era, the United States seems to be progressing along the path of strong individual religious faith, but with an equally strong determination to keep religion and government separate while protecting and respecting all faiths. While the U.S. and Europe have seemed to be moving in opposite directions regarding religion, paradoxically they are now actually moving toward each other. Ironically, the politically active religious extremists of the Bush era have provoked a rise in secularism in America while at the same time the dramatic increase of Muslim immigrants and Islamic extremists in Europe has contributed to the effort to restore Christian influence, which Pope Benedict XVI has made a major theme of his papacy. As Americans are attempting to re-secularize America, Europeans appear to be attempting to re-Christianize Europe.

America's secularist upswing probably began in the 1990s as a reaction to fundamentalist Christians who were very politically active, along with others on the conservative right, against abortion, gay marriage, and later, stem cell research. Their political support of President Bush's election led to his famous faith-based initiatives where public monies were distributed to religious groups to help the needy. At the same time, in a paper written for the *American Sociological Review* in 2002, two Berkeley sociologists, Michael Hout and Claude S. Fischer, found that the percentage of Americans who claimed that they had "no religious preference" had doubled in less than 10 years, rising from 7 percent to 14 percent of the population.[24] However, Hout and Fischer believe that this increase is not a result of growing atheism. Americans, they wrote, were distancing themselves from organized religions as a "symbolic statement" against the religious right.[25]

This new secularism is a reaction to the Bush era and opposes any efforts to mix faith with politics. Chances are that it will increase in the next decade, especially among young Americans. Still, only extreme secularists fear some sort of American theocracy, and Americans have never completely separated God from politics. The United States will continue to be a very religious nation, while Europeans are unlikely to move toward a much greater mix of religion and politics.

The Future of American Exceptionalism

Americans are increasingly expressing a distinct preference for multilateralism, rather than the unilateralism of the past—thus, the years of America's midlife crisis may be coming to an end. Furthermore, with the rise of India and more particularly China, America's status as the sole superpower may be challenged in the coming decades. Throughout the past decade, there has been a constant mumbling in America warning that increasing Chinese economic and military might could harm the U.S. and its interests. One may suspect that the American can-do nature and an unwavering belief in American exceptionalism would cause Americans much grief, real and existential, when considering China's rise. Yet the opposite has been the case. A recent poll found that only about a third of Americans believed that the U.S. economy would always be larger than China's; a strong majority believed that China's economy would equal the U.S. Perhaps even more strikingly, few Americans see this as threatening. Only a third believes this would be negative, and most Americans see such equilibrium as a good or neutral thing.[26]

So, we may ask, what is the future of American exceptionalism? Of course, the national culture of the United States is exceptional, as are all national cultures in different ways. It is a result of unique historical experiences and waves of exceptional immigrants. The physical, social, economic, and political environment nurtured these internal cultural characteristics to create what today is an "exceptional" country.

Current American exceptionalism appears to be balanced by increased humility and a belief that we are interdependent with the rest of the world. While America will gradually withdraw from its role as the world policeman and the sole economic and military superpower and cede its (sometimes self-appointed) identity as the exceptional international nation, it will not shed its identity as the exceptional domestic nation, where each individual's future is not determined solely by their social, familial, or ethnic background, but by their industriousness and ability, and where people of all stripes and origins come together to form a unique and ever-changing tapestry where their personal identity is not limited to just "American"—but can be hyphenated in whatever way the individual desires.

While Americans are often overly idealistic or utopian—and perhaps naïve—they are also incredibly pragmatic and are willing to draw the ideas of others into the American bubble of exceptionalism in order to succeed. We freely draw from the experiences and ideas of others who may not share our ideology if this helps us solve practical economic or political problems facing the nation. During the 1980s, when the Japanese economy seemed to be soaring because of their emphasis on collectivist values, many American companies began to develop "quality circles" where all employees joined together to discuss the quality of their product, the importance of teamwork and collaboration, and the need to view the organization as a great extended family. These ideas are still incorporated into many corporate training programs and into our educational system.

Public policy is not based solely upon some kind of American ideology or set of moralistic admonitions. Few leaders wake up in the morning and ask themselves, "What would a capitalist do about this problem?" During the Cold War, Erich Fromm commented that the only people who take communism seriously are capitalists and the only people who take capitalism seriously are communists. That is, we make policy based upon our pragmatism . . . *and* our basic values and beliefs.

With regard to the exceptionality of America's role on the world stage, while the country may gradually become more and more unexceptional and may act more multilaterally and less asymmetrically, the country's exceptional domestic condition and experience may translate to an enduring international exceptionalism relative to other nations. America's history of relative inclusiveness and integration, along with its continuing, generally successful experiment in the coexistence and unity of people from highly diverse origins, may serve as a model to other countries. Many European countries, with their difficulties dealing with immigrants—particularly those from outside Europe—could benefit from studying the American experience. Similarly, as greater economic power comes to China and India, the American experience could be instructive, as various ethnic groups, empowered and impelled by newfound economic mobility, interact to a greater and greater degree and with a greater chance for conflict. If these countries and regions heed and apply the lessons of the American experience, it could be in the service of greater harmony and egalitarianism globally, which in fact is just how America's founders conceived of the country's mission.

Concluding Thoughts

We began this book with the premise that the only way to truly understand the behavior of the American people and their public policies is to get inside the cultural shoes of Americans. Furthermore, we have argued that you really cannot begin to predict where America is going unless you clearly understand where we've come from and what we've experienced as a people.

An understanding of the culture of Americans allows us to explain the country's present behavior and reasonably predict its future. Understanding a country's culture allows us to be both reflective—why did the country do that?—and predictive—what might the country do?

Therefore, it is with confidence that we can judge that the current period in American history is the country's midlife crisis—when the trauma of 9/11 tossed the country into panicked actions incommensurate with its cultural and national developments. As this book goes to press, we believe that America is coming to the end of its midlife crisis and is on the cusp of a bold, mature stage in its development. It is in this new phase that the country will more fully come to terms with its station in the world and its development as a people. The nation will return, as always, to the core cultural values of Americans and it will become a more willing partner and peer of other nations, though America will always find safety in the oceans that stand between it and Asia and Europe.

Although many Americans are unaware of their own culture, and people from other countries are not even sure if there is an American culture, we have tried to show that a unique, robust, and clearly identifiable mainstream American culture exists, which is shared by all. Common historical experiences, widely shared core values, and a strong national identity bind Americans together, especially during times of crises. Unfortunately, the assumption that Americans have no culture results in an incoherent understanding of American public policy and national behavior.

The dominant culture includes many very distinct and unusual so-called "Old World" European values and beliefs, which took root in the New World. The seeds of British legality and individual rights grew in a new soil separated from the rest of the world by two vast oceans. This provided an opportunity for these seeds to germinate and grow without much interference from the rest of the world. There were centuries of conflict within the United States and with other countries that tested the resolve of Americans to preserve and grow these beliefs and values, but these conflicts only served to nourish and strengthen the civic culture.

There are hundreds of ethnic, racial, national, religious, and regional differences among Americans, all of which are respected and valued. One can retain his or her ethnic, racial, national, religious, regional, gender, and even sexual identity and still be a red-blooded American. Multiculturalism doesn't mean assimilation *or* separatism. You do not need to give up your differences to be an American. This pluralism and unity did not come easily. It took centuries to finally allow for equal rights and opportunities for all Americans regardless of their secondary cultural identities. It was this process that made the country exceptional and created within it the unique American values that form the American culture.

The trauma and impact of 9/11 have been as dramatic as World War II, and the war in Iraq has lasted longer than World War II. The years since 9/11 have been among the most contentious and trying in American history. We have tried to demonstrate by bringing together various disciplines and fields of study, such as intercultural relations, cultural anthropology, sociology, political science, economics, psychology, and history, that this difficult period may challenge Americans to demonstrate that they sincerely believe and practice the national cultural values that are truly "American." As a nation, we cannot really lay claim to such civic virtues as protecting individual liberties and democratic practices unless these virtues can withstand the fear of terrorism over time. This will be the real test of American exceptionalism.

Notes

Introduction

1. Americans surveyed for the same poll, however, had much more difficulty distinguishing between their opinions of the Iranian government and the Iranian people. Twelve percent of Americans had a favorable view of the Iranian government, but only 29 percent of Americans had a favorable view of the Iranian people. Steven Kull, et al., "Public Opinion in Iran and America on Key International Issues," *www.WorldPublicOpinion.org*, January 24, 2007, p. 13.
2. The United States fought the Persian Gulf War in 1990 and 1991 to free Kuwait from Iraqi occupation. Many other countries supported this war as they supported the effort to bring to justice those responsible for 9/11. The invasion of Afghanistan on October 7, 2001 escalated American involvement in the Middle East. However, when the United States attacked Iraq on March 20, 2003, it no longer had the support of most of the rest of the world.

Chapter 1

1. Arthur M. Schlesinger Jr., "Folly's Antidote," *The New York Times*, January 1, 2007.
2. Freud used the iceberg analogy to describe personality, but it has also been used by various cultural anthropologists to explain overt and covert culture (Ralph Linton, *The Cultural Background of Personality* [New York: Appleton-Century-Crofts, 1945]), or explicit and implicit culture (Clyde Kluckhohn, *Mirror for Man* [New York: McGraw-Hill, 1949]), or external and internal culture (Edward T. Hall, *Beyond Culture* [Garden City, NY: Anchor Press/Doubleday, 1977]). We suspect that Hall was influenced by the earlier thinkers and his experiences as a staff member at the National Institutes for Mental Health when he first writes about the iceberg analogy in his

classic book *The Silent Language* (Greenwich, CT: Fawcett Publications, Inc., 1959), pp. 64–6.

The model presented here suggests that there are various layers to the "iceberg" and, just as the unconscious shapes the conscious mind in Freudian theory, the hidden part of culture shapes the external aspects of culture. Previous authors have not used the layers or suggested the ranking within the iceberg. This graphic was first used in the paper and presentation by Gary R. Weaver and Phil Uncapher, "The Nigerian Experience: Overseas Living and Value Change," SIETAR Conference, Vancouver, BC, Canada, March 11, 1981.

3. See Edmund S. Glenn, *Man and Manhood* (Norwood, NJ: Ablex, 1981) and Rosalie A. Cohen, "Conceptual Styles, Culture, Conflict and Nonverbal Tests of Intelligence," *American Anthropologist*, Vol. 71 (1969), pp. 828–856.

4. Marshall Singer, *Perception and Identity in Intercultural Communication: Abridged and Revised Edition* (Boston: Intercultural Press, 1998).

5. J.W. Bagby, "A Cross Cultural Study of Perceptual Dominance in Binocular Rivalry," *Journal of Abnormal & Social Psychology*, Vol. 54 (1957), pp. 331–334.

6. According to Samuel Huntington, "the great divisions among humankind and the dominating source of conflict will be *cultural*. Nation states will remain the most powerful actors in world affairs, but the principal conflict of global politics will occur between nations and groups of different *civilizations*." (emphasis added) Huntington does not distinguish between cultures and civilizations. Samuel Huntington, "The Clash of Civilizations," in Gary R. Weaver, ed., *Culture, Communication and Conflict: Readings in Intercultural Relations*, Revised 2nd Edition (Boston: Pearson Publishing, 2000), p. 472.

7. Ironically, with the end of the Cold War, Huntington looked backward from the conflict of nation states based upon ideology and nationalism to a world of wars between mutually exclusive religions similar to the Holy Crusades. See Samuel P. Huntington, *The Clash of Civilizations and the Remaking of World Order* (New York: Simon & Schuster, 1996).

8. For example, see Seymour Martin Lipset, *The First New Nation: The United States in Historical and Comparative Perspective* (New York: Basic Books, Inc. Publishers, 1963).

9. Nancy Adler believes that stereotyping is natural and allows us to initially sort out the complexities of trying to understand another culture. Stereotypes can be effective or ineffective depending upon whether we know we are stereotyping and are willing to discard the stereotype when it is no longer useful or accurate. While her definition of an "effective stereotype" is roughly the same as our definition of a "cultural generalization," we think all stereotypes inhibit understanding because the concept of a stereotype does not allow for exceptions regardless of whether the stereotype is "effective," "positive" or "negative." Nancy J Adler, *International Dimensions of Organizational Behavior: 4th Edition* (Cincinnati: South-Western, 2002), pp. 81–83.

10. Kenneth E. Boulding, *The Image* (Ann Arbor: The University of Michigan Press, 1956) and Ralph K. White, *Nobody Wanted War: Misperception in Vietnam and Other Wars, Revised Edition* (New York: Doubleday/Anchor, 1970).

11. See Singer, *Perception & Identity in Intercultural Communication*, pp. 13, 30, 33–34.

12. Angus Campbell, Philip Converse, Warren Miller, and Donald Stokes, *The American Voter* (Chicago: University of Chicago Press, 1960).

13. Donald P. Green, Bradley Palmquist, and Eric Schickler, *Partisan Hearts and Minds: Political Parties and the Social Identities of Votes* (New Haven: Yale University Press, 2002).

14. Hall, *Beyond Culture.*

15. See T.W. Adrono, et. al., *The Authoritarian Personality, Part One and Part Two* (New York: John Wiley & Sons, Inc., Science Editions, 1964) and Erich Fromm, *Escape From Freedom* (New York: Holt, Rinehart and Winston, 1941).

16. Alkman Granitsas, "Americans are Tuning Out the World," YaleGlobal, November 24, 2005, http://yaleglobal.yale.edu/display.article?id=6553.

17. Richard Armey quoted in Mathew Engles, "Senior Republican Calls on Israel to Expel West Bank Arabs," *The Guardian*, (May 4, 2002). p 2.

18. We are using the term "empathy" as a variation of Ralph K. White's concept of "realistic empathy" in his anthology *Psychology and the Prevention of Nuclear War* (New York: New York University Press, 1986), pp. 550–553. White's definition is primarily cognitive and psychological. We have broadened the scope to also include culture. It is very difficult, if not impossible, to separate the psychological from the cultural. In the following pages, we are adopting the phrase "realistic cultural empathy" within a culture-and-personality framework. Other concepts that are similar to "realistic cultural empathy" include Glen Fisher's use of the term "mindsets" in his book *Mindsets: The Role of Culture and Perception in International Relations* (Yarmouth, ME: Intercultural Press, 1988, 1997).

19. The purpose of this book is not to garner sympathy for the United States, but rather to encourage readers to empathize with the American people.

20. In many countries, people focus on the past to explain the present. For example, over the past three decades there has been a bloody civil war in Sri Lanka with Hindu Tamils fighting Sinhalese Buddhists. Suicide bombing of innocent civilians was commonplace throughout this war. Within a two or three week period, a plane was blown up on the tarmac of the airport killing at least 40 passengers and a terrorist blew up the telecommunications center in Colombo, killing dozens of people. When I (Weaver) asked a Singhalese colleague at the University of Colombo why Tamils would do this, he explained that they were "newcomers" to the island of Ceylon and they didn't quite "fit in." Moreover, he said, this was retaliation for an incident where a number of Tamils were killed. Later in our conversation I realized that when

he said they were "newcomers" he meant they arrived hundreds of years ago and the incident he was referring to took place at least thirty years earlier.

21. Arthur M. Schlesinger Jr., "Folly's Antidote."

Chapter 2

1. During the twentieth century, 36 million immigrants entered the United States, but an estimated 12 million people exited. Ivan Chermayeff, Fred Wasserman, and Mary J. Shapiro, *Ellis Island: An illustrated History of the Immigrant Experience* (New York: Macmillan Publishing Company, 1991), p. 276.

2. Remarks of George Gerbner, Dean Emeritus, The Annenberg School for Communication, University of Pennsylvania in his keynote address celebrating the anniversary of the founding of the International Communication Program at American University, Washington, DC, November 4, 1995. The German World War II movie *Das Boot* ("The Boat") is considered one of the finest German movies ever made and yet it is certainly one of the most tragic. All of the sailors in a German submarine perish. This is the tragic reality of war: it is brutal, soldiers do cruel things to others, and death is random. This is in stark contrast with the American melodramatic John Wayne movies where the Americans are all heroes and often do not get killed. For many young boys, war is seen as something fun or "cool." Dropping grenades on the German high command trapped underground in *The Dirty Dozen* or spray-painting Nazis red with your Thompson in *The Longest Day* were depicted in black and white, melodramatic fashion. "And there was that Hollywood thing where the hero ran through blizzards of fire and somehow was never touched, because, after all, he was the hero." Stephen Hunter, "Spielberg's War: It's Hell," *Washington Post*, July 24, 1998.

3. This reaction to the word war is similar to the reaction many Jews have to the overuse, and casual use, of the word holocaust. While all ethnically motivated killing is abhorrent, when the word is used to describe any ethnic conflict, it demeans the systematic slaughter of 6 million Jews during World War II.

4. Robert Hay Lifton and Richard A. Falk, "On Numbing and Feeling," in Gary R. Weaver, ed., *Culture, Communication and Conflict: Readings in Intercultural Relations*, Revised 2nd Edition (Boston: Pearson Publishing, 2000), p. 404–7.

5. Until the September 11, 2001 attacks, the Oklahoma City bombing was the deadliest terrorist act on U.S. soil. There were 168 people killed, including at least 20 children. Within days of the blast, Timothy McVeigh and Terry Nichols were arrested and investigators found that they were sympathizers of an anti-government militia movement that was opposed to gun control, increased taxes, and U.S. membership in the U.N. Their primary motive

was to avenge the so-called Waco (Texas) incident in 1993 and the Ruby Ridge (Idaho) incident in 1992 when the FBI and ATF used deadly force to arrest Americans with illegal guns.

6. Among the many daytime court television shows are Judge Judy Sheindlin ("Judge Judy"), Judge Greg Mathis ("Judge Mathis"), Judge Marilyn Milian ("People's Court"), Judge Glenda Hatchett ("Judge Hatchett"), Judge Larry Joe Doherty ("Texas Justice"), Judge Mablean Ephraim ("Divorce Court"), and Judge Joe Brown ("Judge Brown"). These are among the most popular television shows in America today. James Hibbard, "Verdict's in on Court Shows; Law Strips Exhibit Significant Growth Over Last Year," *Television Week* (April 19, 2004), p. 8.

7. To attract large audiences, the American television news industry has combined information with entertainment to produce "infotainment." Coming from the other direction, some advertisers have created the "infomercial," entire television programs devoted to promoting a product, but presented in the guise of a regular TV news or information program.

8. Dozens of studies have found this dramatic increase in stories regarding violence and crime on national broadcasts, such as Dennis T. Lowry, Tarn Ching Josephine Nio, and Dennis W. Leitner, "Setting the Public Fear Agenda: A Longitudinal Analysis of Network TV Crime Reporting, Public Perceptions of Crime, and FBI Crime Statistics," *Journal of Communication*, Vol. 53, No. 1 (March 2003), pp. 61–73 and Daniel Romer, Kathleen Hall Jamieson, and Sean Aday, "Television News and the Cultivation of Fear of Crime," *Journal of Communication*, Vol. 53, No. 1 (March 2003), pp. 88–104.

9. Mike Wendling, "Statistics Confirm Huge London Crime Wave," CNSNEWS .com, April 18, 2002.

10. Deborah Tannen, *The Argument Culture: Moving From Debate to Dialogue* (New York: Random House, 1998), pp. 3–4.

11. Before 1866, citizenship was not defined in the Constitution or in any federal statute. As a matter of practice or common law, it was assumed that anyone born in the United States was a citizen, except slaves. However, the Civil Rights Act of April 9, 1866, which became the Fourteenth Amendment two years later, made this a matter of national law. "All persons born or naturalized in the United States, and subject to the jurisdiction thereof, are citizens of the United States." Today, there are some who want to ship undocumented Mexicans back to Mexico. However, if their children were born in the United States, the children are American and cannot be forced to leave with their parents. A few politicians have suggested that the fourteenth Amendment ought to be changed to avoid the possibility of sending law-abiding, undocumented Mexican parents home without their children.

12. Fareed Zakaria, "Europe Needs a New Identity," *Newsweek* (November 21, 2005).

13. See Marc Pachter, "American Identity," *eJournal USA: Society & Values* (Washington: Department of State, 2005), pp. 3–7.

14. See R. Roosevelt Thomas, Jr. "The Concept of Managing Diversity," *The Bureaucrat*, Winter 1991–1992, pp. 19–22.

15. *Public Papers of Presidents of the United State: Lyndon B. Johnson, 1965.* Vol. 2, entry 301 (Washington, D.C.: Government Printing Office, 1966), pp. 635–640.

16. See Orlando Patterson, "The Paradox of Integration," in Gary R. Weaver, ed., *Culture, Communication and Conflict: Readings in Intercultural Relations*, Revised 2nd Edition (Boston: Pearson Publishing, 2000), p. 99.

17. Jeremy Rifkin, "Thanks, Mr. President," *The Guardian*, April 26, 2003.

18. Robert Kagan, "Cowboy Nation," *New Republic*, December 10, 2006.

19. Robert Samuelson, "Myths and the Middle Class," *The Washington Post*, December 27, 2006, p. A19.

20. According to the UN Gini Index.

21. See Thorstein Veblen's *Theory of the Leisure Class* (1899) and Rick Tilman, *Thorstein Veblen and His Critics, 1891–1963* (Princeton: Princeton University Press, 1992). In contrast with Karl Marx's view that the lower classes would somehow overthrow the upper classes, Veblen believed that there was no need to have classes because the lower classes strive to become higher classes and there is fluidity between classes. To this extent there is a classless society in the United States.

22. Frank Newport, "Questions and Answers about Americans' Religion," Gallup, December 24, 2007, http://www.gallup.com/poll/103459/Questions-Answers-About-Americans-Religion.aspx; Ira M. Sheskin and Arnold Dashefsky, "Jewish Population of the United States, 2006," in David Singer and Lawrence Grossman, eds., *American Jewish Year Book 2006*, Volume 106 (NY: American Jewish Committee, 2006); "Muslims in America: Middle Class and Mostly Mainstream," Pew Research Center, May 22, 2007, pp. 9–14. See also "U.S. Religious Landscape Survey 2008," The Pew Forum on Religion and Public Life, 2008.

23. Barry A. Kosmin, Egon Mayer, and Ariela Keysar, "American Religious Identification Survey 2001," The Graduate Center of the University of New York, p. 12.

24. According to the 2000 U.S. Census.

25. According to the 2000 U.S. Census.

26. Theo Summer, quoted by Anne-Marie Slaughter, "Earning It," *Foreign Policy* (July, 2007).

Chapter 3

1. Thomas Cahill, *Bill Moyers Journal*, "Bill Moyers talks with Thomas Cahill," December 28, 2007, PBS Television, http://pbs.org/moyers/journal/1228 2007/transcript1/html.

2. Leon Festinger, *A Theory of Cognitive Dissonance* (Stanford, CA: Stanford University Press, 1957).

3. The idea of a melting pot is actually much older and is even found in Creve-coeur's 1783 "Letters from an American Farmer." Among German immi-grants, there had been much talk of a *Schmelztiegel* (melting pot) as early as the middle of the nineteenth century. There is also an obscure, posthu-mously published text originating from around the 1850s by Emerson in which he wrote about a "smelting pot."

4. This letter can be found in the manuscript division of the Library of Con-gress. It was written January 3, 1919 to Mr. Richard K. Hurd, 59 Liberty Street, New York. Theodore Roosevelt often spoke of the Irish as an inferior race of people and he strongly believed the Asians should not be allowed to enter the U.S. In 1924 the state of Virginia passed a law that prohib-ited whites from marrying anyone with "a single drop of Negro blood" and marriage between whites and blacks was illegal in thirty-eight states. In the same year, Congress passed the Immigration Act, a series of strict anti-immigration laws calling for the severe restriction of "inferior" races from southern and eastern Europe. In the 1950s, almost half of the states had mis-cegenation laws and Virginia did not change its law until 1967. While the original laws were directed wholly against black white unions, the legislation was expanded to include unions between whites and Mongolians, Malayans, Mulattos, and Native Americans. See Ellis Cose, "One Drop of Bloody His-tory," *Newsweek*, February 13, 1995, p. 70 and the Association of American Law Schools, ed., *Selected Essays*, p. 278.

5. On the other hand, Roosevelt was also a populist who broke up trusts of wealthy businessmen. He is also credited with being the very first environ-mentalist president who was responsible for establishing many of the na-tional parks that still exist today.

6. An early version of this discussion can be found in Gary R. Weaver, "Amer-ican Identity Movements: A Cross-Cultural Confrontation," *Intellect*, March 1975, pp. 376–380. It is also in Gary R. Weaver, ed., *Culture, Communication and Conflict: Readings in Intercultural Relations*, Revised 2nd Edition (Boston: Pearson Publishing, 2000), p. 60–65.

7. When we grow up in a particular culture, we unconsciously learn the cultur-ally accepted values, beliefs, and behaviors as part of a particular family. This is the process of *enculturation* and it takes place implicitly and informally. *Acculturation* is the process by which we learn our secondary cultures, usu-ally through an explicit, conscious, and more formal manner than the way we learned our primary culture. Immigrants are already enculturated to their home culture and must acculturate to the United States' dominant cul-ture. The process of being fully accepted into the culture and treated as an equal to all others is the process of *assimilation*. People of color could ac-culturate to the mainstream American culture by accepting its values, be-liefs, and behaviors, but they were often excluded because of their race and

therefore could not assimilate. On the other hand, some white immigrants could easily be assimilated by simply fitting into the mainstream cultural cookie cutter, but they refused to fully acculturate—the Amish are one example of this. For a further discussion see Andrea L. Rich and Dennis M. Ogawa, "Intercultural and Interracial Communication: An Analytic Approach" in Gary R. Weaver, ed., *Culture, Communication and Conflict, Revised 2nd Ed.*, (Boston: Pearson Publishing, 2000), pp. 54–59.

8. United States immigration officials often changed the names of immigrants because they couldn't pronounce many non-English names and many of the immigrants were illiterate.

9. In *Loving v. Virginia*, 388 U.S. 1 (1967), the Supreme Court declared Virginia's anti-miscegenation statute, the "Racial Integrity Act of 1924," unconstitutional, thereby overturning *Pace v. Alabama* (1883) and ending all race-based legal restrictions on marriage in the United States.

10. There are eight protected classes of people under the various civil rights in employment laws that have been passed since 1964: race, sex/gender, skin color, national origin, religion, age (everyone over 40), disability, and reprisal (anyone who alleges discrimination based on membership in one of the seven other classes who is victim of reprisal). Senator Strom Thurmond tried to keep the 1964 Civil Rights Act from becoming law by adding protection against discrimination based upon sex/gender, which was not included in the original legislation. Supposedly, Senator Thurmond believed that raising the specter of "your daughters going off to war" would keep the bill from passing. Furthermore, he thought this would show the absurdity of treating a majority of Americans (approximately 52 percent) as a minority. The legislation was passed to include women and some would argue that, as a class of citizens, they may have benefited the most from the Civil Rights Act.

11. The terms "liberal" and "conservative" are used in the typical American jargon where the liberal position would be one of more federal government involvement in issues of welfare and social justice. The conservative view is usually one of less government involvement in welfare and social justice, more emphasis on the rights and responsibilities of the individual, and greater influence of the private sector in the economy. In many parts of Europe, liberal and conservative are used in almost the reserve fashion.

12. *The Autobiography of Malcolm X* (New York: Ballantine Books, 1999), p. 169.

13. This has also been referred to as the "deficit" model by the African American psychologist Gerald Gregory Jackson, "The Roots of the Backlash Theory in Mental Health," *Journal of Black Psychology*, Vol. 6, No. 1 (August 1979), pp. 17–45.

14. It has become politically correct to refer to American Indians as "Native Americans." However, few natives of America would use this term because it was invented by the United States government and it is not accurate. Anyone born in the United States is a "native" American, which is the reason those who oppose immigrants are often referred to as "nativists." Most

American Indians know that is was a mistaken label perhaps given by early settlers who thought they had discovered the East Indies. While some American Indians will use the term "American Indian," most simply refer to each other in terms of their tribal affiliation. Thus, one could be called a Zuni, Hopi, Apache, or Menominee. The overall term American Natives has also recently become more popular among American Indians.

15. On May 26, 1830, less than six months after Jackson assumed the office of President, the Indian Removal Act of 1830 was passed by the Twenty-First Congress. After four months of heated debate, Jackson signed the bill into law.

16. "My original convictions upon this subject have been confirmed by the course of events for several years, and experience is every day adding to their strength. That those tribes can not exist surrounded by our settlements and in continual contact with our citizens is certain. They have neither the intelligence, the industry, the moral habits, nor the desire of improvement which are essential to any favorable change in their condition. Established in the midst of another and a superior race, and without appreciating the causes of their inferiority or seeking to control them, they must necessarily yield to the force of circumstances and ere long disappear." From Jackson's fifth annual message to Congress on December 3, 1833.

17. Polk and Jackson were both born and raised in southwestern North Carolina and then migrated to Tennessee. Jackson was known as "Old Hickory" and Polk was nicknamed "Young Hickory." Polk was the eleventh president and he served from 1845–1849.

18. The policy of Manifest Destiny led to the war with Mexico in 1846. It ended with the Treaty of Guadalupe Hidalgo in February of 1848 with Mexico. The treaty gave the United States control over Texas and California, and much of the so-called Southwest Territory which today includes New Mexico, Arizona, Nevada, Utah, and parts of Colorado and Wyoming.

19. Ironically, casinos have been a benefit to some American Indian tribes because the laws regarding gambling are local or state. There is no federal law against gambling. To settle the Indian Wars with hundreds of tribes, treaties were signed between tribes and the federal government. Of course, the only entity that could sign a treaty is another country. American Indian tribes were treated as foreign governments and only in the fast few decades have American Indians living on reservations been allowed to vote in federal elections. Some tribes have actually gone to the United Nations in efforts to be declared separate nations with their own passports. Many tribes realized that local gambling laws could not be enforced on reservations which had either federal or tribal jurisdiction. Thus, some began building casinos with the requirement that at least 40 percent of the profit would be devoted to building schools and roads or other community development projects. While this has improved the way of life for some tribes, most tribes do not have casinos and the majority of American Indians still live in abject poverty.

20. "Let me tell you just a little something about the American Indian in our land. We have provided millions of acres of land for what are called preservations—or reservations, I should say. They, from the beginning, announced that they wanted to maintain their way of life, as they had always lived there in the desert and the plains and so forth. And we set up these reservations so they could, and have a Bureau of Indian Affairs to help take care of them. At the same time, we provide education for them—schools on the reservations. And they're free also to leave the reservations and be American citizens among the rest of us, and many do. Some still prefer, however, that way— that early way of life. And we've done everything we can to meet their demands as to how they want to live. Maybe we made a mistake. Maybe we should not have humored them in that wanting to stay in that kind of primitive lifestyle. Maybe we should have said, no, come join us; be citizens along with the rest of us. As I say, many have; many have been very successful." Ronald Reagan, "Remarks and Question-and-Answer Session with Students and Faculty at Moscow State University," May 31, 1988, http://www.reagan .utexas.edu/archives/speeches/1988/053188b.htm.

21. In South Africa, it was customary to consider anyone with one drop of white blood as "coloured" whereas in the United States, if a person had one drop of "black" blood in his or her ancestry, you would be considered black. In New Orleans, those of mixed white and black ancestry were often called "mulatto," but throughout most of American there was no term which indicted a mixture of races. One was either white or black. "Colored," in American English, simply meant black.

    Since the 1960s, the words "Negro" and "Colored" are not used to describe Americans of sub-Saharan African ancestry. An important aspect of the black cultural or national identity movement of the 1960s was the right of people of color to decide what they wanted to be called rather than allowing the dominant white society to label them. Especially among young black activists of the 1960s, the label black American was used as a matter of racial pride. In the 1980s, Jesse Jackson popularized the phase African-American. The terms are often used interchangeably. Other ethnic and racial groups also began to identify themselves in terms of their differences. For example, many Mexican-Americans use the term "Chicanos" and other Latin American immigrants will use labels such as "Latinos." Along with the "Gay Liberation Movement" of the 1970s many homosexuals use the label "Gay" as a matter of pride in their sexual orientation.

22. See Orlando Patterson, "The Paradox of Integration," p. 95–100.

23. Amaad Rivera, Brenda Cotto-Escalera, Anisha Desai, Jeannette Huezo, and Dedrick Muhammad, "Foreclosed: State of the Dream 2008," United for a Fair Economy, 2008, p. 6, using U.S. census bureau statistics for 1968 and 2005.

24. Angelina KewalRamani, Lauren Gilbertson, Mary Ann Fox, and Stephen Provasnik, "Status and Trends in the Education of Racial and Ethnic

Minorities," Institute of Education Sciences, National Center for Education Statistics, September 2007, http://nces.ed.gov/pubsearch/pubsinfo.asp?pubid=2007039.

25. Aditi Balakrishna, "Class of 2011 Admits Beat Lowest Odds," *The Harvard Crimson*, April 2, 2007, http://www.thecrimson.com/article.aspx?ref=517944.

26. http://web.mit.edu/facts/enrollment.html.

27. Jean Pfaelzer, *Driven Out: The Forgotten War Against Chinese Americans* (Random House, 2007).

28. See Noel Ignatiev, *How the Irish Became White* (New York: Routledge, 1995).

29. For sixty-one years, the Chinese were excluded from entering the United States and becoming naturalized citizens. During the gold rush in the 1840s, white miners and prospectors imposed taxes and laws to inhibit the Chinese from success. Racial tensions increased as more and more Chinese emigrated, occupied jobs, and created competition on the job market.

30. Sociolinguist Thomas Kochman describes the difference between structural and cultural pluralism in "Black and White Styles in Pluralistic Perspective," in Gary R. Weaver, ed., *Culture, Communication and Conflict: Readings in Intercultural Relations*, Revised 2nd Edition (Boston: Pearson Publishing, 2000), pp. 283–4.

31. People of Mexican ancestry often refer to themselves as Mexican-American or Chicano. This is not a racial identification because Mexicans and all Hispanics come in a variety of all colors. They are the largest group of Hispanics in Los Angeles and Chicago. While the United States government often used the term Hispanic to describe anyone who came from Latin American, each group has its own self-identity depending upon location, ancestry, nationality, and so on. For example, in Miami there is a large Cuban immigrant population and many could term themselves Cubanos or Cuban-Americans. In Washington, D.C. the largest groups come from such Central American countries as El Salvador, Honduras, Panama, and Guatemala. They usually refer to themselves as Latinos. The largest group of Hispanics in New York City is from Puerto Rico and the second largest group is from the Dominican Republic. They refer to themselves as Puerto Ricans or sometimes even a New York Ricans, and Dominicanos. On the other hand, there are many in Texas or New Mexico who use the term Hispanics as a self-identity to make clear that they arrived before recent Mexicans. Generally, it is up to each group or individual to decide what label they use to identity themselves and it clearly is not a matter of "blood."

32. "Fact Sheet: Korean Americans and Comprehensive Immigration Reform," Asian American Justice Center, http://www.advancingequality.org/files/cir_kor_fact.pdf.

33. Samuel P. Huntington, *Who are We?: The Challenges to America's National Identity* (New York: Simon & Schuster, 2004), p. 61.

34. For an excellent distinction between the concept of assimilation and acculturation, see Andrea L. Rich and Dennis M. Ogawa, "Intercultural and

Interracial Communication: An Analytic Approach," in Gary R. Weaver, ed., *Culture, Communication and Conflict: Readings in Intercultural Relations*, Revised 2nd Edition (Boston: Pearson Publishing, 2000), pp. 54–59.

35. Maria Sacchetti, "Immigrant parents struggle to keep their children bilingual," *The Boston Globe*, July 22, 2007.

36. Shirin Hakimzadeh and D'Vera Cohn, "English Usage Among Hispanics in the United States," Pew Hispanic Center, November 29, 2007.

37. Samuel P. Huntington, "The Erosion of American National Interests," *Foreign Affairs*, Vol. 76, No. 5 (September/October, 1997), pp. 28–49.

38. Charles William Maynes, "The New Pessimism," *Foreign Policy*, Fall, 1995, pp. 32–49.

39. Pew Research Center, "Muslim Americans: Mostly Middle Class and Mainstream," May 22, 2007, http://pewresearch.org/assets/pdf/muslimamericans .pdf.

40. Karina Fortuny, Randy Capps, and Jeffrey S. Passel, "The Characteristics of Unauthorized Immigrants in California, Los Angeles County, and the United States" (Washington: The Urban Institute, March 2007).

41. Public Agenda, "Now That I'm Here: What America's Immigrants Have to Say About Life in the US Now," 2003, p. 11.

42. Leon Festinger, *A Theory of Cognitive Dissonance* (Stanford: Stanford University Press, 1957). More pathological forms of this principle can be found in the brainwashing of prisoners or even college fraternity and sorority hazing. Interestingly, the less the reward for the changed behavior, the greater the likelihood people will change their beliefs. Another consequence of cognitive dissonance is that in-group membership becomes stronger and the in-group/out-group distinction becomes greater. A college student who has gone through some hazing is likely to remain very loyal to the group. Unconsciously a new fraternity brother believes "I must love this group of guys or why would I have gone through the humiliation of hazing."

43. Public Agenda, "Now That I'm Here: What America's Immigrants Have to Say About Life in the US Now," p. 13.

44. The New York Times/CBS Poll, May 18–23, 2007.

45. For example, Pew Research Center, "Democratic Leaders Face Growing Disapproval, Criticism on Iraq," June 7, 2007, http://people-press.org/reports/ pdf/335.pdf.

46. Public Agenda, "Now That I'm Here: What America's Immigrants Have to Say About Life in the US Now," p. 17.

47. Jill Lepore, *A is for American* (New York: Alfred A. Knopf, 2002), p. 18.

48. Lepore, *A is for American*, p. 22. A popular, though likely apocryphal story known as the Muhlenberg Legend, contends that German was but one vote away from becoming an official language of the United States in Pennsylvania, and that the decisive vote was cast by a bilingual immigrant from Germany. While this legend is not true, it is true that in 1794 Germans living in Virginia petitioned Congress that some U.S. laws be written in German as

well as English. While this petition was denied, it is a distant ancestor to the current debate over providing official government documents in languages other than English, particularly Spanish.

49. Lepore, *A is for American*, p. 37.
50. National Opinion Research Center, "General Social Survey Codebook," http://webapp.icpsr.umich.edu/GSS/.
51. According to the 2000 U.S. Census.
52. Public Agenda, "Now That I'm Here: What America's Immigrants Have to Say About Life in the US Now," p. 23–4.

Chapter 4

1. There are hundreds of books and essays written on American exceptionalism. Some variation of the phrase is routinely used in political speeches today. Alexis de Tocqueville made the assertion that Americans were exceptional in his writings in the 1830s, but there are many contemporary writers who also write about it. To name only a few—Michael Ignatieff, ed., *American Exceptionalism and Human Rights* (Princeton: Princeton University Press, 2005), Seymour Martin Lipset, *American Exceptionalism: A Double-Edged Sword* (New York: W.W. Norton & Company, 1997), Kim Voss, *The Making of American Exceptionalism: The Knights of Labor and Class Formation in the Nineteenth Century* (Ithaca: Cornell University Press, 1993).
2. Sociologist Seymour Martin Lipset has written extensively about the similarities and differences between the national and civic cultures of the United States and Canada. For example, see his *Continental Divide: The Values of the United States and Canada* (New York: Routledge, 1990).
3. When Columbus first arrived in America, it is estimated that there were ten times as many American Indians as there are today. Over 90 percent died from diseases that Europeans brought with them. According to the 2000 census, American Indians and Alaskan natives make up 0.7 percent of the American population or 1,878,285 of an overall population of 281 million. They include over 500 different tribes and clans and have among the highest rate of poverty, unemployment, and suicide of all Americans today and about half still live on reservations around the country. Many American Indian children were forced to attend federal Indian schools where they were forced to give up their native languages and learn only English. When Europeans began to colonize Australia in the late eighteenth century, there were approximately 300,000 aborigines who were members of perhaps 500 different linguistic and cultural groups. A policy of assimilation was carried out between 1910 and 1970 which required aboriginal children to be removed from their homes in the Northern Territory and either put in orphanages or placed in white families. Today there are about 228,000 in Australia or 1.5

percent of the 16 million Australians. Their rate of unemployment and infant mortality rate is three times the national average. Their suicide rate is six time the national average and an adult life expectancy is 20 years below the national average.

4. This really was a matter of some kind of Orwellian double think. The Reagan Administration supported the government of South Africa because it was anti-communist and supported the U.S. in the Cold War. However, the Afrikaner government also oppressed black and colored South Africans in its racist policies.

5. See Daniel Yankelovich, *New Rules: Searching for Self-Fulfillment in a World Turned Upside Down* (New York: Random House, 1981).

6. After a 40-year-old highway bridge in Minneapolis collapsed on August 1, 2007, dropping 50 cars and trucks into the abyss and killing 13 people, a nationwide study found that engineers had given 74,000 other bridges in the United States the same rating as the fallen span: "structurally deficient." Congress established a "bridge fund" and allocated $1 billion to inspect and repair deficient bridges, about $13,500 per bridge. In the same bill, Congress voted to spend $7.4 billion on such earmarks as a National First Ladies' Library in Canton, Ohio; a project to improve "rural domestic preparedness" in Kentucky; and a high-speed ferry to the remote Matanuska-Susitna Borough in Alaska. William Falk, "You Must Remember This," *New York Times*, December 27, 2007.

7. Arthur M. Schlesinger, Sr., *New Viewpoints in American History* (MacMillan, 1922), p. 2. Interestingly, Schlesinger's very next sentence reads: "Since the red-skinned savage has never been a potent factor in American development, the whole history of the United States . . . is, at bottom, the story of the successive waves of immigration and of the adaptation of the newcomers and their descendants to the new surroundings offered by the Western hemisphere." This reflects the long-held bias, mitigated but by no means exterminated today, towards the ignorance of the history—and indeed the presence—of the pre-Columbian peoples who populated the United States.

8. The first known sale of slaves in America occurred in Virginia in 1619. By 1780, just under 700,000 slaves lived in the US. Fifty years later, in 1830, their number had shot up to over 2 million. And, on the eve of the Civil War, roughly 4 million slaves were held in bondage in America.

9. Mary K. Geiter and W.A. Speck, *Colonial America: From Jamestown to Yorktown* (New York: Palgrave Macmillan, 2002), pp. 26–7.

10. Calvinism is named after its founder, John Calvin (1509–1564), a French theologian. Calvinism emphasizes the centrality and involvement of God to all events in life, and has been popularly summarized as ascribing to the so called "five points of Calvinism:" total depravity (people are disposed to serve themselves rather than God or their fellow); unconditional election (God has decided from time immemorial to save certain elected people for His own reasons); limited atonement (Jesus died to redeem the sins of the

elect and no one else); irresistible grace (God's grace in saving the elect trumps the elect's attraction to ungodly pursuits); and perseverance of the saints (the elect cannot truly stray from their faith or be condemned for their sins).

11. Puritanism was an English religious reform movement which began in the sixteenth century. Influenced by Calvinism and gaining many adherents among the middle class, many of the first immigrants to America were Puritans, including the Pilgrims and the Quakers.

12. J. Franklin Jameson, ed., *Original Narratives of Early American History: Johnson's Wonder-Working Province, 1628–1651* (New York: Charles Scribner's Sons, 1910), p. 23.

13. Quaker is the popular name for the Religious Society of Friends. They refused to pay tithes to the state church in England, to take oaths in courts, or to show any special sign of respect to the king or nobles. Quakers were conscientious objectors who refused to engage in combat during wartime and they were advocates for the disadvantaged including slaves and prisoners. They agitated for an end to slavery and for improvements in living conditions in penitentiaries and in treatments in mental institutions. They were strong egalitarian and democratic individualists who believed that every man and woman has a direct access to God, there is no need for a priestly class or churches, and every person is of equal worth including men and women and slaves or free people. In Cromwell's England they were seen as enemies of the crown and state and during the second half of the seventeenth century, over 3,000 were imprisoned in English jails, and hundreds died in cells. When they fled to the American colonies in the mid-1600s, Quakers were viewed as dangerous heretics in many of the colonies. They were deported as witches, imprisoned or hung. Most found a sanctuary in the Rhode Island colony, which had been founded on the principle of religious tolerance. William Penn (1644–1718) and other Quakers played a major role in the creation of the colonies of West Jersey (1675) and Pennsylvania (1682). These colonies were noted for their toleration of minority religious groups.

14. Today, about 70 percent of Americans live in urban areas, and more than 40 percent are in areas of 1 million people or more. In 1990, according to the U.S. census, the farm population was about 4 million (under 2 percent of the population), a figure that has steadily declined since the first national census in 1790, when over 90 percent of all Americans were farmers.

15. The head of a family had to be twenty-one years of age, a citizen or someone who had filed a declaration of intention to become a citizen, and a person who had never taken up arms against the United States or given aid or comfort to its enemies. If you served in the army or navy of the United States you also were considered eligible. Filing to own the one hundred and sixty acres of land simply required a registration fee of ten dollars.

16. Frederick J. Turner, "The Significance of the Frontier in American History," *Annual Report of the American Historical Association for 1893* (Washington:

U.S. Government Printing Office, 1894). Also see David Brooks, *On Paradise Drive: How We Live (and Always Have) in the Future Tense* (New York: Simon & Schuster, 2004).

17. See Walter LaFeber, *The New Empire: An Interpretation of American Expansion, 1860–1898* (Ithaca: Cornell University Press, 1963), Chapter II. LaFeber maintains that Turner's thesis, and the idea that America would need to look beyond its current boundaries to avoid ruptures in its body politic or national character, influenced both Theodore Roosevelt and Woodrow Wilson, two American presidents of the early twentieth century who were both heavily involved in international issues and led America's engagement on the world stage.

18. John O'Sullivan, "Annexation," *Democratic Review* 17 (July and August 1845), p. 5.

19. Cited in Robert W. Johannsen, et al., *Manifest Destiny and Empire: American Antebellum Expansionism* (College Station: Texas A&M University Press, 1997), p. 16.

20. There is a very popular country and western song which ironically reflects these values and the cowboy image. One stanza of the song has the phrase, "they're always alone, even with someone they long." The title of the song is "Mommas, Don't Let Your Babies Grow Up to be Cowboys." The irony is that the opposite of this is true—most American mothers want their babies to grow up to be cowboys. They want their children to succeed and if they are to be successful in the United States they must be enculturated to the values of the dominant society, including the cowboy values. The man on horseback is not only a symbol of individualism but also action.

21. Jim Yarley, "Vicarious Consumption: Boots Made for Walking on Pennsylvania Avenue," *New York Times*, May 13, 2001.

22. See Lawrence Harrison, *The Pan-American Dream: Do Latin America's Cultural Values Discourage True Partnership with the United States and Canada?* (New York: Basic Books, 1997) and Lawrence Harrison and Samuel Huntington, eds., *Culture Matters: How Values Shape Human Progress* (New York: Basic Books, 2000).

23. German economist and sociologist Max Weber wrote *The Protestant Ethic and the Spirit of Capitalism* in 1904 and 1905 as a series of essays. The original edition was in German and was entitled: *Die protestantische Ethik und der 'Geist' des Kapitalismus*. David McClelland was a social psychologist who provided extensive "scientific" evidence of Weber's contention that Protestant capitalist values were essential to develop an entrepreneurial and democratic motive or drive amongst citizens. Among the underlying "needs" was a need or drive to achieve as an individual. His most famous book was *The Achieving Society* (Princeton: Van Nostrand, 1961).

24. Indeed, reality matched appearance fairly well for a long time. In 1650, America had just over 50,000 inhabitants (free and slave); by 1700, that number had increased to over 250,000, still a very small number given the size of the land available. The area of the thirteen colonies, at independence,

was approximately 860,000 square miles. When the first census was taken in 1790, the United States was found to have just under 4 million people, making for a population density of about 4.5 people/square mile. (The current U.S. population density is about 80 people/square mile, for comparison's sake.) *Historical Statistics of the United States*, Part 1 (Washington, D.C.: U.S. Department of Commerce, 1975), p. 8 and *Historical Statistics of the United States*, Part 2 (Washington, D.C.: U.S. Department of Commerce, 1975), p. 1168.

25. The Dutch settlers were among the first to view all as equal regardless of their backgrounds. New Amsterdam (today known as Manhattan) was the first and most important multicultural center in America. While Boston and, later, Philadelphia developed along distinctly English lines, New Amsterdam was pluralistic from the beginning. In 1643, with about 500 settlers, director Willem Kieft told a visiting Jesuit priest that 18 languages were spoken. In fact, according to some estimates, this "Dutch" city was never more than 50 percent Dutch in its population. The other major groups included Germans, English, Africans, Scandinavians, French, and Jews. From this tiny mix of peoples would come the structure of New York City. The British were much more hierarchical and had only begun the transformation to a constitutional monarchy when the original colonies at Jamestown and Plymouth were founded. And, the King was definitely not equal to the average colonist in New England.

26. Alvaro Vargas Llosa, "The Individualist Legacy in Latin America," *The Independent Review*, Vol. 8, No. 3 (Winter 2004), pp. 427–438.

27. Today, some Americans might express this viewpoint with the question, "If you had the cure for cancer, wouldn't you want to share it with the rest of the world?"

Chapter 5

1. The term was first coined by Max Weber in his book *The Protestant Ethic and the Spirit of Capitalism*, which was published in 1904.

2. Adam Smith, *Wealth of Nations*, edited by C.J. Bullock, ed., The Harvard Classics Vol. X (New York: P.F. Collier & Sons, 1909–1914).

3. The term "liberal" in everyday usage refers to those who are socially liberal and believe the government ought to actively protect individual rights and promote equality of opportunity. The term "conservative" usually refers to those who believe that government ought to be more limited and the political and economic system should operate in a free market manner with little interference from government.

4. "Italy floats raising retirement age," BBC, August 25, 2003, http://news.bbc.co.uk/2/hi/europe/3180011.stm

5. Stephanie Rosenbloom, "Please Don't Make Me Go On Vacation," *The New York Times*, August 10, 2006.

6. An exception to this seems to be tombstones where people are often identified as "son of" or "wife of." On the other hand, only immediate family
members usually visit cemeteries to view the tombstones of loved ones.

7. Center for American Values in Public Life, People for the American Way
Foundation, *American Values Survey*, August 9–23, 2006.

8. The Pew Research Center, *Trends in Political Values and Core Attitudes:
1987–2007*, p. 15.

9. National Security Advisor Dr. Zbigniew Brzezinski was also referred to as
"Doctor." He was also a renowned academic and foreign-born. In many
countries such as Germany and Japan, it has been common to have multiple
titles that indicate status, position, academic accomplishments, ancestry,
and so forth. But, times have changes. For example, although Chancellor
Angela Dorothea Merkel of Germany has a Ph.D. in structural linguistics,
her proper title is simply Madame Chancellor (*Bundeskanzlerin*). In Japan,
the use of honorific language (called *keigo*) to elevate a person or humble
oneself has fallen out of use in many companies and especially among young
Japanese. The practice today is simply to add the suffix *–san* (Mr.) to their
names. Normitsu Onishi, "Japanese Get Word From on High: Drop the
Formality," *New York Times*, October 30, 2003.

10. The research of anthropologists Kluckhohn and Strodtbeck in the 1940s and
1950s with the Harvard Values Project led to the proposition that we can
distinguish cultures based upon their basic concerns or "value orientations."
Among the five orientations they found to be most important was the concern for activity—"being" or "doing." People from "being" cultures tend to
believe that relationships are more important than accomplishing great
things whereas those from "doing" cultures believe that hard word and effort will lead to reward and that a what a person accomplishes is a measure-
ment of his or her worth. "Being" cultures tend to be nonwestern while
"doing" cultures tend to be Western. Kluckhohn and Strodtbech found that
the U.S. usually ranks among the highest in "doing." Hofstede ranked the
U.S. highest on "individualism" (in contrast with "collectivism") of all other
countries. F.R. Kluckhohn and F.L. Strodtbeck, *Variations in Value Orientations* (Evanston, IL: Row, Peterson, 1991) and Geert Hofstede and Geert Jan
Hofstede, *Cultures and Organizations: Software of the Mind*. 2nd ed. (New
York: McGraw-Hill, 2005).

11. Deborah Tannen, *You Just Don't Understand: Women and Men in Conversation* (New York: Morrow, 1990).

12. See Geert Hofstede, *Cultures and Organizations* (Cambridge: University
Press, 1991) and Geert Hofstede, "Cultural Constraints in Management
Theories," *Academy of Management Executive 7*, No. 1 (1993), pp. 81–94.

13. His concept of individualism is very similar to David McClelland's "need for
achievement" which focuses on individual, entrepreneurial personality traits
with an emphasis on delayed gratification and a future time orientation.
McClelland, *The Achieving Society*.

14. Seymour Martin Lipset, the monumental political sociologist who died on New Year's Eve 2007, was the scholar most responsible for the phrase "American exceptionalism" entering modern political discourse. Lipset, *American Exceptionalism: A Double-Edged Sword.* Also see David M. Potter, *People of Plenty: Economic Abundance and the American Character* (Chicago: University of Chicago, 1954).

15. Political economist and social critic Thorstein Veblen (1857–1929) saw the negative aspect of this. He theorized that the "conspicuous consumption" of the leisure class would lead to economic collapse. (*Theory of the Leisure Class*, 1899). He is often credited with being the intellectual source of increased government involvement in the *laissez faire* economy after the Great Depression of the 1930s.

16. This statue is found in Meridian or Malcolm X Park in Washington D.C. She had a large sword in one hand which was stolen. Some would argue that this theft has Freudian overtones.

17. "Masculinity stands for a society in which social gender roles are clearly distinct: Men are supposed to be assertive, tough, and focused on material success; women are supposed to be more modest, tender, and concerned with the quality of life. . . . Femininity stands for a society in which social gender roles overlap: Both men and women are supposed to be modest, tender, and concerned with the quality of life." From Geert Hofstede, *Culture's Consequences: Comparing Values, Behaviors, Institutions, and Organizations Across Nations*, 2nd ed., (Thousand Oaks, CA: Sage, 2001), p 297.

18. The Pew Research Center, *Trends in Political Values and Core Attitudes: 1987–2007*, p. 12–14.

19. Janet Kornblum, "Study: 25% of Americans have no one to confide in," *USA Today*, June 22, 2006.

20. Shankar Vedantam, "Social Isolation Growing in U.S., Study Says," *The Washington Post*, June 23, 2006, p. A3.

21. This is not true of African Americans. The typical African-American lives closer than 200 miles from their nearest relative.

22. "Tests show students learn basics in history, civics," www.cnn.com.

23. "Whether scientist or criminals, mountain climbers or hot-dog skiers," says Farley, "all are driven by temperament, and perhaps biology, to a life of constant stimulation and risk taking. Both the socially useful and the socially appalling Type Ts (for thrill seeking personality types)," he says, "'are rejecting the strictures, the laws, the regulations—they are pursuing the unknown, the uncertain'" John Leo, "Looking for A Life of Thrills," *Time Magazine*, April 15, 1985.

24. McClelland, *The Achieving Society*. In his study he found that moderate risk-taking often led to success in the United States but not extreme risk-taking or gambling.

25. Andy McSmith, "The Big Question: Why do wealthy Americans donate so much to charity and wealthy Britons so little?" *The Independent*, June 27,

2007, http://news.independent.co.uk/world/politics/article2714116.ece and Christopher Shea, "Who Gives?" *The Boston Globe*, December 10, 2006, http://www.boston.com/news/education/higher/articles/2006/12/10/who_gives/.

26. McSmith, "The Big Question: Why do wealthy Americans donate so much to charity and wealthy Britons so little?"

27. Although Americans receive tax breaks for making charitable donations, studies have shown that it is unlikely that these tax incentives have much effect on giving. In fact, giving has stayed at fairly constant levels despite changes in the size of the tax relief. See "Sweet Charity," *The Wall Street Journal*, December 24, 2005, http://www.opinionjournal.com/weekend/hottopic/?id=110007728.

28. Bureau of Labor Statistics, "Volunteering in the United States, 2006," January 10, 2007.

29. Bureau of Labor Statistics, "Volunteering in the United States, 2006," January 10, 2007.

30. This number does not include the almost 375,000 congregations in the US. http://nccs.urban.org/statistics/quickfacts.cfm.

31. http://nccs.urban.org/statistics/quickfacts.cfm.

32. Beth Walton, "Volunteer rates hit record numbers," *USA Today*, July 7, 2006, http://www.usatoday.com/news/nation/2006-07-06-volunteers_x.htm.

33. Cited in Samuel Eliot Morison, *The Oxford History of the American People* (New York: Oxford University Press, 1965), p. 764.

34. Eric Foner and John A. Garraty, eds., *The Reader's Companion to American History* (New York: Houghton Mifflin, 1991), p. 869.

35. As was mentioned earlier, Roosevelt strongly believed that immigrants ought to give up their differences and adapt to the dominant culture and he had strong biases against non-Northern European immigrants. But, he was also the champion of the "working man" who fought against the oppression of the lower and middle class workers and the greed and corruption of large conglomerates, trusts, and the wealthy.

36. Bly was a wholly remarkable American for her time, or indeed any time. The year after she got herself committed to Blackwell's Island, she set the world record for the fastest time in circling the globe, clocking in at just over 72 days.

37. This is something de Tocqueville observed.

Chapter 6

1. This saying was popularized by the very melodramatic 1945 war movie entitled *God Is My Co-Pilot* which was based on an autobiography by the same title written by General Robert Lee Scott Jr., a retired United State Air Force

officer who described his experiences with the famous Flying Tigers in China and Burma during World War II.

2. Everyone was not equal in Aristotle's Athens. For example, slavery was fully accepted and slaves could not become citizens.

3. The historian Gertrude Himmelfarb, *The De-Moralization of Society: From Victorian Virtues to Modern Values* (New York: Alfred A. Knopf, 1995), notes that what Victorians called virtues we call values.

4. It is not uncommon for people to confuse the Declaration of Independence and the Constitution. The Declaration was a document that dissolved the relationship between the colonial power (England) and the colony (America). It is quite clearly a revolutionary treatise. The Constitution, on the other hand, was written to create a new government and a sovereign country. While the Preamble to the Constitution contains some of the same admonitions and assertions about individual freedom that are found in the Declaration, they are very different documents with very different purposes.

5. In the past two decades, the federal government has assumed more power over criminal behavior. For example, many crimes involving drugs are now "federal crimes" that can lead to the death penalty. Also, there is now a Department of Education that reports directly to the President. Since 9/11 the federal government has also held both American and foreign prisoners who were accused of being involved in terrorism. Before 9/11, if someone were arrested for terrorism, it probably would have been considered a criminal activity that would be adjudicated at the local or state level rather than at the federal level.

6. AP, "Five Vermont Towns Vote to Impeach Bush," March 7, 2006.

7. *The Book of Virtues: A Treasury of Great Moral Stories*, sometimes just called *The Book of Virtues*, is an anthology edited by William Bennett in 1993 and published by Simon and Schuster. This book was turned into a PBS animated television series. Note that his values do not include fairness and justice.

8. *The Coming Crisis in Citizenship: Higher Education's Failure to Teach America's History and Institutions*, Intercollegiate Studies Institute, Wilmington, Delaware, http://www.americancivicliteracy.org/report/summary.html.

9. On September 8, 1892 a Boston-based youth magazine, *The Youth's Companion*, first published a short, 22-word recitation of "The Pledge to the Flag" for school children to use during activities following the month of commemoration for the 400th anniversary of Columbus' discovery of American. It has become a profession of loyalty and devotion to not only the flag, but also the way of life of Americans.

10. *Millersville School District v. Gobitis (1940)*.

11. *West Virginia State Board of Education v. Varnette (1943)*.

12. This list includes Tennessee (Butler Act) and Arkansas (Epperson v. Arkansas).

13. http://www.ala.org/ala/oif/bannedbooksweek/challengedbanned/challengedbanned.htm#wcb.

14. http://www.nytimes.com/2006/05/21/books/fiction-25-years.html?ex= 1305864000&en=d3f9cc78ce4c00b7&ei=5088.
15. http://www.ala.org/ala/oif/bannedbooksweek/bbwlinks/100mostfrequently .htm. School boards banning *Huckleberry Finn* also may be extracting vengeance on Twain for his famous saying, "In the first place God made idiots. This was for practice. Then He made school boards."
16. Today there are more than 4,000 universities and colleges in the United States. Most are state and local institutions.
17. Alternatively, they could sell the granted land and use the proceeds to found universities elsewhere in the state.
18. See C. P. Snow, *The Two Cultures and the Scientific Revolution* (New York: Cambridge University Press, 1959) and Robert M. Hutchins, *The Learning Society* (New York: Frederick A. Praeger, Publishers, 1968).

Chapter 7

1. Some scholars in international relations theory would call this an "isomorphic approach" to understanding the growth of a nation or the international system of nation states. It also falls under the rubric of "historical sociology." See Raymond Aron, "Conflict and War from the Viewpoint of Historical Sociology," in *The Nature of Conflict (Studies on the Sociological Aspects of International Tensions)* (International Sociological Association, UNESCO, Paris, 1957), pp. 177–203.
2. Reinhold Niebuhr, *Moral Man and Immoral Society* (London: Scribner's, 1941).
3. The nation grew dramatically between the end of the Civil War in 1865 and the end of World War II in 1945 in terms of industrialization and economic and geographic expansion. The population swelled dramatically with waves of immigrants from non-Protestant and Northern European countries. Most importantly, this new country began to expand its involvement with the rest of the world. The U.S. grew not only in terms of expanded territory and commerce, but also in its involvement with the rest of the world and its global military adventures.
4. World War II began on September 1, 1939 when Germany invaded Poland. However, the U.S. did not formally enter the war until Pearl Harbor was attacked on December 7, 1941.
5. In the United States, Calvinists formed the Protestant denomination of Presbyterians while the Anglican Church of England became the Episcopal Church.
6. Harvard professor Stanley H. Hoffman might characterize the childhood period as a time of idealist utopianism and the adolescent period as a time of cynical realism. In a somewhat Hegelian dialectical manner, the synthesis

of these two opposites might be seen as utopian idealism. "Suggestions for the Study of International Relations," in Stanley H. Hoffman, ed., *Contemporary Theory in International Relations* (Englewood Cliffs, NJ: Prentice Hall, Inc, 1960), p. 189.

7. Quoted in Robert Kagan, "Cowboy Nation," *New Republic*, December 10, 2006.

8. Unilateralism was also central to American foreign policy during the war against the Barbary Pirates and the Spanish-American War during which the U.S. did not enter into formal alliances with other nations.

9. Through such restrictive legislation as the Townshend Acts, the Sugar Act, the Currency Act, and the Stamp Act.

10. http://press-pubs.uchicago.edu/founders/documents/v1ch8s38.html.

11. Upon entering office as President in 1801, Jefferson had been "appalled to discover that tribute and ransoms paid to Barbary had exceeded $2,000,000, or about one-fifth, of the entire annual income of the United States government." Thomas Jewett, "Terrorism in Early America," *The Early American Review: A Journal of Fact and Opinion on People, Issues and Events of 18th Century America* (Winter/Spring, 2002).

12. The United State Marine Corps, a branch of the Navy, fought the major battles in these wars which led to the line, "to the shores of Tripoli" in the opening of the Marine Hymn sung by all U.S. Marines. Due to the hazards of boarding hostile ships, Marines' uniforms had a leather high collar to protect against cutlass slashes. This led to the nickname "Leatherneck" for U.S. Marines. Col. H. Avery Chenoweth, USMCR (Ret.) and Col. Brooke Nihart, USMC (ret), *Semper fi: The Definitive Illustrated History of the U.S. Marines* (New York: Sterling Publishing Company, Inc, 2005).

13. This was the first real internationalist foreign policy. However, it was not a war against a state but rather one in which the enemy were thugs and criminals who used terrorism to force nations to pay tribute to win back their citizens and ships. Ironically, the situation was remarkably similar to 9/11. Those who attacked the United States in 2001 were terrorists, not members of a national army. Before the American Revolution, the British protected American ships from pirates and during the Revolution, the French provided protection. As a newly independent state, the U.S. was forced to protect itself and this conflict did not involve an alliance with other nations, although all nations who were victims of piracy refused to pay tribute and fought the pirates.

14. Unfortunately, on July 3, 1988, Iran Flight 655 was shot down by the *USS Vincennes* on the Bandar Abbas-Dubai rout, which resulted in the loss of life of 290 civilians from six nations including 66 children. There were 38 non-Iranians aboard.

15. Though by the time the treaty was signed, the Napoleonic Wars—which were the impetus for these two things in the first place—were over, thus rendering the continuance of these two policies unnecessary from the British perspective.

16. Grant was one of many famed Civil War figures who fought in the Mexican-American War. Other notables included Robert E. Lee, William T. Sherman, George McClellan, Stonewall Jackson, Jefferson Davis, Ambrose Burnside, and James Longstreet.

17. Cited in Howard Zinn, *A People's History of the United States* (New York: HarperCollins Publishers, 2003) p. 299.

18. Paul Johnson, *A History of the American People* (New York: HarperCollins Publishers, 1998), p. 613.

19. Twain in *New York World*, October 6, 1900.

20. This is usually referred to as "The Tampico Affair" of 1914.

21. The Quasi-War with France (1798–1800) is another, much more minor, exception.

22. "As a youth he experienced a characteristic 'awakening,' believing himself one of the elect. He retained throughout his life what he termed 'faith, pure and simple', and an accompanying conviction that he was chosen to lead, to teach, and to inspire." Johnson, *A History of the American People*, p. 627.

23. Johnson, *A History of the American People*, p. 648.

24. Even as recent as the 2008 Republican Presidential primaries, a relatively minor and libertarian candidate, Ron Paul, campaigned on a policy of "fortress America." He strongly believed that the U.S. could withdraw from all international military engagements and foreign alliances unless it was directly attacked by another nation. From his perspective, when the U.S. is engaged as an internationalist foreign policy, the federal government becomes too powerful and American self-interests are compromised.

25. Morison, *The Oxford History of the American People*, p. 990.

26. Morison, *The Oxford History of the American People*, p. 1000.

27. Johnson, *A History of the American People*, p. 769.

Chapter 8

1. Since two American University alumni and one current AU professor are writing this book, it is incumbent upon us to mention that Kennedy made this remark at his 1963 commencement address at American University, during which he also announced the first atomic weapons treaty between the US and USSR.

2. Francis Fukuyama, *The Great Disruption: Human Nature and the Reconstitution of Social Order*, (New York: Free Press, 1999).

3. A more anthropological version of this fear is found in Colin Turnbull's *The Mountain People* (New York: Simon & Schuster, 1972). In his study of the Ik in Uganda he raises the question as to how enduring our values really are. He describes a tribe of people who are starving and show no compassion for others, and especially the elderly, because they are overwhelmed with their

individual need to survive. Furthermore, if we apply Abraham Maslow's famous hierarchy of needs theory, if such basic needs as food or water cannot be met, then humans care little about such higher order needs as liberty, democracy, and concern for others.

4. Robert D. Putnam, *Bowling Alone: America's Declining Social Capital* (New York: Simon and Schuster, 2000). This was originally an essay that was published in the *Journal of Democracy*, Vol. 6, No. 1 (January 1995).

5. James Surowiecki, *The Wisdom of Crowds* (New York: Doubleday, 2004).

6. The famous mythology of a violent gun culture in the American frontier may actually be an exaggeration. Richard Shenkman has written that some of the most famed bloody towns of the Old West were actually anything but: Dodge City, site of many Westerns, had its all-time high homicide rate of five people killed in 1878. Deadwood, South Dakota and Tombstone (where the legendary gunfight at the OK Corral occurred) had respective highs of four and five people killed in a single year. Cited in Robert Spitzer, *The Politics of Gun Control*, Third Edition (Washington, D.C.: CQ Press, 2004), p. 10.

7. The majority of gun-related deaths in the U.S. are suicides. The incidence is greatest in southern and western states. Firearm homicides are much greater in many other countries such as Mexico, Brazil, Thailand, Guatemala, Columbia, Estonia, and Russia.

8. Cited in Spitzer, *The Politics of Gun* Control, p. 1.

9. Gallup Poll, "Death Penalty," http://www.galluppoll.com/content/default.aspx?ci=1606.

10. Gallup Poll, "Death Penalty," http://www.galluppoll.com/content/default.aspx?ci=1606.

11. By 13 percent. Joseph Carroll, "Who Supports the Death Penalty," November 16, 2004, http://www.deathpenaltyinfo.org/article.php?scid=23&did=1266.

12. Harris Poll, "Majorities of U.S. Adults Favor Euthanasia and Physician-Assisted Suicide by More than Two-to-One," April 27, 2005. Also GSS website and results: http://www.icpsr.umich.edu/GSS.

13. Amy Burdette, Terrence Hill, and Benjamin Moulton, "Religion and Attitudes toward Physician-Assisted Suicide and Terminal Palliative Care," *Journal for the Scientific Study of Religion*, 2005, Vol. 44, No. 1 (Mach 2005), pp. 79–93.

14. Cited in Sydney Ahlmstrom, *A Religious History of the American People*, Second Edition (New Haven: Yale University Press, 2004), p. 386.

15. Pew Global Attitudes Project, "Among Wealthy Nations . . . America Stands Alone in its Embrace of Religion," December 19, 2002.

16. Public Agenda, "Religion and Public Life: 2000–2004," p. 6. See also "U.S. Religious Landscape Survey 2008," The Pew Forum on Religion and Public Life, 2008.

17. Public Agenda, "Religion and Public Life: 2000–2004," p. 6.

18. Pew Research Center, *Trends in Political Values and Core Attitudes: 1987–2007*, p. 30.

19. "Did Humans Evolve? Not Us, Say Americans," *New York Times*, August 15, 2006.

20. Barry Kosmin and Egon Mayer, "American Religious Identification Survey 2001," p. 12; The Pew Forum on Religion and Public Life, "Religious Demographic Profile: United States," http://pewforum.org/world-affairs/countries/?CountryID=222. See also "U.S. Religious Landscape Survey 2008," The Pew Forum on Religion and Public Life, 2008.

21. Robert Putnam, "Bowling Alone: America's Declining Social Capital," *Journal of Democracy*, Vol. 6, No. 1 (January 1995), pp. 65–78.

22. This was a period when many joked that American ambassadors were the "undertakers for the world" because at all the embassy parties they looked like undertakers in their black suits.

23. The practice of use formal titles is changing in Japan and it is common to simply address a superior with the title *san*. See Norimitsu Onishi, "Japanese Get Word From on High: Drop the Formality," *New York Times*, October 30, 2003.

24. The Dutch researcher Geert Hofstede found that Americans ranked the highest on his dimension of "individualism" as opposed to "collectivism" in his study of over 60 IBM offices around the world. He also found that the "power distance," as reflected in the gap between subordinates and superiors, is much less in the U.S. than most other countries. Hofstede and Hofstede, *Cultures and Organizations: Software of the Mind*.

25. The phrase "Joe Six-Pack" is often used to describe an ordinary, hard-working, masculine American man who buys a cheap "six pack" of beer rather than an expensive bottle of wine. The beer is usually domestic and it is often assumed that the wine is foreign.

26. Examples of the right portraying the left as elite can be found in such books as Bernard Goldberg's *Arrogance: Rescuing America from the Media Elite* (New York: Warner Books, 2003) and Laura Ingraham's *Shut Up & Sing: How Elites From Hollywood, Politics, and the UN are Subverting America* (Washington: Regnery Publishing, 2003) The notion of a sinister, liberal elite Democratic party has been rebutted by Thomas Frank in his book *What's the Matter with Kansas?: How Conservatives Won the Heart of America* (Metropolitan Books/Henry Holt & Company, 2004).

27. Richard Benedetto, "Who's More Likeable, Bush or Kerry?" USA Today, September 17, 2004.

28. Patrick Buchanan (*The Death of the West: How Dying Populations and Immigrant Invasions Imperil Our Country and Civilization* [New York: St. Martin's Press, 2002]), Lou Dobbs of CNN, and Samuel Huntington (*Who are We?* [New York: Simon & Schuster, 2004]) all have become very popular among Americans who have a strong belief that illegal and legal Mexican immigrants may be undermining the traditional values and the foreign policy of the United States.

29. Lincoln went before Congress to ask for the temporary suspension of the writ of *habeas corpus* until the end of the Civil War. Southern spies were arrested in Baltimore and it was vital that their arrests were kept secret to allow the government to find other spies. When the war ended, the writ was restored.

30. Abraham H. Maslow, *Toward A Psychology of Being* (Princeton: D. Van Nostrand, 1968).

31. It seems that some who designed American foreign policy towards Iraq may not agree with Maslow. The policy of the United States appears to be to establish and support the higher-order needs of "liberty" and "democracy" before the needs for food and water, safety and security have been fully met.

32. In December of 2001, 64 percent of Americans felt that it was a good idea "for the president to have the authority to make changes in the rights usually guaranteed by the Constitution" during "wartime." In contrast, by August of 2006, this number declined to 36 percent.

33. New York Times/CBS Poll, August 17–21, 2006.

34. Pew Research Center, "Trends in Political Values and Core Attitudes: 1987–2007; Political Landscape More Favorable To Democrats," p. 61.

Chapter 9

1. Gail Sheehy, *Passages: Predictable Crisis of Adult Life* (New York: Bantam, 1977).

2. This is also known as the Second Gulf War, Operation Iraqi Freedom, or the occupation of Iraq—a military conflict that began on March 20, 2003 with the U.S.-led invasion of Iraq.

3. Pew Research Center, "Trends in Political Values and Core Attitudes: 1987–2007," p. 21.

4. Peter Singer, *The President of Good and Evil* (New York: E.P. Dutton, 2004).

5. See Gary R. Weaver, (dissertation) *The American Public and Viet Nam: An In Depth Study of the American People During Times of International Conflict* (Washington: American University, 1970).

6. Pew Research Center, *Trends in Political Values and Core Attitudes: 1987–2007*, p. 19. Fewer "completely agree" with this statement. This is probably the effect of Iraq, etc. But, they have not flipped and decided to disagree with the statement.

7. Chicago Council on Foreign Relations, "Worldviews 2002: American Public Opinion & Foreign Policy," p. 11.

8. The Chicago Council on Global Affairs, "Global Views 2006," p. 6.

9. 49 percent agreed, 47 percent disagreed. Pew Research Center, *Trends in Political Values and Core Attitudes: 1987–2007*, p. 21.

10. The Chicago Council on Global Affairs, "Global Views 2006," p. 16–18.

11. Pew Research Center, *Trends in Political Values and Core Attitudes: 1987–2007*, p. 21.

12. Article I, Section 8 of the Constitution provides that only Congress has the power to declare war. One of the founders' greatest concerns was that they might unintentionally create a president who was too much like the British monarch, whom they despised. They allayed that concern in part by assuring that the president would not have the power to declare war.

13. See Amy Chua, *Day of Empire: How Hyperpowers Rise To Global Dominance—and Why They Fail* (New York: Random House, 2008).

14. http://www.galluppoll.com/content/default.aspx?ci=4729. There remain two groups, however, who Americans still have trouble accepting as presidential candidates: atheists and homosexuals. Americans are evenly split about whether or not they would consider voting for an atheist as president (in 1958, only 18 percent would consider voting for an atheist). A slight majority—55 percent would consider voting for a homosexual as president (in 1978, only about a quarter of Americans would have given such a candidate consideration.).

15. http://www.galluppoll.com/content/default.aspx?ci=1687.

16. Pew Research Center, *Trends in Political Values and Core Attitudes: 1987–2007*; Political Landscape More Favorable to Democrats," pp. 39 and 42.

17. http://www.galluppoll.com/content/?ci=28072.

18. In 1991, King was beaten by officers of the Los Angeles Police Department who apprehended him after he led them on a high speed chase and physically resisted arrest. The beating was captured on film. A mostly white jury acquitted the majority of the police officers on charges of excessive use of force, setting off massive riots in Los Angeles. In 1999, Amadou Diallo, an African immigrant in New York City, was shot 19 times by police who believed that he matched the profile of a serial rapist and that he was attempting to draw a firearm. Diallo's death set off demonstrations against police brutality and racial profiling (the use of racial and ethnic characteristics to determine a person's likelihood to commit a crime).

19. Isabel Sawhill and John E. Morton, "Economic Mobility: Is the American Dream Alive and Well?" The Economic Mobility Project, 2007. See also Julia B. Isaacs, Isabel V. Sawill, and Ron Haskins, "Getting Ahead or Losing Ground: Economic Mobility in America," The Brookings Institution, 2008.

20. See Jeffrey Reiman, *The Rich Get Richer and the Poor Get Prison: Ideology, Class and Criminal Justice, 8th edition* (Boston: Pearson, 2007) There are more prisoners in prison in the United States than any other country. The number of African-Americans in prison is far more than the proportional amount of African-Americans in the U.S.

21. Generally, poorer school districts often, but far from always, result in poor schools. Poorer districts mean that there is less money to go towards supplies, new resources and facilities, and towards attracting and retaining enough teachers to provide an adequate teacher to student ratio. Of course, it is easier for wealthier families to afford private schools and colleges. However, there may be a movement brewing on the university level (with schools

like Yale and Harvard in the lead) to provide more financial aid to less wealthy students.

22. A late eighteenth century treaty between the US and the Barbary states noted that "'as the government of the United States is not, in any sense, founded on the Christian religion,' there should be no cause for conflict over differences of 'religious opinion' between countries . . . The treaty passed the Senate unanimously." Jon Meacham, "A Nation of Christians Is Not a Christian Nation," *New York Times*, October 7, 2007.

23. See Ross Douthat, "Crisis of Faith," *The Atlantic*, July/August 2007, p. 38.

24. Michael Hout and Claude S. Fischer, "Explaining the Rise of Americans with No Religious Preference: Generations and Politics," *American Sociological Review*, Vol. 67, No. 2 (April 2002), pp. 165–190.

25. This seems to be increasing especially among the young. In a Pew Research Center survey, it was found that 20 percent of 18 to 25-year-olds reported no religious affiliation, up from 11 percent in the late 1980s. And, books such as Kevin Phillip's *American Theocracy*, which portray the religious right as a threat to traditional American values, have become popular.

26. The Chicago Council on Global Affairs and WorldPublicOpinion.org, "World Publics Think China Will Catch Up With the US—and That's Okay," May 25, 2007, http://www.worldpublicopinion.org/pipa/articles/ views_on_countriesregions_bt/366.php?nid=&id=&pnt=366&lb=btvoc There is a Zogby poll that counters these findings at: http://www.zogby .com/news/ReadNews.dbm?ID=1314. These counter-results are likely the result of how the survey questions in the Zogby poll are negatively worded.

Index

within cultures, 9, 11
egalitarianism and, 186–189
ethnic, 19
fear of terrorism and, 189–193
race relations and, 210–211
regional, 19
religious, 181–182
dot-com industries, 116
Douglas, Stephen A., 93
*Driven Out: The Forgotten War
Against Chinese Americans*
(Pfaelzer), 65
dualism, 26–27, 30–34, 203–204

E

economic development, 95–96, 99,
102
economic mobility, 35, 91, 102, 129,
159, 215
Economic Policy Institute, 43–44
education
in civics, 128, 135–144
evolution and creationism in, 141,
186
immigrants and, 91–92
integration of, 135, 144
local control in, 134–135, 144
national policy in, 142–143
private vs. public, 144
race and, 63, 64, 211
school prayer and, 186
education, higher, 138–139, 143–144
Edwards, John, 211–212
egalitarianism, 98, 186–189
Eisenhower, Dwight D., 85, 135,
139–140
elitism, 188–189
emergency powers, 144–145
Emerson, Ralph Waldo, 105, 127
empathy, cultural, 16–19, 221n
enculturation, 9–11, 225–226n

The End of History and the Last Man
(Fukuyama), 41, 172
England, 25, 156–157, 158
English language, 14, 69–70, 76–78
English-only movements, 50
entertainment, 29
environmental issues, 42, 85, 134,
200, 207
Equal Employment Opportunities
Commission (EEOC), 39
equality, 37, 57, 187–188, 189–191
Espionage Act, 164
Europe
immigrants in, 36, 215
national identity in, 39–43
as not-American, 41–42
reasons for migration from, 86–87
tragic worldview in, 26–34
European Commission, 40
European Union (EU), 39–43
euthanasia, 180–181
Evangelicalism, 182–183, 212
evil, 27, 203–204
evolution, 88, 141, 186
exceptionalism, 1–2, 79–100
America as example and, 1–2
beginnings of, 89–90
cowboy values and, 94–95
development of, 98–100
foreign policy and, 152–153
future of, 213–215
geography and, 95–98
immigrants' belief in, 73
imperialism and, 45–46, 161–162
individualism and, 90–93, 109–113
isolationism and, 13–14
Manifest Destiny and, 59–61
melting pot image and, 50
War of 1812 and, 156–157
Executive Order 11246 (1965), 39
expansionism, 151–153, 157, 158 *See
also* Manifest Destiny